The Mental Road
to the Major Leagues

The Mental Road to the Major Leagues

A Guide for Rising Ballplayers

KELLY J. PFAFF *and*
PEDER N. PIERING

McFarland & Company, Inc., Publishers
Jefferson, North Carolina, and London

LIBRARY OF CONGRESS CATALOGUING-IN-PUBLICATION DATA

Pfaff, Kelly J.
   The mental road to the major leagues : a guide for rising
ballplayers / Kelly J. Pfaff and Peder N. Piering.
      p.   cm.
   Includes bibliographical references and index.

   ISBN 978-0-7864-6563-7
   softcover : acid free paper ∞

   1. Baseball—Psychological aspects.   I. Piering, Peder N.
II. Title.
GV867.6.P43   2012
796.35701—dc23   2011050001

British Library cataloguing data are available

Front cover photograph and design by Jennifer Kuhn.

Manufactured in the United States of America

*McFarland & Company, Inc., Publishers
   Box 611, Jefferson, North Carolina 28640
   www.mcfarlandpub.com*

Table of Contents

Preface 1

ONE—Growing Up with Baseball 7
TWO—Getting Noticed 23
THREE—Draft or College 43
FOUR—The Apprenticeship 59
FIVE—AAA 84
SIX—The Call-Up 113
SEVEN—Winter Ball 130
EIGHT—The Show 150

Appendices
    A: Psychological Characteristics of Peak Performance 169
    B: Understanding and Using Imagery in Sport 172
    C: Relaxation Techniques for Regulating Arousal 176
    D: Vital Skills for Generating Energy 178
    E: Goal Setting: The Game Within the Game 180
    F: Patterns of Distorted Thought and Maladaptive Thinking 183
    G: The Performance Triad: Thought, Feeling and Action 186
Bibliography 189
Index 193

Preface

"You don't have a soul. You are a Soul. You have a body."—C.S. Lewis

SOME OF OUR GREATEST achievements are born out of our deepest challenges. It is human nature to want to bury the past, to eliminate the moments of struggle and recklessness that blacken our present achievement. Yet the adversity, not the successful moments, makes us fuller, deeper, more complex creatures. Without the thorn of adversity, we would never know the exhilaration of relief and triumph.

I became interested in the topic of adversity one summer while I observed the wicked struggle of a young major league pitcher. It was 2008 at Miller Park in Milwaukee, and Manny Parra was on the mound for the Brewers. On paper, and throughout his minor league career, Parra appeared to be a prodigy. He was left-handed, had a fastball that could clock 95 miles per hour, and had excellent command of all his pitches. Yet, when he stepped onto a major league mound, time and time again he lost it. His face fell into that same grim expression every time his coach jogged out to chat with him. After the talk he'd throw a few good pitches, maybe get a strikeout, then definitely give up a home run or two.

Watching him, I felt his humiliation. Why? Because everyone believed he had the potential to be a contending major league pitcher. They gave him chances—and he blew them. He had the stuff, but (as the media loved to put it) he was a headcase.

I realized through that study that the mind is powerful. Even when our bodies are perfectly aligned, and all the pieces are in place, a troubled mind can sicken our resolve. So I started wondering: What is the team doing to help this struggling pitcher?

That was when I discovered sport psychology. I found out that there actually were ways for athletes to train their minds for competition. And it wasn't mystic or weird—it was a type of wisdom that, if mastered, could

1

influence someone's entire life. Players who incorporate sport psychology into their routines have been able to set goals and meet them, to gain more confidence, and to control their thoughts.

After writing an article for *Milwaukee Magazine* about the Milwaukee Brewers, I was inspired to do a much larger study of the subject of sport psychology throughout major league baseball. In this pursuit, I found many people willing to discuss how moments of adversity helped them to grow stronger as players and as people. I was privileged to find four major league players—Adam Pettyjohn, Justin Lehr, Brandon Snyder, and Vinny Rottino—willing to go more in depth, to give a full account of what it took for them over the years to become major league baseball players. Through these stories I was able to discover the topics that are universal to anyone pursuing baseball as a career—from college scholarships to meager minor league salaries, from getting traded to getting injured. The most resounding theme for these players, however, was the importance they placed on preparing their minds for competition. Anyone who fights his way to the big leagues understands the dedication it takes—and the tricks the mind can play—during the ascent.

Working with clinical and sport psychologist Dr. Peder Piering, I endeavored to tell the story of the journey—not just the journey of a player's career, but also the journey of his mind.

Baseball, of all occupations, proves the fascinating power of the human mind. Take the story of Rick Ankiel—once a major league pitcher with a 3.50 ERA, until he reached the postseason with the Cardinals and mysteriously lost the ability to control the ball. Or more recently, Jarrod Saltalamacchia, a talented young catcher who suffered Steve Blass disease (inability to accurately throw the ball) while recovering from injury. These are players who possess the talent and the technique, but somewhere along the way something had gotten into their minds. Stories like these (and baseball is filled with many more) prove that the mind, not the body, has the strongest control over a person.

Today, more than half of all major league teams have sport psychologists on staff. More and more articles are being written about how major league players like Chris Dickerson have worked with sport psychologists to overcome mental challenges they were facing (Sheldon, par. 5). And in 2008, three major league baseball players (Khalil Greene, Dontrelle Willis, and Joey Votto) were placed on the disabled list for non-physical reasons.

The power of the mind is real and baseball has been an important arena in which people have witnessed and acknowledged this power.

Those who pursue major league baseball may have been dedicating the majority of their lives to the sport, but that will not always be the case. In a lifespan, a player's baseball career is a small percentage of all that he will experience and accomplish. Yet baseball can give someone some of the greatest tools he can use throughout his life. Most of all, baseball can give someone the opportunity to learn about himself, understand his mind, and learn how to control the battles raging on the inside.

In this book, we have integrated sport psychology theory and techniques along with the personal testimonies of ballplayers. Alongside these testimonies we explore various social issues players must face throughout this journey. Each chapter blends these three areas to provide a comprehensive picture of this experience.

While working on this book, I have had the opportunity to interview a range of people, including high school and college baseball players, minor league and major league players, coaches and managers at all levels, sport psychologists and consultants, player development staff, sports agents, parents, lawyers and professors. Speaking with such a range of people, I have found that the book's topic is relevant to anyone impacted by baseball. For fans who love baseball, this book provides a look into the details the average person cannot observe from merely watching a game. It provides insight into players' lifestyles, what they experience during competition, political issues they must encounter, and the challenges they face as celebrities. For athletes and parents, the book discusses the many choices they need to make in order to pursue elite baseball, from baseball academies to showcases, from college selection to professional contracts. Many people today understand the prominent role that sports hold in American culture. For this reason, the book considers some of the dilemmas this trend has created—from unethical recruiting in Latin American countries, to steroid abuse, to suffering college graduation rates.

Most importantly, the book considers the intangible elements of the game: the emotion of a pitcher after throwing a no hitter, the painful memory of a hitter after striking out, the imagination of an outfielder who pre-plays a fly ball, and the confidence it takes for somebody to step up to bat and hit a grand slam. These are the unseen parts of baseball's visual display; these are the parts that give baseball its life and vitality.

—KELLY PFAFF

Because Competition Can Be a Beautiful Thing

Historically, many ideas have provided us with a foundation for our modern-day theories on the association between mind and body. These ideas served as the roots for what we now know as the field of sport psychology.

The mind-body dichotomy and the perceived separation between the two was originally referred to as dualism. The origins of dualism are found as far back as Pythagoras in the late sixth century B.C. Dualism held that humans have physical bodies and nonphysical souls. Body and mind were viewed as separate. Dualism proposed a clear distinction between the physical world and the soul or metaphysical world.

On the opposite end of the spectrum was monism. Monism stated that a single material principle is adequate to explain reality and that mind and body are the same. The mind exists only by the function of the body and its interaction with the environment. In the third century B.C., Plato's student Aristotle offered the position that the soul and the body constitute a single cohesive entity.

In approximately 1487, Leonardo da Vinci used the theories of the Roman architect Vitruvius to create "The Proportions of Man" or "Vitruvian Man." Vitruvius was a proponent of the Sacred Geometry of Pythagoras. He designed temples based on the proportions of the human body, believing them to be perfect. He believed the extended limbs of the human body fit perfectly into both the circle and the square. According to Pythagorean tradition, the circle represented the spiritual realm and the square represented our material existence. The human body represented the fusion of matter and spirit, which was reflected in its proportion. Today the image of the Vitruvian Man represents health and fitness—an image of a balanced, healthy man.

To me this is a powerful image that represents the balance between our material and spiritual existence. When I look at the Vitruvian Man, I see what the human body is capable of when mind, body, and spirit function as one. While philosophy and physiology represent the polar opposites in the contrast between mind and body, psychology has emerged somewhere between these two to study the relationship between mind and body.

Although scientists have been studying the psychological aspects of sport for more than 100 years, the field of sport psychology has been until most recently underutilized. Sport psychology is one paradigm that embraces this connection between mind and body. Sport psychologists have come to recognize the more integrative view that mind and body exist together. They do not function as separate entities and they never have.

With an emphasis on the dynamic that is mind and body, sport psychology has become an increasingly recognized discipline that enhances our knowledge in the areas of health and human performance. When mind and body function in harmony, an athlete is capable of tapping into what many have referred to as "intangible" qualities. While in this mental and physical state, an athlete can achieve the ultimate high and experience thrilling moments that result in peak performance. Unfortunately these relatively rare and elusive moments are difficult to repeat if they aren't fully understood. With specific knowledge of the psychological characteristics necessary to experience these moments and the mental strategies it takes to achieve them, the field of sport psychology has made what was once intangible, tangible. An athlete who possesses greater awareness of what he or she is striving for is able to bring about these magical moments with more frequency.

In the game of baseball there are managers, batting coaches, pitching coaches, and baserunning coaches. Players are provided with strength and speed specialists. They also have access to expert nutritionists, financial planners, and time management counselors. Each of these areas touches on the mental aspects of sport and life indirectly, but there is a lack of direct focus on the mental aspects of the game. Dedication to disciplining the mind as a primary function is needed. Utilizing the mental techniques and strategies of a sport psychologist is one way to fill that need.

The area of applied sport psychology has made great strides in recent years, yet this growth has been hindered because people still don't know what it is. Sport psychology has been misunderstood. To clarify, let me start by stating what sport psychology is *not*. This is not Freudian psychoanalysis. We do not lay you on a leather couch and ask you questions about your mother. This is not the Psychology 101 course you took in college and it goes far beyond Pavlov's dog. There are no sock puppets or primal scream therapies. Finally, you won't hear us ask, "Yes ... but how do you 'feeeeeel' about that?" In the field of sport psychology a cigar is just a cigar.

There is also a stigma attached to the word *psychology*. This is true especially in the world of sport where the perception of strength and mental discipline is paramount. An athlete may fear seeing a sport psychologist because it may be seen as weakness by coaches and teammates. Even worse, they may have to acknowledge some weakness in themselves.

Not only is sport psychology rooted in scientific research, it is also common sense. There is no mystery to it. In my experience I have worked with athletes ranging from professional and elite status to those with recreational interest. I have found that the higher you climb the competitive ladder, the more important the mental aspects of the game become. From traditionally American team sports like football, basketball, and baseball, to more global sports like soccer, hockey, and rugby, the athletes I work with require mental discipline to excel. With individual sports ranging from tennis and golf, to ironman and speed skating, I believe the same mental principles apply. Even in sports where there is a unique interaction between man and machine as in auto racing, or between man and beast as in equestrian events, I have realized these mental tools can be tailored to the distinct needs of any athlete in any sport.

With over ten years of formal education and over ten years of experience as a sport psychologist, I have come to believe in this simple premise: Where your mind goes your ass will follow. Sport psychology is about providing you with the mental links to athletic excellence. It helps you take advantage of the most powerful weapon you have: your mind. With access to the theories, techniques, and tools of modern sport psychology, you can better understand and improve your mental game.

As a sport psychologist, my expertise lies in the area of human performance and what I like to call "The Psychology of Excellence." The greatest barriers in our pursuit of this excellence are often psychological. Through the psychology of excellence you can break through these barriers and find the courage to follow through with your vision. With greater ability to direct your mind and inspire your passion, you can truly access the power within.

My philosophy on sport and competition may best be described by considering the myth of Prometheus. Prometheus is a figure in Greek mythology, and his name is associated with endurance and strength of will. It was written that Zeus gave Prometheus the task of creating man. In completing this task, Prometheus allowed man to stand upright, like the gods, so he could gaze upon the stars. Prometheus also lit his torch at the chariot of the sun and brought down the gift of fire to man. This fire provides us with light in the darkness and warmth in the cold. It also serves as the fire in our soul that gives us the ability to endure the human condition. We are all flawed in some way. We all struggle at times. We must all overcome obstacles. This fire allows us to survive, strive, and thrive throughout our lives. Each of us has access to this gift of fire ... but not everyone knows how to use it.

Sport is an amazing arena that can fuel this fire where it can burn brightly for all to see. I have always loved sport and always will. When you choose to compete in sport, you choose to accept a challenge, to take a risk. This is a worthy pursuit that allows us to test our own will alongside others who are testing theirs. Through this interplay of passion and determination, we are somehow better for being a part of it. When the experience is pure, those involved are given the opportunity to engage in meaningful struggle and overcome the obstacles within. Teammates have a chance to join as a unified force and rise to the occasion as one. Through competition in sport, opposing forces actually promote strength in the other and push each other to new limits.

With this challenge of competition and the spark that sport provides, you can elevate your experience and ignite your life. As a sport psychologist I appreciate the opportunity to be a part of these moments and to help bring them about.

I do what I do because competition can be a beautiful thing.

—PEDER N. PIERING

ONE

Growing Up with Baseball

Man, unlike any other thing organic or inorganic in the universe, grows beyond his work, walks up the stairs of his concepts, emerges ahead of his accomplishments. — The Grapes of Wrath

ADAM PETTYJOHN READ ABOUT the Oakland A's in the newspaper. Hailing from Exeter, a farming community in California's Central Valley, he didn't have cable TV, ESPN *SportsCenter*, or season tickets. Instead he collected and traded cards of his favorite players, memorized their statistics, and then went outside and played ball with his brothers. After his parents split when Adam was four, he and his brothers would go to visit their dad in the San Jose area. Occasionally, they'd get tickets to A's games where Adam could watch Jose Canseco and Mark McGwire tear open a game with their home runs; that was when he got his first taste of baseball's intensity and excitement.

In the Central Valley, a narrow region swelling through the heart of the state, foods such as peaches, almonds, avocados, and oranges grow in the rich, heavily irrigated soil. In the summer, temperatures can get hot, even stifling, but the winter months rarely dip below freezing. Today, nearly 40 percent of the Valley's population is Latino, second only to Los Angeles within the state. Many immigrants are able to make a decent living, moving from farm to farm as the harvest dictates. It was also a place for Adam's family to find affordable housing.

Growing up in Exeter, Adam and other kids in the neighborhood would play every kind of sport—football, basketball, baseball—and with the Valley's mild climate, they'd play year-round. In a small town, traffic was never an issue, so the streets would be their playing fields. As a young boy, Adam took a liking to baseball. His brother would catch him when he started pitching, both in baseball and as a receiver in football. At first they played pickup games in the neighborhood—games that could end as serendipitously as they

7

would begin, games regulated by peer pressure, dinner calls, and cars driving down the street.

Neighborhood games turned into Little League for Adam at age seven. The coaches he worked with were talented but did not push too much. For him Little League was pure entertainment, especially as he began excelling beyond the talents of his teammates. His brother, if anyone, pushed him to get out and take 25 more swings before quitting, and soon, with the extra practice, he began to see the difference it made in his game.

Exeter High School, which enrolled 1,200 students from four neighboring towns, was known for having a winning volleyball program, but in general all sports had a big following. This is where Adam, along with another left-handed pitcher, developed his fastball and his changeup. Ray Strebel, the high school's pitching coach who had worked with Adam during winter league, gave Adam his first glimpse of the possibility of professional baseball. During his junior and senior years, scouts came around and Adam filled out their information cards. But from the beginning he was up-front with the coaches and the scouts. "My attention was more focused on going to college and getting an education, not getting drafted," Adam recalls. "I knew I wasn't done maturing physically, I still had a lot to learn about the game, and mentally I had to get stronger."

Adam knew he had talent, though, especially when he joined a travel team and started playing guys from different parts of the country. Because Exeter was a small town, the team usually played teams no more than 30 miles away. However, the summer after Adam's senior year of high school, his team played in the AAU tournament in Florida where Adam dominated. There, Adam realized that "players in other states put their pants on one leg at a time, too."

In high school, especially as a left-handed pitcher, Adam had great success, especially his senior year, where, he says, "It seemed like every game I was flirting with a no-hitter into the sixth inning." During one game, Adam's father was sitting in the stands with his former high school coach, who said, "I've been watching your son for two or three years, and watching your son pitch this year, it's like men among boys." The other boys looked like they belonged in high school on a small-town field. For Adam, though, it was a different story, for according to the coach, "It looks like he just doesn't belong here."

About 200 miles south of Exeter, Justin Lehr grew up outside of Dodger City, but he went to more Angels games as a kid. According to Justin, "The Angels weren't as good so the tickets were cheaper."

Even though West Covina was only twenty miles east of Los Angeles—home of Hollywood, Disneyland, and A-list celebrities—the most glamorous experience he had at age five was pitching to his father in the driveway. Although his father was not a huge baseball fan, he was a fan of Justin being a fan. Justin, even if he had never played, would still have loved the game. He sat down and watched games on TV, and was always interested in the postseason. As a boy he told his father he wanted to be a professional baseball player; his father was amused but told him eventually he'd get interested in girls.

Justin's three sisters followed their own athletic pursuits. His oldest sister played men's water polo in high school, and his youngest sister went to Cal State Fullerton on a softball scholarship. Once he went pro, Justin would throw light bullpens to his youngest sister, and later her husband, who had had his own minor league stint with the Phillies.

Unlike other parts of the United States, West Covina and the Los Angeles area was flooded with baseball talent. Being drafted out of high school was not uncommon for many players; although a few played beyond college, many could claim they had played on the same teams with those who would become major league baseball players.

When he started playing travel teams and high school ball, Justin was greatly influenced by coach Mike McCarthy, someone who had played in the minors and coached half a dozen major league players throughout his career. With McCarthy, Justin first gained the notion that he really could become a professional player. McCarthy was the kind of coach who would teach every kid how to reach the highest level of his talent. Justin, who never claimed the status of phenom among his peers, appreciated how his coach valued his talent. He affirmed that Justin had a place in baseball, a belief that he would carry with him into his professional career.

A pivotal moment for Justin was at age fourteen when he received a business card from his first major league scout, an associate with the Kansas City Royals. Then he started getting letters from colleges, both because he had been noted in *Baseball America*'s list of prospects, and also because recruiters regularly scoped the area for baseball talent. He was drafted out of high school as a catcher in the 15th round, but declined the offer to take advantage of a scholarship with UCC Santa Barbara.

At this point, Justin found his family supportive of his endeavor to become a professional baseball player. They knew the idea was risky, especially since nobody else in his family had played professionally. But they also knew he had talent. His father was especially supportive. "I got the majority of my dad's down time. He would always watch me play, and he helped me out financially when he could," Justin remembers.

With family support, the uphill climb to the big leagues seemed like a much less daunting task. As a young man, Justin was ready to do whatever it would take to carve out his place in the game.

Brandon Snyder got intentionally walked all the time during his amateur days. "I would get really frustrated," he says, "because I wanted to hit."

As a boy he had problems with the Little League system. Coaches were always moving him up a level, afraid he'd hurt the other boys. And of course there were the intentional walks. "One of the Little League coaches told me I'd get intentionally walked during every at-bat. The next game that's what happened, so I just stopped going," Brandon recalls.

As an aspiring baseball player, Brandon had a bit of a head start. Some of his earliest memories were in the Oakland A's clubhouse where his father Brian played major league baseball for two years. "That was my first taste of baseball, and that's when I really fell in love with the game," Brandon says.

Throughout his father's professional career, Brandon, his older sister, and his mother would watch Brian's home games, then wait for him to come home again when he was on the road. While Brandon remembers his father being gone a lot, "he'd always bring something back for us when he returned."

Born in Las Vegas when Brian was playing with the Las Vegas Stars, Brandon experienced over ten different cities in his early life. When Brian ended his professional career in 1991, the family settled near Chantilly, Virginia. By then Brandon was five.

Northern Virginia, although not known particularly as a baseball area, has been growing in reputation during the 2000s. Although difficult to compete with areas that boast year-round baseball, especially Florida and Texas, the public school system is one of the best in the country, and with these schools come excellent baseball programs. The area is a strange mixture of old families and highly transient implants working in the progressive fields of technology, national defense, and politics. The roads are multi-laned, the traffic rated some of the worst in the nation; regardless of the high concentration of people and cars, Northern Virginia rarely feels urban. Even the drive down Pennsylvania Avenue in Washington, D.C., past the White House is hedged with rows of cherry blossoms, along with gray marble water fountains. Going out of the city, it doesn't take long to find lush green trees, fields, and far enough to the west, the Blue Ridge Mountains. This pastoral setting hosts several minor league teams—the Frederick Keys, Aberdeen Iron Birds, Potomac Nationals—and of course two major league teams, one of which (the Baltimore Orioles) drafted Brandon in the first round out of high school.

"I wasn't even thinking about it until about a month before the draft my senior year," Brandon says. "If anyone asked me, I'd tell you to go get your college education. Not because I don't think I've made the right decision, but because I don't think it's as easy for most people as I think it was for me."

Brandon grew up in a house with a professional baseball player. Likewise, he was surrounded by a tight-knit, loving family. During his youth,

Brandon's father let him make his own mistakes and then helped him learn from them. After retiring from professional baseball, Brian opened his own baseball academy, and Brandon spent most afternoons after school working out at the academy. In the offseason, professional players would come by for batting practice. As Brandon recalls, "That's how I started using wood bats from an early age. The pros would take BP and crack a bat, so I'd snatch it up. I was eight-years-old and swinging a 34-inch bat and thinking I was hot snot."

He began playing on his dad's academy team and traveled up and down the East Coast to compete. As a freshman, he started getting letters from colleges. By his junior and senior years, he was getting four or five letters a day. Before the draft he had decided to take a full ride to Louisiana State, one of numerous universities that had offered him full tuition. Ironically, his best baseball year was his freshman year, simply because he actually had a chance to hit. Once again, by the time Brandon reached his sophomore year, nobody would pitch to him, "so I started swinging at anything and started striking out. I talked to my dad to figure out what I could do."

His senior year his goal was to hit .500, regardless of the pitches he saw. In 22 games he reached his goal with some good hitting, but at the same time he walked 30 times. It was a test in patience. By his senior year he had learned to make the most of his situation, even if in his mind it wasn't ideal.

Thirty miles south of Milwaukee, Vinny Rottino grew up in Racine, a diverse working class community, situated directly on Lake Michigan's western shore. S.C. Johnson Wax, a corporation that produces cleaning lines such as Windex, provides a large number of jobs for people in the community. As a boy, Vinny played every sport he could, and loved going to the parks to play sandlot baseball or touch football with his friends. In the summers his family would go camping in Wisconsin or fly out to New York City to visit his father's relatives. After school, he would practice hitting with his father by the factory behind their house. Sometimes his father would take him to County Stadium where he watched players like Paul Molitor and Robin Yount build their reputations as baseball legends. It had always been a dream of Vinny to become a professional baseball player. If he had the opportunity, he wanted to follow his dream.

Wisconsin winters can be cold and long. For a good five months, waiting outside for the bus requires multiple layers of hats, scarves, boots, and long underwear. Children at recess go outside to play king of the hill on snow mounds, or on a Saturday afternoon chisel and pack elaborate snow forts that could withstand major seismic forces. There aren't any earthquakes in Wisconsin, though—only twisters on hot summer days when the sky turns cold, or flooding in the spring when the massive thaw finally releases and overfills sewers and streets. Spring is when kids are supposed to play baseball, and at any one point in March or April, a game could turn snowy, rainy, or just too cold for hitting. In a land of seemingly perpetual winter, 60 degrees in April feels like summer, a good occasion to fire up the grill and have some beer and brats and, of course, lots of cheese.

Not many scouts make their way through Wisconsin, though. It's too cold, for starters. Usually any sort of Wisconsin baseball talent moves out of the state as quickly as possible, aiming for an Arizona State or a University of Miami. Then there was Vinny, brimming with talent, playing on a college summer team as a junior in high school and earning all-state accolades. On a college scholarship to LaCrosse, he led the team in RBIs and home runs his junior and senior years. Loyal to Wisconsin, home and family, he didn't have serious baseball intentions until late into his college career. By then Vinny was on his way to graduating from a Division III school where only a handful of scouts had visited, mainly for the beer and brats. After his senior year when he didn't get drafted, he was on his way to the baseball afterlife. At that time one of his former coaches, Jack Schiestle, told him he should give a Brewers tryout camp a shot. Vinny felt like it was his last opportunity and he could put his mind at ease once he had done all that he could.

People who are born in Wisconsin tend to stay in Wisconsin, and because of that cherish tradition, religion, and strong family values. Those foundational beliefs keep Wisconsin strong; they also keep it somewhat unmovable, reluctant to change. So when Vinny talked to his family about becoming a baseball player rather than continuing pharmacy school, he was initially faced with reluctance. He was exchanging the opportunity for a steady income and a relatively stable future for a path that was completely uncertain. They knew he loved baseball, though, and that he still had a chance to play professionally.

After the tryout, the Brewers signed him—not necessarily because of his performance (he went 2-for-17 at the plate) but because he was a competitor and he was a teamplayer. All of Wisconsin was suddenly coming to his rescue—the hard work, the discipline, the 9-to-5ing it day in and day out, and the unpretentious, realistic attitude. His parents, mourning the passing of pharmacy school, now rejoiced with Vinny in the pursuit of his lifelong dream.

That spring, rather than being released, he was invited to play in spring training where he could work on perfecting his swing. He worked hard, taking more at-bats after practice, spending long hours on defense. He listened to his coaches, too, learning from their experience and knowledge of the game.

The next year Vinny made it to rookie ball; he had transformed his swing and put up some great numbers. Through his unlikely start, he proved that baseball, perhaps unlike any other game, is achievable even for the player who is not loaded with talent. "This is probably the most incredible thing about baseball—you can make yourself into a major league player," Vinny says about his experience. "Obviously there's some baseline of talent you have to have, but basically if you work your tail off, you can make yourself into a major league player. There's a number of players who have done that."

For him, 2004 was only the beginning of the hardest work he had ever done. Still, it was baseball. To Vinny, it was worth it.

For many players, the years of growing up with baseball can be some of the most endearing. A young person is free to say something like, "I want to be a major league baseball player" and still draw admiration rather than scorn. Usually those players destined for pro ball dominate on their teams when they are young, and so learn to enjoy praise and affirmation when they are playing. For young people, baseball can be a pure passion, one untainted by financial concerns or politics.

Not until they get older will young players begin to realize some of the pressures they will face when they try to pursue a baseball career. According to Justin Lehr, "There are so many challenges for somebody trying to play baseball. It's easy to look at the money and the glamour—but very few guys even get that far."

Before experiencing what it is really like, many young people want to rush into baseball careers if they think they have the talent. Their desire is admirable, but those in the game know that desire alone cannot fulfill their dreams. As Ted Power, the pitching coach for the Reds' AAA affiliate, states, "Many guys think it's just about talent. If you've grown up with the talent, then you can make it to the big leagues. Really, it's so much more than talent."

Obviously, physical talent does play a significant role in a player's success. Very few people, especially left-handers, can throw five pitches with accuracy like Randy Johnson. Few people can compete with Carl Crawford's speed or Prince Fielder's power. These players won their spots and kept them because of their physical talent.

Yet, what many young people cannot perceive, especially as they are still waiting to experience the range of hardships life has to offer, are the mental challenges of the game.

Most people agree that baseball is one of the most mentally challenging sports. Anyone who has grown up with baseball, intimately familiar with the landscape of nine innings, recognizes how the game can play with the mind. Players have so much down time. Every three outs they go back to the dugout; for three hours they stand in the outfield, sometimes only making one or two plays. The mind can wander.

Likewise, players use deception in baseball to gain an advantage. A pitcher's curveball could come in looking high, but dive at the last second to be strike three. A baserunner could fake to second, but then really run on the next pitch, fooling the pitcher. Deception is one of baseball's essential strategies, yet it can become confusing and frustrating, turning the mind in on itself.

Another reason baseball is so mentally challenging is because failure, rather than achievement, is often highlighted. A pitcher's ERA indicates how many times he failed to keep the hitters from scoring; a player's one mis-step—an E6—gets carved into the record books, not his ten other successful plays.

For somebody to develop into a great baseball player, he must learn how to control his mind, something that can often be a player's worst enemy. Ironically, baseball has been a game that has not prepared players for mental performance.

Justin Lehr has experienced this throughout his pitching career: "Say you've had a bad game, the first thing the coach is going to say is let's go take some swings. The reality is, I don't know how much of that is a problem. Everything steers back to maintaining mechanical adjustments because that's what people know. They never really deal with what I think is the biggest problem. When you have no confidence, ultimately that is a bigger problem than mechanics."

Very few players are willing to admit when they struggle with confi-dence, and even fewer coaches are willing to address such a taboo subject. For somebody like Justin, his love of the game pushed him to seek the counsel of a sport psychologist. "It's like another coach, but he knows how to help you deal with the struggles you're having in your mind," says Justin. But he quickly learned that the term "psychologist" could be misleading to many people.

Contrary to popular belief, players who consult sport psychologists or performance enhancement coaches don't need "fixing." They don't neces-sarily have to have a problem in order to work on improving their mental game. For many players who resist dealing with the mental aspect of the game, though, seeing a sport psychologist is a last resort. "There's a stigma attached to it," says Vinny Rottino, who also worked with a sport psychologist when he was with the Brewers. "Guys think that they will be admitting that they are weak."

Stigma or not, athletes in today's society face some of the toughest men-tal pressure of any profession, mainly because of the American idea that winning is everything. The cultural mindset promotes that only one winner is possible, so everyone else must fall into the category of "loser." Along with the victory of athletic competition, society links "winning" with wealth, status, attractiveness, and popularity—all indicators of a successful person, someone who is acceptable to society. For most people operating under these definitions, success will be largely unattainable. In fact, much of what we see as "winning" or "success" is contrived through endless highlight reels. The media and today's technology condition people to skip to the "good parts," seek immediate gratification, and affix on athletes' top moments. In reality, the "good parts" are few and far between. People who attempt to achieve the glory of highlight reels will never be satisfied, because they are chasing an illusion.

To counteract society's message, athletes should strive to develop disciplined minds, ultimately a way of thinking that cannot be challenged by society's perspective. A disciplined mind goes beyond what some players call "mental toughness," which often boils down to suppressing emotion or working harder. Developing a disciplined mind begins when an athlete acknowledges the presence and power of his non-physical self—his mind, his spirit, and his emotions. He adapts his thinking so that he can approach competition, and life, with confidence and optimism. When a person is confident, he believes in his athletic abilities, thereby generating a positive view of himself. He understands his capabilities and believes he can perform a certain skill successfully. In this sense, he has control over his performance and can expect the best possible outcome. If he is optimistic, he will focus on the most hopeful aspects of a situation.

Over time and with practice, an athlete can develop a confident mindset. With this mindset, he can approach competition with an "I can and I will" attitude. He will begin to look for situations, rather than avoid them, in which he can rise to the challenge. Even if these situations threaten failure, he can be optimistic by recognizing and seizing opportunities found in the moment. Likewise, he can come away from competition with a positive outlook, a mindset that allows him to use what he learned to directly impact his future.

To build confidence, though, a player must be willing to subject himself to moments of adversity, moments that most people tend to avoid. According to Vinny Rottino, "If you go up to bat in a clutch situation and you think, 'I really hope I don't strike out,' you're already handicapping yourself. Your body has the tendency to do what your mind is thinking."

Aside from helping in game situations, a disciplined mind can aid a player in the "rest" of the game, as well—the social pressures and lifestyle challenges he will face. Many players aiming for a major league career come from relatively typical, middle class American families. Nobody in their family has been famous, wealthy, or ever done an interview on TV. Yet, these young people may become celebrities very quickly, handed millions of dollars before they've even had to work long hours to pay off a home mortgage. They have to grow accustomed to being watched, no longer by a few bleacher rows of fans, but upwards of 40,000 people. They are criticized and heckled, always expected to earn every penny of their inflated salaries.

More often than not, the events off the field will keep an athlete from achieving his dreams on the field. Although a narrow margin of players reach the "good life" of big league play, 99 percent of players fight through minor league conditions in order to be given a shot. These conditions include a low salary, long hours traveling, long hours traveling by *bus*, and being away from home.

When they turn pro, much of the affirmation of their youth vanishes as coaches and managers only see players in one of two ways: in or out. For some players this may be the first time their athletic ability has been challenged, and they struggle to cope. For years, they have had success at their sport, and either consciously or subconsciously they have learned to define themselves based on their athletic performance. When they experience failure for the first time, their confidence can be shaken to the core, especially if they have nothing else (relationships, interests, or beliefs) to define who they are. This is especially true of elite athletes who often times have been dominant throughout high school, college, and even most of the minor leagues. Since they don't understand how failure feels, they have no tools for coping with failure.

This is why it is important for athletes who are so immersed in their sport to develop an identity beyond baseball.

Steve Shenbaum, director of Game On, a media training and communication company, works with elite athletes to develop a self that exists outside the game.

"The biggest challenge for players who are preparing for the draft is that they spend the majority of their time becoming the best players they can be, so there's not a lot of time to practice day-to-day life skills," says Shenbaum. "They miss out on the skills that 'civilians' practice on a daily basis. And the first thing that goes is the quality time it takes for them to build self-awareness, to develop their minds and their lives beyond their sport."

To help players bridge this gap, Shenbaum has them engage in what he calls "continuing education," which might include looking at the day's news headlines on their laptop or reading a book or magazine — something a little more than playing a video game, yet a little less than reading *War and Peace*.

"These guys have great lives *aside from baseball* that they sometimes forget about," Shenbaum notes. "They travel to Europe, they speak three different languages, they are the oldest of four brothers, they just got married, they love to hunt. I try to get them to gather these other parts of their lives, and to turn to them, especially when baseball becomes a grind."

Another often times puzzling aspect of professional baseball is the fact that it is a business. This can be emotionally challenging, especially for young players who have risen through the ranks of Little League and travel teams, forming loyalties and friendships that they think will last a lifetime. In pro ball, team loyalty and friendship play a major role in players' lives and business on the field; however, a player must be cautious not to get too attached to anyone or any team.

Adam Pettyjohn, who has played on seven different teams in his eleven-year professional career, learned within his first two years that it isn't worth it to pay attention to the front office: "You have no control of whether they trade you, release you, promote you, demote you. The quicker you figure out you have no control, the better off you are."

An organization's decision to trade or release a player *may* have to do with a player's talent. At the same time, an organization may trade a player whom they would like to keep, but they need a player who can play a different position. Sometimes teams acquire a surplus of catchers or relievers, but they need a good center fielder. A player who has been traded often has no idea what goes on behind the curtain.

According to Adam, the organization that traded you rarely even contacts you: "The new GM who acquired you will call you up and welcome you. The old organization doesn't even call you. To them, the trade's done and they're looking for their new player to come in."

In reality, players who try to figure out the system often end up being frustrated or bitter. They begin to think they understand how certain people think or feel about them, solely based on their perceptions. This can be a dangerous mindset, especially because people's perceptions are often inaccurate, frequently projections of their own insecurities. Likewise, this sort of thinking can lead to compulsive behaviors. As Adam says, "Too many guys read all the papers and all the team web sites. All that does is cause you stress and makes you depressed if you're struggling. The only thing that does is work you out of the game because you're trying to control something that is out of your control."

Compulsively searching the internet or reading the headlines reinforces negative thinking, creating a vicious cycle that becomes more and more difficult to break. A player's motive may be natural—he wants answers—but the answers aren't "out there." Rather, the athlete should focus on controlling what he can control—that is, his own mind.

The other aspect of the business of baseball lies in the draft picks an organization makes. In a perfectly democratic game, every player should have an equal opportunity to develop his talent and rise to the big leagues. For the most part this is true. Until you talk about first-round or second-round draft picks.

According to Brian Snyder, whose son Brandon was tempted away from college with a $1.7-million signing bonus, an organization's top draft picks will be given more opportunity to succeed: "It's human nature. Everybody can say they want to give everybody an equal chance, but your future as an organization is based on how well your draft picks do."

So did his son deserve the Orioles' first-round pick?

"Now Brandon has a certain amount of pressure to prove everybody right," Brian says. "But I don't think anybody would ever doubt that Brandon would be a good player and a good teammate. The team has to ask if the player is going to continue to be driven, even after he thinks he's arrived. Brandon is very focused on what he wants to do."

It can be frustrating for some players (those who aren't first-round picks) to see preference given to players like Brandon. The best players, however, do not let what they see as "unfair conditions" taint their desire and ability to achieve. Everyone naturally would like to encounter ideal conditions in life; however, a pursuit for ideal conditions can become someone's excuse for why he has not realized his potential. Every player needs to work within the circumstances he's given. Coaches do treat players differently; and athletes efforts and achievements are not always recognized; and the breaks of the game do seem to favor the opposition. Coming to grips with this and learning to stay composed is one of sport's many valuable lessons. A responsible attitude, even amid "unfair" conditions, will impress coaches and managers far more than a draft selection.

Brandon, likewise, understands this reality: "Just because you're a first rounder doesn't mean you'll make it to the major leagues. And it certainly doesn't mean you'll stay there. You have to earn it."

Regardless of many challenges and roadblocks along the way, professional baseball can yield many great rewards, not only for players, but also for fans and other staff involved with the game.

So what exactly is it about the game of baseball that people find so intriguing? The game is a form of entertainment, a creative pursuit, even an art. People tend to get uncomfortable, though, discussing sports and art in the same sentence, generally because the traits associated with each group seem to be diametrically opposed. The artist is the person who is misunderstood by society—strange, spontaneous, and visionary. The athlete, on the other hand, fulfills the prototypical figure in society—physically well-formed, liked by peers, admired for qualities of teamwork and courage. Although many of these ideas that people hold about artists and athletes may be true, both groups originate from the same bloodline. Artists and athletes both exist in order to entertain and enrich the lives of others; they really have no practical purpose whatsoever, and if they all disappeared overnight, society would still be able to eat, perform surgeries, and remove trash on a regular basis. But we like to watch *CSI*, read a John Grisham book, and play fantasy football for one simple reason: we like to play. Not only do we like to play, but we need to play. According to Melinda Wenner in "The Serious Need for Play," adults as well as children need a certain amount of play in their lives: "Adults who do not play may end up unhappy and exhausted without understanding exactly why" (Wenner, p. 29). Without relaxation and a verifiable "pastime," people tend to be less effective in their work and their lives lack a depth and richness that entertainment provides.

Apart from the many kids involved in group sports, many adults enjoy the "play" of sports vicariously. That is, they watch, discuss, analyze, coach — but do not perform. That does not mean, however, that all the benefits go to the players, and those sitting around talking about them go home empty-handed. Watching a sport is equivalent to reading a book or watching a movie. You don't have to be a writer or an actor in order to appreciate those forms of entertainment. You probably enjoy them in a different way from the "artists" (including athletes) who perform, but, clearly, you become engaged and connected. If this weren't the case, people wouldn't throw things at the TV when a six-foot-something college basketball player in March misses a free throw.

Watching, rather than participating, can be a pleasurable experience because, especially for adults, it provides an opportunity to watch life unfold without having to put forth any effort, at least for a certain amount of time. The other minor twist on the situation, though, is that the "life" of the game is not really life. Although the game resembles real life, and it's filled with people who lead real lives and look and act like the rest of us (for the most part), it is still contrived, a mere imitation of the gears and cogs of each day. The game is like looking at the room you see in the mirror, rather than looking at the room itself. It is slightly separated from reality, and because of that, it gives us the opportunity to reflect and compare the situation to real-life circumstances. After all, the game tinkers with people's emotions. How many times has someone left a losing game with a heavy heart, all because of a bat and a ball and some leather gloves? It's the same feeling you get on a Sunday night, with Monday coming in only a few short hours to signal the weekend's over.

One more reason it is good for people to enjoy entertainment is that we can learn to appreciate something beautiful. Beauty is hardly limited to super-models and red roses. Really, beauty amounts to representing something in its truest form. In the case of sports, especially professional sports, athletes represent what Howard Gardner refers to as "kinesthetic intelligence" in its truest form. Their natural way of learning and experiencing the world is through their bodies. It is an intelligence that proves useful in the trades, in the laboratory, and in the operating room, as well. For athletes, though, they are using their bodily intelligence for no good purpose other than to express the beauty of the human form and its physical capabilities. We may "pretend" athletes have a purpose (e.g., to hit a home run or pickoff the runner on first), but it only matters within the context of the game. What matters beyond the context of the game, though, is the beauty of physical intelligence. Especially when that physical intelligence breaks down (e.g., when somebody dislocates a shoulder or pulls a muscle), we can appreciate what a gift it is.

With all these benefits to society, we have to believe that professional baseball players are doing something right. At the same time, what they're doing is not easy. From a young age, serious baseball players have had to make decisions that young people typically do not need to make. Players also have to learn how to make sacrifices in order to keep their baseball dream alive.

Kyle Weldon plays baseball at Miami University in Ohio and has realized from a young age the additional sacrifices he needs to make in order to be serious about his sport. Those sacrifices include taking care of his body, getting enough sleep, eating well, and avoiding alcohol and drugs.

At Miami University, the coach reinforces the message that his players should make smart choices in their free time. Many players listen to the message, but not all of them. "It's important to get the team leaders on track with making smart decisions," Kyle acknowledges. "If they start doing stuff on the weekends, then other guys are going to feel pressure to do it, too."

For Kyle, sometimes the best way for him to avoid the temptation is to take the 45-minute drive home on the weekends. It was the same way for him at the high school he attended in Cincinnati. In order to make the right decisions for his career, he had to be selective in his social life: "I had a batting T set up in the garage. Sometimes if I knew there was a party with drinking, I'd stay home and work on hitting."

The friends he's chosen, many of them fellow teammates, hold each other accountable, too.

"Some guys can handle going out two or three nights a week and still perform well on the field," Kyle says. "Many guys can't, and when they do stupid stuff, it's going to show in their game."

When Brandon Snyder decided on a career in baseball his sophomore year in high school, he too had to make the decision to devote most of his time to baseball rather than partying with his friends. By the time he graduated, most of his friendships shifted from high-school friends to baseball friends, the people with whom he spent the majority of his time. Did this come as a sacrifice to him? "At first a lot of people criticized me. But eventually they saw the reason for it."

Both Brandon and Kyle attribute strong family support as a major factor in helping them make the right decisions. At the same time, they have both developed close relationships with teammates and coaches who share their values and goals. According to Brandon, "As long as I can take care of what I need to do, take care of my body, take care of my business and play baseball, I can have a lot more fun that doesn't include all of that stuff."

Those decisions can be difficult for anyone, let alone young people, to make. And yet those decisions only mark the tip of an iceberg of challenges people face when they pursue a career in baseball. For somebody who has grown up with baseball, and who sees a professional career in his future, he will not be daunted by the many challenges. Rather, the challenges fuel his energy.

Vinny Rottino is an example of a player who has thrived amid the struggles of the game: "Baseball is unlike any other game because it's a game of failure. It's something that really tests your confidence, and even players with less than record-breaking talent can be winners if they believe in themselves. It's a sport where you can be as good as you want to be with incredible amounts of work and desire and passion."

Baseball is a game, too, where sometimes appearances can be deceiving. When Dustin Pedroia, the Red Sox's second-round draft pick in 2004, came to his first big league camp, teammate Gabe Kapler recalled how unimpressive Pedroia looked: 5'8", a little out of shape, with somewhat of an ugly swing. Regardless, when Kapler watched Pedroia on the field, he could tell the only message going through the kid's head was that "I'm the best player out on this field." Pedroia's confidence defined his game, and he now holds several awards, including Rookie of the Year (2007) and MVP (2008).

Such confidence can be breathtaking—for some people it is a gift, a genetic predisposition combined with a certain upbringing. For others, confidence may not come easily, or they may struggle to maintain confidence on a day-to-day basis. In either case, players regularly will face moments that will give them reason to doubt their ability. The confident player, then, is not necessarily someone who always "wins" or dominates in his performance (although this could be the result of a confident attitude). Rather, confidence consists of a way of thinking, how somebody responds to certain moments. Although game situations will fluctuate, a player's confidence should not waver. The best way for a player to maintain a confident attitude in every situation is to treat every opportunity as important, not just "when it really matters." In a confident player's mind, every moment matters, from the first inning to the ninth, from the first game of spring training to Game Seven of the World Series. That way he establishes a routine—he can make batting practice the same as a ninth-inning, game-winning at-bat. When he sees those situations the same way, he relieves his mind from the pressure that game situations can impose.

Baseball is a game that proves again and again how powerful the mind can be. Often times it proves this power in a negative sense. For instance, Justin Lehr sees the power of the mind at work in pitching, sometimes with amusing results: "My favorite is when a pitcher hits a batter. You realize how strong your mind is because he's thinking, 'Don't hit this guy again.' Then the next pitch he smokes him. How does that happen? You're thinking, 'Don't hit this guy' and your arm goes right towards him."

In order to achieve peak performance, a player must learn how to control his mind. Because he hears so many different messages from a variety of sources—the media, family, and fans—a player must proactively speak to himself with productive messages. He must first begin by acknowledging his own voice, and identify the messages he is communicating to himself. According to Trevor Moawad, director of the Performance Institute at IMG Academy, "Athletes at the subconscious level, twenty-four hours a day, are advertising to themselves at 400–1,000 words a minute, sending messages like 'I can't do this, I can't believe I'm having these issues.' They're basically running their own campaign in their mind." If this campaign is negative, then their thoughts will hinder their ability to succeed. Taking control of these negative thoughts can be the first step to success for many athletes.

This was a step Justin Lehr took early in his career. Justin says learning how to manage his thinking made a powerful impact on his success on the mound: "When I'm having a bad outing, the game sort of speeds up in my mind. Thoughts pop into my head like, 'Wow, I gave up a three-run homer to this guy, I'm going to lose.' These thoughts can overwhelm you when you're trying to perform at a high level. Something I learned, though, is that these thoughts are normal. It's a waste of time for me to try to stop these thoughts from coming. What I learned instead was how to deal with these thoughts when they entered my head."

This is a technique Moawad teaches to athletes at IMG Academy: "For one negative thought, you need to counteract it with ten positive thoughts. When an athlete takes control of that simple step—when he stops criticizing himself—then he can have success."

This is a lesson for anyone, not just baseball players, and yet it can be one of the most challenging steps for a person to take. We have a tendency to compare ourselves to others, to want what they have, and believe that "what you see is what you get." Yet the human mind, as well as the will and ability to perform, is much more complex than how TV shows and movies portray it.

Baseball, too, is complex—not just the innings and the pitches, but the promotions and the demotions, the looks and the releases. At first glance, being a major league baseball player may seem to be anyone's dream come true. In many ways it is. But it can also be a person's greatest test, a constant pressure to perform and compete. The rewards can be phenomenal. But what does it feel like once you've made your last play or thrown your last pitch? In the words of Scott Sanderson, who had an eighteen-year career as a major league pitcher, "It was a relief."

Two

Getting Noticed

How do you know you're going to do something, until you do it?—The Catcher in the Rye

EVEN THOUGH BASEBALL played an important role in Adam Pettyjohn's life, he tried to maintain a balanced perspective. At age seventeen he was a pitcher with a lot of promise, but he could also see himself earning a teaching degree, eventually teaching at the college level where he could also coach on the side. Baseball was his passion, but he also held it loosely as one of the many possibilities—the possibility with the least guarantee. As Adam says, "My parents always emphasized the importance of education. If I could play baseball, great. But I needed to get a decent education."

With that in mind, Adam never pressed himself to find opportunities for baseball. In fact, he told his high school coach to turn away pro scouts. He knew he wanted to go to college. "I had a lot more developing to do, physically and emotionally. I knew I wasn't ready for pro ball," Adam says. Rather than fearing he might go unnoticed, Adam continued to do what he did best—play ball—and worked on developing as a person and a player before he took on the burden of planning his career.

Still, he knew the realities of the game. Players like Alex Rodriguez had to do very little to get noticed. But for somebody from Exeter, Adam would need to work a little harder if he wanted to earn a spot. As he recalls, "I just knew I had to do first things first. It wasn't worth worrying about all of that when I wasn't ready to play anyway." Adam knew better than to look for promises that he had no reason to believe would come true. Instead, he needed to focus on each day, the here and now, pitch by pitch.

When Adam played, he knew that the scouts were around. He'd see them behind home plate when he pitched, clocking his speed. When his travel team began taking him down the coast, closer to Los Angeles, more scouts would appear. College recruiters were around, too, representing prestigious programs at Stanford, Fullerton, Pepperdine, and UCLA.

He knew that he was going up against some of the best baseball talent in the state and that baseball coaches had fewer than twenty scholarships to distribute to their teams. Sometimes pitchers got full rides, but they usually threw harder stuff than Adam did.

Another option Adam considered was playing at a junior college. The program might not be as glamorous as some of the UC schools, but it would be smaller, which meant he could pitch more often. He could work towards a degree and transfer, or, if he got drafted, turn pro. A lot of baseball players went the community college route to buy some time before going pro; unlike at a four-year college, they didn't have to wait until junior year to get drafted.

"It's a tough decision to make," Adams says. There are so many different ways you can go, and you want to pick the one that's right for you."

The same scouts who saw Adam also looked at Justin Lehr who lived closer to Los Angeles. When he played in high school, scouts would get a look at him while they were considering older players who were eligible for the draft. Justin, like many of his friends, had his sights set on pro ball. He realized from an early age that living in southern California, he had an advantage. "My parents were involved in helping me get noticed, but coming from the LA area, it wasn't really difficult to draw attention," Justin says.

Over the years, California has produced major league baseball talent, including legendary players Randy Johnson, Ted Williams, Barry Bonds, Tony Gwynn, Jim Edmonds, and C.C. Sabathia. In many ways, California is baseball's promised land, filled with wealth and opportunity.

Because California is so rich in talent, the area is filled with hitting facilities, academies, and camps. Many of these facilities are run by former players and provide individual work for athletes who hope to distinguish themselves.

Another benefit to California: it's a year-round baseball state. Players don't just have to rely on warm, summer weather to keep honing their skills. In December through March, temperatures range from 59 to 79 degrees and although occasionally rainy, conditions still support relatively regular play.

Although Justin's parents were supportive of his pursuit of baseball, they didn't go to extreme measures to prepare him for the game. He attended college camps in the summers, but beyond that developed his baseball skills through his high school and community-based teams. According to Justin, "You really just need good coaching, and you don't necessarily have to pay big money to get that. Parents can go way over the top with paid lessons. They don't know enough about the sport, or think their kid's going to be the next Babe Ruth."

The other thing a player needs is determination. Never a night went by when Justin wasn't outside, throwing pitches, swinging the bat, taking ground balls. Although he would funnel into a pitching role eventually, when he was young he learned every aspect of the game, and at one point did more catching than pitching. Baseball was an after-school constant, a summer obsession. From an early age, it had become a way of life.

Brandon Snyder's home, Northern Virginia, was not a year-round baseball community, and the talent wasn't as deep as the Southern states. Still, it was an area of opportunity, mainly because of the quality, attractive baseball programs sprinkled throughout the region. Although not a baseball metropolis, players still had access to top competition from other regions.

Brandon played on a competitive team at Westfield High School, where players were routinely drafted or earned scholarships at Division I colleges. Because many families were interested in and able to provide opportunities for their children, the area was rich with independent travel teams and baseball academies. Players serious about baseball attended showcases in Florida, Georgia, and Texas.

Brandon realized he did not have a typical experience growing up, either as a boy in his father's clubhouse or as a teen at his father's hitting facility. In part, he was already on the radar because of his father's career. As he recalls, "I consider myself extremely lucky—not everybody has the opportunities I had."

He didn't attend a lot of showcases because he didn't need to. Scouts knew about Brandon already for years. To get a full ride to college, all he had to do was play baseball the way he did. "My dad made me fill out every questionnaire," Brandon says. It was a respect thing. You show them respect because you never know if the coach at Lee High Valley Community College will be the coach at LSU next year."

Brandon also received attention from professional scouts, at least one from every major league team. He filled out their paperwork and completed psychological evaluations for a majority of them, some that consisted of hundreds of questions. At age seventeen, Brandon was more preoccupied with professional opportunities than most adults are ten years into their careers. The details never wore him down, though; to him it was part of the fun.

Vinny Rottino knew that good baseball was limited by good weather. Unlike other outdoor sports, baseball requires certain weather conditions in order for the ball to be visible, and the field playable. So much of the game depends on mechanics and technique, which is why historically baseball originated as a summer sport.

In Wisconsin, summers are beautiful, but they steal in and out so quickly. Players like Vinny were limited to a much shorter playing season, which meant fewer games of baseball, fewer throws, fewer hits, and fewer opportunities. There's a reason year-round states like California produce the largest percentage of professional baseball players each year. Yet, to exclude cold-weather states would be limiting. Players like Curtis Granderson, Jayson

Werth, Joe Mauer, and Jason Jaramillo are just a few of the players who got their first looks in states like Minnesota, Wisconsin, Illinois, and Michigan.

Where he grew up in Racine, Vinny played as much baseball as he could, but that usually amounted to about thirty games a year. He, too, had good coaches, and they also had connections, mostly regional and at the college level. Getting noticed in Wisconsin was tougher and, compared to other parts of the country, a lot more rare. As Vinny says, "Wisconsin is not a hotbed of baseball. You look at how many major league players are from Wisconsin and it's just a handful."

In cold-weather states, players have to rely on indoor facilities to stay in the game when the snow flies. In Vinny's case, he threw himself into multiple sports to build his strength and athleticism. Still, baseball was the sport he was most passionate about.

"My dad loved baseball and that rubbed off on me," Vinny remembers. "He grew up in the Bronx and watched Mickey Mantle play, and he loved following the Brewers, too."

Even though geographically his chances weren't as good, Vinny believed that players who had talent would get looks, no matter where they lived. He didn't concern himself with showcases and scouts, but just worked hard at playing on the teams in his community, which in the summers included American Legion ball and community recreational leagues. He believed that there were many different roads people took to make it to the major leagues. In his hometown community of Racine, he believed that he was taking one of those roads.

Getting noticed as an athlete can be a frustrating, exhausting process. To complicate matters, it is a process that must be broached by teenagers who are already going through a host of adjustments physically, emotionally, and socially. Although talent, naturally, is a deciding factor of whether a player gets signed, many people in the game would acknowledge that luck or being in the right place at the right time can be equally as important. Because of this uncertain element, more and more people today, especially those not well connected to the game, invest a great deal of time and money into the process of getting noticed. In some cases, players, because they (or their families) are so preoccupied with marketing their talents, enjoy less time exploring the game, relaxing, and having fun. Baseball is a serious business now for many teenagers, a pursuit that has changed the lifestyles and values of many families, and that will continue to enforce incredible pressure on those considering a life in the game.

Pursuing a creative career can be extremely challenging, and baseball is no exception. The demand for talent is always much lower than the supply, making most creative fields highly competitive. At the same time, opportunity is limited by society's ability to accommodate leisure, relaxation, and the meaningful reflection cultivated by the arts. Employment is sporadic, frequently pays very little, and can be accompanied by poor working or living conditions.

So what is the best approach for someone to take who wishes to pursue a career in baseball?

Those who are in the game have gone through differing experiences based on a variety of factors: where they live, how talented they are, and what year they started playing. In professional baseball, opportunities have always been available for those with talent and a good work ethic; yet, the culture of competitive sports has gained such incredible momentum in the past two decades that many players and families are turning towards the private sector to cultivate and showcase their talent. After all, there is a lot of money involved in the form of scholarship dollars or signing bonuses, and many parents find the cost of lessons, time, and travel a worthy investment that they will eventually reap a return on. Realistically, however, "95 percent of people don't get anything out of baseball financially," according to Justin Lehr. Ironically, the other 5 percent earn more than enough to feed a small country, or several small countries. That's the game within the game of baseball, and nobody's particularly complaining.

But as the competitive sports industry continues to gobble up family dollars, the grassroots, community-based teams are at risk. The other thing at risk, some would argue, is our children's childhoods. The Tiger Woods story is inspiring, very American and self-made. Yet Tiger Woods, like Ghandi or the Beatles, is somewhat exceptional. Today, more and more people want to be the exception. That drive to be the best athlete of this generation has placed a great deal of strain on children and their families; it also has changed the look of the game and what steps players have to take to get noticed today.

Rick Saggese, a baseball coach and mentor who works with kids in Naples, Florida, sees firsthand the pressure some teenagers are under to succeed in the game. According to Saggese, "Baseball has become a global sport now, not just America's pastime. You're competing against a much bigger pool of players than you were twenty years ago. If players want to make it to the next level, they need to market themselves."

For most high school kids, attending multiple showcases is an important step in the marketing process. At showcases, they are able to display for both college and professional scouts their "tools"—hitting (for power and average), baserunning, fielding, and throwing. Saggese, who operates a baseball facility called Think Outside the Diamond, recommends that his clients who want to play college ball attend two to five showcases after their sophomore year. When he had played high school ball in the early '90s, college recruiters showed up at games in order to watch prospects play. Now, they only attend the games of players they know are rated as top prospects. Other players who hope to have a chance need to go to the showcases in order to draw their attention.

For some players and families, showcases have provided great opportunities; they are a tangible step parents can take to help their child succeed. Many parents look at the dollars they spend on showcases (at least $500 per showcase, not including travel expenses and lodging) as an investment into their child's future.

This is how it worked for Patrick Arnold, drafted in the 15th round in 2007 out of high school by the Washington Nationals. Arnold states, "Let's put it this way—if I hadn't attended [showcases], I probably wouldn't have been drafted."

Patrick's dream to play baseball was shaped both by his love of the game as well as his battle with cancer from infancy. Although the doctors were able to remove the cancerous tumor when he was a baby, his parents steered him away from rough contact sports like football or hockey that could have posed health risks. He started working on baseball from a young age, and his father, who had played college baseball and served a career with the marines, helped Patrick structure his workouts. As Patrick recalls, "He taught me that when you do something, you do it perfectly." That meant Patrick didn't get his allowance until he did his baseball activities; he had to keep his school grades up, as well.

When he underwent a series of additional surgeries at age thirteen, the doctors told him he would never be able to pursue baseball as a career. For Patrick, that only fueled his determination to get bigger and stronger, and to play at the next level.

Similarly, Adam Moore, a 6th round pick for the Seattle Mariners in 2006, relied on showcases to advance his career. Many of the showcases he attended were hosted by Northeast Texas Community College, a junior college Adam attended on a scholarship out of high school. "At every showcase, there were about 20 college scouts, 40–50 pro scouts," Adam remembers. "Showcases are very big in people's careers." For Moore, showcases helped him secure a scholarship so that he could continue playing college ball, and get in position for a professional draft in a few years.

Moore also worked out at D-Bat Baseball Academy near his home in Dallas, Texas; it was through the academy that he learned about many of the showcases. Many baseball academies have travel teams that players can join in order to play more competitive baseball and increase their chances of getting noticed.

Although showcases, academies, and travel teams have become the path of many families in America today, they can put a lot of strain on the family as well as the player. Young people are being pushed like never before, primarily because of the money at stake. Colleges and private corporations have taken advantage of parents' desire to give their children every chance, and so the showcases they organize have become tremendous money-making opportunities. As youth baseball leans towards the business rather than the non-profit model, the powers-that-be bring completely different interests to the experience. They may believe in the "greater good" as non-profit organizations do, but they also believe in financial opportunity.

Jay Coakley, professor of sociology at Colorado State University and author of definitive textbook *Sports in Society*, sees the showcase model as a "win win" situation for many people, including the businesses that coordinate them. According to Coakley, "The entrepreneur makes money, the players get seen, the colleges and teams save money on recruiting."

Yet, this trend, fueled by dollars, excludes underprivileged talent; it puts in motion a widening divide between families who can afford to fund their child's opportunity and those who cannot.

For those families who are in the business of creating a superstar, the dynamics of their family life become influenced, consciously or subconsciously, by the money at stake. Sports, for these families, *must* be a priority. Coakley comments: "More of the everyday lives of families are revolving around sport participation than ever before. These are often times not enjoyable times—it is traveling to and from practices and tournaments. Sometimes you get a nice vacation with it, but often times it's just tedious."

According to Coakley, much of the reason for the trend lies in parents' motives to be "good" parents according to contemporary cultural definitions. A good parent is somebody who designs his child's future, sometimes in spite of society. It's up to parents to advocate the interests of their child and provide their child with ample opportunities to succeed. If parents are unable to provide their child a shot at his dream, then somehow they have failed as parents.

Coakley goes so far as to say that parents are using sports as a site for establishing their moral worth. "All of a sudden they feel that it's their moral obligation to go to every tournament regardless of whether they have the money," Coakley says. "They're scratching by on other things, sacrificing things maybe related to academic development, so they can get to the tournament."

Although these motives may appear admirable, it is important for parents to allow their children to develop a sense of ownership over their sport. Without ownership, an athlete, especially at the elite level, will be vulnerable to burnout.

Brian Snyder and his wife made significant sacrifices of time and money so their boys could develop into baseball players, and yet they tried to provide their children with an environment that was optional, something they could embrace or decline.

"It's easy for me to say that the money doesn't matter because my kids have done well," Brian says. "Families have to make big sacrifices, though. We traveled for nine consecutive years, and all of our family vacations were centered on baseball. But we never did all that to get a scholarship. If you're going to do that, why don't you go up to Atlantic City and put your money on black or red."

In Brian's mind, parents cannot look at their investment into athletics as a deposit on a much larger return: "If you're focused on the money you're spending, that pressure trickles down to the kids' shoulders, and that becomes a very bad situation. The whole purpose of why we did it was to help our sons follow their passion. We wanted them in an environment with other kids who are like-minded and goal-oriented. We felt that was a healthy learning process that is going to help them throughout life."

Not all families, though, take such an idealistic approach to their child's sports. When they invest in teams, lessons, and tournaments, parents want their efforts to pay dividends in the end.

In his book *Game On: The All-American Race to Make Champions of Our Children*, Tom Farrey writes about the extent to which some parents will go to ensure their child has a chance to make the team or, in many cases, secure the college scholarship. One family he followed in Concord, Massachusetts, spent more than $10,000 a year per twin on ice hockey even though they were only seven-years-old.[1] Although theirs was an extreme case, it cannot be denied that in today's youth sports culture, parents have to put out regular amounts of cash in order to give their child a chance.

In reality, the chance of a high school athlete becoming a professional in any sport is less than 1 in 10,000. In light of this, a career in a professional sport, or even participation at the college level, is an unrealistic goal for the majority of young athletes. There is nothing wrong with an athlete setting these goals and pursuing them—in fact, it is important to dream big and be creative when he's young—but it is critical for a young person to realize that sport only occupies a portion of his life. Other aspects of life—making friends, achieving in school, growing spiritually, and spending time with family—create a healthy balance in a person's character.

Although some people would argue kids should devote their energy to studying rather than playing, it cannot be denied that sports provide many valuable lessons that the classroom lacks. In sports, people can learn about the world and where they fit within the world. They can keep their bodies healthy, develop social skills such as cooperation, and learn how to lead and follow. In many ways, children's play serves as an apprenticeship for later in life when children become adults and enter society. With an opportunity to learn skills such as concern for others, self-sacrifice, and assertive behavior, childhood athletes can grow into well-adjusted, reliable adults who can positively impact their communities.

The danger creeping into youth sports today, however, is that the professional model (focused on winning) is invading the amateur model (focused on developing the athlete). Unfortunately, the trend has influenced college coaches to identify prospects at younger and younger ages.

Amanda Paule, assistant professor of sport management at Bowling Green State University, has conducted research on college athletic recruiting practices among 30 Division I colleges. In her findings, she found overwhelmingly that if an athlete is being recruited by a big college program, the college has identified that person by age 12–13. Through showcases, college recruiters are able to narrow down their searches. Identifying talent at showcases is more cost effective for colleges; likewise, they can observe young athletes within a highly competitive environment.

Although this trend may be good for colleges, it can cultivate the wrong environment for young athletes. As Paule comments, "At 12–13 you should still be having fun, not worrying about college scouts. It becomes a problem when too many adults get their hands in there and it stops being fun for the kids."

When athletes are raised or coached to believe that to be successful they must win, they never experience the freedom to fail, make adjustments, and persevere regardless of the results. As a result, they will lack the ability to tolerate failure and setbacks because in their mind these are unacceptable behaviors. Paule remarks, "We're almost preparing children to fail when we focus so much on athletics at such young levels. We should be focusing more on academics at that time and allowing children to develop skills through their athletic experiences."

There are many benefits when a child plays on developmental rather than highly competitive teams. This child will still learn that winning is important, but he will not see winning as a primary concern. He will understand that his role on the team is to develop into the best athlete he can be and to gain a variety of quality experiences. He will develop friendships, face adversity in a non-threatening environment, and learn to cope with failure in a positive manner.

The mistake some parents make is that because *they* want their child to play baseball in college, they assume their child will want and appreciate the goal, too. By investing so much of their own interest in their child's efforts, parents rather than their child are assuming ownership of the achievement. Though well intentioned, the result is that children feel no sense of connectedness and responsibility for their efforts. In this case, competing could be little more than an obligation, and its only purpose to earn another trophy.

Brandon Snyder appreciates that his parents never pressured him into playing: "Baseball was never forced down our throats. It was something I saw my father do, it was something my grandfather had done, and I wanted to do it, too. My dad created a positive environment through baseball and his academy. That appealed to me. It was just something I wanted to be a part of."

A player who owns his sport loves to play and values the process of achieving. He is the first person to arrive at the ballpark and the last person to leave, and usually goes beyond what is expected of him. He seems to enjoy the grind, the endless and tedious repetition to become successful. External rewards such as trophies, attention, and social status may be nice, but they are not a necessary form of validation. No matter what the conditions, he just loves to compete, to learn something new, and to challenge himself.

This attitude is obvious in players like Adam Pettyjohn who return to the ballpark day after day, year after year, no matter what the conditions. He says, "As long as I have a uniform, I'll compete. Of course I'd like to get more time in the big leagues, but I can enjoy competing anywhere, no matter where I'm at."

Some players, however, cannot muster as much contentment as Adam, in part because they've acquired a habit of avoiding undesirable circumstances or adversity. These sorts of players, when they do not work well with a coach or other teammates, try to avoid the confrontation and might even try to switch teams. Because they do not want to feel frustrated or angry, they avoid the situation entirely. The result, in many cases, is a person who is restless, discontent, and critical of himself and others.

In Northern Virginia, David Carroll, a coach at Battlefield High School, has seen this trend in some parents who, when they disagree with a coach or other parents, will break off and form their own independent team. Unfortunately, the trend has caused animosity in the community, a subject Carroll has had to address with parents in order to encourage them to be realistic about their child's future.

"They can't figure out that some day, all the kids will be going to high school together. Their dads can't go out there and start another high school team," Carroll notes. "If their kids are going to be successful, the dads are going to have to admit their faults and put aside their differences."

Because so many people in America long to be professional athletes, often they begin specializing in a sport from a very early age, even as young as a five-year-old in some cases. People assume that the sooner a child specializes in his or her sport, the better chance of developing into a top athlete. However, specialization does not have a guaranteed "winning" effect on a child. Coakley criticizes the trend of specialization for children, feeling it "keeps [children] from developing skills across sports, limits identity development, and limits the breadth of their social interactions."

When an athlete specializes at a young age, he runs the risk of becoming a "one-dimensional" person, someone who identifies solely with the values and standards of his sport. When a one-dimensional athlete succeeds, he views himself as worthwhile, competent, and valued; if he fails, however, he will feel anxiety, worthlessness, helplessness, and even despair because his sport is the only thing he is invested in. More, if a one-dimensional athlete faces an injury or some other setback, he is vulnerable to an identity crisis. He may ask, Who am I? What value do I have? This is because the primary basis for his identity has been removed. An athlete who pursues one sport single-mindedly may be able to achieve celebrity status and wealth in that sport on the surface, but beneath he will likely struggle with discontentment, failed relationships, and limited interests. Or worse, he may not have achieved his dream, and then live a life of unrealized ambitions and lifelong dissatisfaction.

The message from professional ball players is often the same, as well. "In the long run," says Vinny Rottino, "it's advantageous if a kid plays multiple sports. It's good athletically to learn all the different skill sets in all the different sports. Ultimately, building athleticism will help someone when he decides to specialize."

Likewise, playing multiple sports allows an athlete to play for fun, where he can develop the ability to deal with loss and failure. David Carroll feels that so many travel teams today are so focused on "beating the brains out of the other teams" that the players are not taught how to deal with failure. "If baseball's a game of failure and you don't learn how to fail, you're going to be miserable and bound to leave the game eventually."

When Carroll played Little League, he felt that the experience had "a little bit of both." Every boy got to play during the regular season, good or bad, but then when the all-star team formed, only the best players competed, and then they played to win.

Parents today, however, are more preoccupied with winning than ever before and can become intensely involved in their child's competitions.

Adam Moore, speaking from his own experiences, sees parents today being far more competitive than when he was playing in school ten years ago. Before reporting to spring training, he had attended a high school basketball game in his hometown, and was surprised to see how much parents yelled at the referees and their children.

"Maybe parents are becoming more intense because they see potential in their child that they didn't have," Moore comments. "The parents might have played, but they want to push their boy or girl because they see the kid's potential, and they want him to do what they weren't able to do."

This idea resonates with Coakley's assertion that parents feel responsible for designing their child's future: "If there's a referee or coach who is making decisions that interfere with your child's development of his dream, it is your moral obligation to get in his face and let him know if he ever does that again, he'll hear from you even louder."

Although it seems like parents are becoming more and more "wacko" as time goes on, they and their children are being placed in a complex situation in today's sports culture.

"They just have a different set of circumstances culturally as parents," Coakley says. David Carroll, who works with parents on a regular basis, agrees that "it's the way that the world is going." Carroll adds, "When I was a boy, if my coach would have called my parents because of my behavior, my parents would not have come back to the coach to complain. They would have grabbed me by the ear, my dad would have taken me back to the woodshed and taken care of it. Now if a kid gets in trouble, it's the coach's fault, it's the teacher's fault. It's a different mindset."

Likewise Coakley, who played Little League during the 1960s, remembers people coming up to his parents saying, "You're really lucky to have Jay as a son." Their congratulations was not based on his parents' involvement in his playing—according to Coakley they might have watched one or two games a season, and "I didn't expect them to be there." Two decades later, when Coakley's son was playing Little League, people would say to him, "You must be really proud," implying that he had a role in developing his son's talent. Today, parents have reached the extreme. "They may say something like, 'How have you created this person?'" Coakley comments. "We've gone from luck, to pride, to creator. That has put massive amounts of pressure on parents."

When parents do all that they can to see their son or daughter win, they can place heavy, even unreasonable, expectations on their child. If a player grows up never meeting someone's expectations, he will begin to hear or develop negative messages that can significantly impact his thinking. He may begin to doubt his ability or, worse, his worth.

At Rick Saggese's facility in Naples, he encounters many young people who struggle with confidence. As a baseball mentor, his goal is to help players both on and off the field to build their confidence, establish goals, and gain life skills. According to him, "Much of the time the problem players face is that they don't believe in themselves."

This may be for a variety of reasons. Many times these athletes have worked with coaches who use punishment and fear as a means to achieve results on the field. Although aversive control works—our entire system of laws is backed up by threats of punishment—it can be damaging within the context of personal relationships. The criminal has no connection to the judge sentencing him to prison. But a player does look to a coach for guidance, mentorship, and leadership. When that trust is jeopardized because of fear—"Coach only wants players who don't mess up—I *can't* mess up"—a player is less likely to perform and more likely to harbor resentment. Many coaches use punishment as a means for conditioning athletic achievement because it can be the fastest way to achieve results. However, they do not take into consideration the side effects this type of coaching can create.

First, punishment creates fear, something that can be a great motivator, but also something that can train an athlete to resent failure. When an athlete is afraid to fail, he cannot enjoy his sport as much, and his likelihood to fail actually increases. An athlete with a high fear of failure is motivated to avoid the "agony of defeat" rather than to achieve the "thrill of victory." Rather than seeing athletic competition as a challenge, the athlete sees it as a threat. When he becomes threatened he can feel anxious, a state of mind that disrupts motor performance and interferes with thinking. He cannot focus on what he needs to do to perform well, and he obsesses about what could "go wrong." Athletes with a fear of failure are more likely to perform poorly in competition, to get injured, to enjoy the athletic experience less, and to drop out of sports altogether.

For somebody like Justin Lehr, his family established a healthy perspective on winning. As Justin remembers, "We were a winning family, my sisters were big competitors, too. But I never felt criticized because I struck out. My parents always supported us."

When an athlete does feel criticized, he is more likely to harbor resentment towards authority figures, such as coaches or parents, because he never feels "good enough" to meet the standard. The more criticism a child receives, the more critical he is of himself, as well. Fear may help him perfect his skills, but it also may lead him to develop an unstable view of himself and others in the meantime.

Saggese works with a variety of players, many of whom have been conditioned through fear. They are often the players who are the most self-condemning. To help them deal with these feelings, he tries to train players to "keep a short-term memory" so that they can learn how to deal with failure and not get frustrated with the game from an early age.

When Saggese works with players, he begins by asking kids to name three people they feel are great players. "It's always Albert Pujols or Derek Jeter. Then I ask them, 'What about you?' Usually they're speechless. That's where we begin. I say to them, 'I think you're a great player. Do *you* believe that?'"

Saggese feels compelled to work with young athletes because when he was a boy, his father not only helped him learn the tools of baseball but also helped him believe in himself as a player. His father took an active role in helping his son by researching the sort of training he needed to do to get better, stronger, and faster at his game. Living in Andover, Massachusetts, Saggese relied on the equipment his father set up in the cellar of their house in order to train year-round. Eventually, his father installed a batting cage in their backyard so he could improve his hitting. Finally, as he approached high school, his family decided to move to Naples so that he would have the opportunity to play year-round. When his father died of a brain aneurism when he was throwing batting practice to his son's team, Saggese felt compelled to carry out his father's legacy of mentorship in the game. His pursuit of baseball ended in college due to a series of injuries, but in 2001 he realized that he still had a role in the game as a coach and mentor.

Realizing the many challenges kids face in today's society as they are developing as baseball players and young men, Saggese says, "If kids don't have success, they end up quitting the sport. But if they learn from a young age not only how to be a good player, but also how to be a good person, they can put everything into a better perspective."

A player's "better perspective" flows from his confidence. In order to develop confidence, a player must develop realistic goals, not goals based on what others expect of him. This can be hard to do, especially for players whose parents have placed high demands on them. Many parents do not realize the pressure they place on their children when they provide expensive, highly competitive opportunities. Although parents may be motivated by a loving desire to see their child succeed, earn people's admiration, and establish a name for himself, the "price" of these opportunities can weigh on a player's mind. When he wins or plays well, then he is worthy of his parents' approval, but when he fails, then he may feel unworthy of their love.

According to IMG's Trevor Moawad, this can be a real stumbling block for players, especially for elite competitors whose parents have provided them with every opportunity to succeed. "Parents can have high expectations, but they should make sure their child knows they love them unconditionally. That's where a lot of athletes get confused."

Even though showcases and the private sector have dominated youth baseball in recent years, those involved in the sport realize there are other chances for players to get noticed.

Brian Snyder, who not only prepared his son Brandon, but also worked with his twin sons Matt and Michael to earn scholarships at Ole Miss, still believes the game will remain in tact regardless of the trends: "They always say the system will find you if you're good enough. You'd like to think that is true."

Vinny Rottino, who never sought the advantages of showcases and attended a Division III college, still made it to the big leagues. In his experience, "Baseball's a really fair game. If you play well, if you continually show you're a major league player, you'll get noticed."

Even though the showcase method is efficient, some people question how effectively recruiters can assess talent in such a setting.

Brandon Snyder, who was invited more than once to the East Coast professional showcase, regularly chose team play over showcase opportunities: "I just played on good teams. I believe that if you play with good players and you're a good player yourself, you will shine on your own stage. You won't have to have that fake persona of someone putting you on a stage."

Coakley concurs, saying, "Showcases are a pretty artificial way to assess talent. Everyone is in it for themselves. You see somebody in a context that is a little bit different from a team context. That's a problem."

Carroll also points out that there are plenty of kids who should not be showcasing, but their parents think they're going to give their child a ticket somewhere by paying for the opportunity. "It's a crazy factor because there are kids who play with travel teams, go to showcases, but then parents don't understand why they can't hold their weight on the high school team."

Carroll, like others, doesn't believe that showcases are the only chance for a player to get noticed. In his view, if a player is in a good high school program with coaching staff who direct players to get in the best physical shape, who practice fundamentals and mechanics, then he can play in college if he really wants to. His talent will get him there. Still, Carroll acknowledges showcases can be important for someone to broaden his options. Without showcases a player may be limited to playing at Division II or III colleges. Likewise, he may not get as many looks from professional scouts.

Those who do turn to showcases, however, need to be careful to select showcases that are legitimate—that is, the ones where recruiters and scouts attend. Because the showcase model has become so prevalent, hundreds of showcases exist, promising young players to get looks from all the right people, but many of them do not deliver on their promises.

In speaking to one father, Carroll found that he signed his son up to attend multiple showcases throughout the summer. Out of the twelve he paid for, only two weekends yielded legitimate recruiters. According to Carroll, "You can count on your hand the showcases that provide players with legitimate looks. If you don't know which are the right ones, you're basically paying to play baseball."

Still, many parents today are eager to get connected to a pipeline their child can use to move up the ranks. Besides showcases, many parents and athletes turn to baseball academies for development and exposure.

Ken Bigler, who operates Bigler Baseball Academy out of Brookfield, Wisconsin, has seen the use of baseball academies grow over the past decade. In many cases, kids aren't even interested in playing college ball, but simply want to make the team at their high school. They have the option of attending academy classes which focus on different skills (hitting, fielding, pitching) over the course of several weeks; many players opt for individual lessons, which allow them to focus on a specific skill with one of the coaches.

From Bigler's perspective, parents are turning to academies because there is a stigma in the youth sports world, the belief that parents need to give their kids a "leg up" through select ball. "Kids with talent still have opportunity," Bigler asserts, "even without academy experience. But if two kids have equal ability, and one played select ball and the other didn't, the coach would go with the select kid. He would assume that kid has been exposed to more game situations, that's he's played more baseball."

Players like Adam, Justin, and Vinny, who played high school ball about fifteen years ago, knew select-ball opportunities were available, but turned to conventional means (playing on teams) for developing and getting noticed. Brandon, however, playing high school ball just six years ago, saw teammates every summer going to different showcases. Likewise, he grew up at his father's baseball academy.

Coakley estimates that "in ten years most of the players in the major leagues will have gone through a pipeline. It's a pipeline you have to go through relatively early in your career because there's a set of transitional points where if you're not in a particular league or with a particular coach, you're not going to make it (except in rare circumstances) to the next level."

Because of the intense competition today, some families even decide to move to a different state to give their child a better opportunity for getting noticed. For Dan Kennon, Deming, New Mexico, a small town thirty miles north of the Mexican border, had the climate for year-round baseball, but it lagged in opportunity. "Not many scouts come through southern New Mexico," Dan says. "I knew that if I wanted more opportunity for a baseball career, I would have to take some steps."

One of those steps included enrolling in a semester at the Pendleton School, the on-campus K-12 school at IMG Academy in Bradenton, Florida. Since its inception in the 1970s, starting as a tennis academy under the direction of world-famous coach Nick Bollettieri, IMG has developed sports legends in multiple sports, including Drew Brees, Eli Manning, Paula Creamer, Andre Agassi, Monica Seles, Freddy Adu, Josh Hamilton, Carlos Quentin, and Ryan Zimmerman.

During his first experience at IMG, Dan questioned whether he wanted to stay. At age twelve, he was the youngest student, a mere 75 pounds, and he doubted whether he could compete with the other athletes. At first, he wanted to return home to be with his friends again. Once he finished the semester, though, he realized the value of attending a place like IMG, especially if he wanted to be a professional athlete. Because of how he handled the semester, Dan believed he was capable of training to become a major league baseball player.

After that semester, Dan's parents decided to enroll him at Pendleton for high school so that he could play on an excellent team and train with the best. At IMG, a familiar stomping ground for recruiters and scouts, Dan would get a lot more attention than he would have back in his hometown of Deming, New Mexico.

Although IMG functions primarily as a sports complex, the presence of Pendleton on campus provides young students with an opportunity that resembles a boarding school experience. Americans are often critical of boarding schools on the grounds that they are elitist and indoctrinating. After all, Holden Caulfield hated his boarding school; Harry Potter had troubles adjusting to his at first, too. The purpose of a boarding school, however, as a self-contained educational facility, offers students the benefits of academic as well as social promotion. The concept of the boarding school dates back to the Middle Ages when wealthy families would send their sons to court to receive training in academics (subjects like Greek, Latin, and geometry), fighting (fencing, sword fighting, and horsemanship), and culture (dancing, playing music, and writing poetry). (Families would send their daughters to court, too, mainly for the purposes of developing social graces and finding a husband of wealth and status.) The modern concept of the boarding school blossomed throughout Europe during the colonial expansion of the nineteenth century; in England, schools like Eton and Harrow sought to educate British boys in the ways of the Empire, cultivating future citizens and leaders of the nation. These schools, and other prominent American schools like Andover and St. Paul's, continue to produce future presidents, professors, and other national leaders.

Undeniably, boarding schools have gone through different phases culturally, but there are many reasons to believe that boarding schools today can be an excellent opportunity for some families to prepare their child for a specific, highly competitive career. The oldest and most renowned schools are the general boarding schools, such as the ones that educated former presidents George W. Bush (a graduate of Andover), and John F. Kennedy (Choate) and influential leaders Brian Cashman (a graduate of Georgetown Prep) and William F. Buckley (a graduate of Milbrook). Some boarding schools specialize, including military academies such as West Point or Florida Air Academy (Prince Fielder's alma mater). Boarding schools exist for artists (Interlochen Arts Academy, for example, which graduated singers Josh Groban and Jewel), equestrians, dancers, and athletes. The purpose of a boarding school is to provide students with a self-contained environment filled with the influences of good teachers and mentors. Students at a specialized boarding school are able to focus primarily on the development of their skill without the usual distractions of adolescent life. Naturally, this model provides young talent with developmental advantages. For the serious athlete a boarding school may be a worthwhile investment, both for the environment it provides as well as the connections and opportunities it affords.

Like many other specialty academies, however, IMG does not offer financial aid. In contrast, schools such as Andover, for instance, offset nearly 50 percent of students' costs; the average financial aid grant per student is

$31,892, a significant portion of the $39,900 tuition that families pay for students boarding at Andover. IMG athletes who attend Pendleton pay one-third more than Andover students—between $50,000 and $60,000 per year. As a result, IMG does not cast a broad economic net; to reap the benefits of the facilities, a family must have money.

So what specifically does IMG (and other boarding schools generally) do that prepares students so completely for elite careers?

In an article from 2001 in *US News and World Report*, Stephen Smith outlined the benefits of attending boarding schools in the following way: they cultivate geographic diversity, they provide conscientious adult supervision, they build positive and fulfilling experiences for students, and they foster social intelligence.[2] These benefits would be useful for a young person on any career path, but they are especially helpful for young people who intend to lead some day through performance and example. With this environment, boarding schools frequently produce well-rounded, mature individuals, sometimes prodigies with an amazing capacity for encountering a complex adult world at a very young age.

JR Murphy is one example of this sort of person.

Born and raised in Bradenton, JR's mom Carolina served as admissions director at IMG, affording JR exposure to the campus and amenities of the academy from an early age. He began participating in summer camps at IMG at age eight and, when approaching high school age, was given the choice of Manatee High School or Pendleton. As JR recalls, "I knew I wanted to play baseball and because I knew about IMG and the Pendleton School, I thought, what better place to play? It wasn't a very tough decision."

As a student at Pendleton, JR functioned much like a college student, with block-structured classes in the morning, and training or competition in the afternoons. In the evenings, he was able to take advantage of directed learning, a time in which he could work with teachers in each of his subjects to make up tests or receive help on class work he might have missed. His senior year, he hit .627 with 11 home runs and 66 runs batted in while leading his team to a 31–1 record and a national ranking (#8). By that time he had tied up a scholarship to the University of Miami and planned to live with family while attending college and playing ball. During the middle of the season, though, more and more professional scouts started showing up at his games, especially after ESPN ranked him as a top ten prospect for 2009. Ken Bolek, director of the baseball academy, forecasted that JR could have a big opportunity in the draft that year, and should consider going pro if that were the case.

Drafted in the second round by the Yankees in 2009, JR decided that a $1.25-million signing bonus and the opportunity afforded by such a high draft pick trumped the scholarship to the University of Miami.

Why, at age eighteen, did JR Murphy think he was ready to enter the professional world? In JR's mind, attending IMG has prepared him to make the adjustment to pro ball. "For me, the minor league schedule hasn't been very different from the schedule I had at IMG. Baseball year round is all I've ever known; the only thing different now is the level of competition," JR says.

He also benefited from IMG's training approach, which not only targets athletic development, but also offers a variety of modules ranging from nutrition to mental conditioning to media training. According to Bolek, "The uniqueness of the program at IMG is that it is totally comprehensive. Part of the responsibility we have to the families is that through competition we hope players are adapting their own life skills that are going to make them better people. This may be the most significant thing we do."

IMG students also go through Steve Shenbaum's program so that they can gain self-awareness, improve communication skills, and learn how to handle the media and fans. These and other skills that athletes can gain at IMG Academy are essential for success in pro ball—they are skills every player can master, but usually in different timing.

For Vinny Rottino, college played a significant role in preparing him for pro ball: "I was able to adjust well to a new environment because I'd already been living at college. I gained a lot of life skills during those four years."

Other factors can prepare a player, as well. When Justin Lehr married his wife Guia the year after he was drafted, he now had the added responsibility of supporting a family and maintaining a marriage. At the same time, he had gained a partner he could turn to throughout the journey. "My wife has been a tremendous support to me. She's helped me over the years work my way towards my dream," Justin says.

Baseball is filled with many different stories of what people have done to become major league baseball players. Robinson Cano learned how to throw a baseball near the sugar cane fields that lined his hometown of Santo Domingo. Andre Ethier attended Arizona State until his junior year when he was drafted in the second-round by the Dodgers. Daniel Nava, after being cut from his college team and overlooked in the amateur draft, eventually earned a spot in the Red Sox minor league system. He made his major league debut with the team in 2010, hitting a grand slam in his first at-bat. Some players turn to independent leagues. Others invest in camps, showcases, and travel teams in order to earn college scholarships. Still others attend academies like Think Outside the Diamond, Bigler Baseball, or even IMG Academy to prepare for a baseball career.

Nobody can say which path is "right" or even most promising. Sometimes the most likely prospects lose their shot because of unforeseen circumstances—injury or organizational changes. The best thing a young person with major league aspirations can do is work within his life and his circumstances. Not everybody gets a scholarship to Fullerton; not everybody hits .600 in high school, either. Pursuing baseball is a day-by-day process, and a long process. Anything worth achieving is rarely easy; in particular, mastery of sport skills (especially baseball) is a long and difficult process.

Although TV highlights make mastery seem easy and instantaneous, it takes years of commitment and dedication, even for elite competitors. Virtually the only thing a person can control throughout the experience is his mind, his will, and his effort. With this under control, a player can take on any situation, any failure or achievement, and see it as just another step in the work that goes into creating a champion.

THREE

Draft or College

Experience is not what happens to you; it's what you do with what happens to you. — Aldous Huxley

As a senior in high school, Adam Pettyjohn investigated colleges to play ball at the next year. He contacted baseball coaches, looking to see if he could secure scholarship money at one of the institutions. Because of California's reputation for baseball talent, competition for scholarship dollars in the state was tight. By graduation, Adam discovered his best option was to attend the local junior college in order to play ball. His situation, after all of his high school success, seemed like a letdown. Yet, Adam was shielded from what could have been a great deal of frustration by his lack of experience, saying, "I didn't know any better so it didn't really bother me much at the time." So he gave the coach at the junior college a verbal agreement that he would play with him the following year.

During the amateur draft that spring, four players at Fresno State were drafted in the 50th round or lower. All signed. That was when Adam's high school coach, Ray Strebel, put in a call to the Fresno State coach, someone whom Ray had worked with when he was at Fresno. Suddenly, Fresno State had a spot and a partial scholarship for Adam. The JUCO coach naturally tried to dissuade Adam from changing his mind. As Adam recalls, "He warned me not to get sucked in by all the nice facilities at Fresno."

Regardless of the facilities, Adam saw an opportunity to pitch as a freshman because of Fresno State's unexpected lack of pitching depth. Moreover, he'd get to play Division I baseball, an elite level of competition that included schools such as Texas, UC Berkeley, UC Long Beach, and Arizona State. All of this would give him more opportunity for getting drafted by the pros.

"Players get noticed all the time at JUCOs and smaller colleges, but scouts definitely give more attention to the Division I schools," Adam says. "If you've got talent to be playing at a Division I school, that speaks for

43

itself and scouts know that. These questions are already on a scout's mind before he sees the kid."

At first college baseball was a tremendous challenge for Adam, something that would later prepare him for pro ball. As a kid from a small town he was used to pitching in front of 200 people; at Fresno State that turned into 2,000. With his first collegiate pitch, he hit the batter in the head. As the season continued, that first pitch became a portent of the struggles he would face. Because he was intimidated by the mammoth competition, Adam's confidence started to deteriorate, and along with his confidence, his willingness to pitch. "It got to the point when I was in the bullpen that I hoped the pitcher would get out of the situation because I didn't want to have to go out there," Adam says.

Three-quarters into the season, the coach pulled Adam aside and talked to him about confidence. He knew Adam's beliefs and he told him when he struggled with his confidence, he should step off the mound and say a prayer. Ask God for more mental focus. As easy as it sounded, it was still tough for Adam to do. That entire season because of his fears, Adam only pitched seven innings, so even getting on the mound was a struggle.

His next outing, he started the game out by walking a batter on four pitches. After that batter, he stepped off the mound and prayed: Lord, help me get out of this situation. The next batter was Adam Kennedy, the Cal State Northridge shortstop who would be the first-round draft pick of the St. Louis Cardinals in 1997. Naturally, Adam was intimidated to pitch to arguably the league's best hitter. He didn't want to surrender another walk, yet feared throwing Kennedy strikes.

Kennedy took the first two pitches out of the zone. Adam, battling with his thoughts, prepared for his third pitch. As he released the ball, he saw Kennedy starting his swing and feared the worst. He heard the ball come off the bat. When he turned to his infield, though, he saw the shortstop scoop up a routine ground ball, dump it to second, then the relay went to first for a double play. Adam was elated.

"That at-bat changed my whole career at Fresno State. As I watched them making the play, I thought, 'That's all I needed,'" Adam says. Before that he had already checked out mentally. He had asked his mother to get him an application to go back to the local junior college, and he had plans for transferring. "That's when God stepped in and said, 'No, these are my plans for you, and I'll be there when you call on me.'"

Adam went on a roll the rest of the season, was assigned to the starting rotation, and eventually went on to pitch a complete game.

Justin Lehr made his college debut at the University of California, Santa Barbara (UCSB), home of the Gauchos and an undergraduate student body of nearly 20,000. Playing Division I ball and earning a degree in sociology was a difficult adjustment for Justin, mainly because his high school had not prepared him for college academics. Rather than teaching the students skills like college writing, Covina Public High Schools were "just trying to get kids to graduate"—a task they accomplished only 50 percent of the time. So while Justin was being groomed on the baseball diamond, he was barely being challenged in the classroom.

"In high school I didn't do any work at home. I breezed through with A's and B's, but I really didn't learn much," Justin says.

When he got to college, he realized, "I'm screwed." It took him ten times longer to do an assignment because of his poor academic training; in addition, he was managing a much more demanding baseball schedule, one that required him to miss classes and travel distances up to 100 miles at a time. In Justin's opinion, "I got accepted because I was an athlete. My test scores alone would not have gotten me into UCSB."

The average SAT score of incoming freshmen when Justin enrolled was 1200, the average GPA 3.8. For athletes like Justin, however, the university expected the NCAA minimum (600 SAT and 2.0 GPA). Once in the classroom, though, athletes were expected to do the same quality of work as regular students.

At first the coursework was challenging for Justin. Like all athletes, he could get tutoring, but nobody was going to take the tests for him. Likewise, UCSB's policy required athletes to maintain a 2.0 GPA every quarter, whereas some universities had cumulative GPA requirements, assessing the athlete's academic eligibility on a yearly rather than quarterly basis.

By sophomore year, through a combination of tutoring, hard work, and common sense, Justin began posting a respectable GPA with regularity. His priority as always, though, was baseball. Notes Justin, "It wasn't until I got into pro ball and started taking classes that I enjoyed college a lot more and actually applied myself."

In his early 20s, he was more concerned about enjoying college life, playing in the College World Series, and getting drafted by the pros. His junior year the opportunity to get drafted came around (the Angels drafted him in the 10th round), but instead of starting his professional career, he decided to transfer for his senior year to the University of Southern California (USC).

For Justin, the one-year transfer proved worthwhile. He played on a more competitive team and made connections on the more prestigious campus that helped him with his baseball career. Even as a transfer student, he moved into a starting pitching role that spring, gaining confidence as he accumulated wins and perfected his arsenal of pitches.

Although still developing as a young pitcher, Justin knew how to win games and he welcomed high-pressure situations so that he could prove his abilities. He believed in his pitches, even after surrendering a hit or a home run. While playing at USC, Justin faced players who were better than him, yet he learned that baseball was a game for many different types of players. Granted, those players who were really physically gifted had better chances of succeeding in the game. Those were the elite players, the A-Rods and Ryan Howards, who rose to the top quickly. For everyone else, though, including Justin, they had the opportunity to hone their skills. Justin would never throw in the upper 90s, but he could perfect his mechanics and learn how to outsmart a batter with his pitches. According to Justin, "That stuff just takes tons and tons of time to develop."

He was given the opportunity to continue developing when, during his senior year, the A's drafted Justin in the 10th round. At that point, 17 credits shy of a bachelor's degree, he decided to start his baseball career.

Brandon Snyder knew what the sacrifices would be if he turned down college in order to begin his professional baseball career. It was pretty clear by his senior year of high school that he was going to get drafted; what was less clear, however, was if he wanted to start his baseball career at age eighteen. He had already earned a full scholarship to LSU. If he would sign with a team instead of go to college, he'd be missing out on the experiences of the college lifestyle, the chance to relax a little before facing major league pressure.

But the Orioles offer, the compliment of a first-round draft pick, was the best any baseball player could hope for. Brandon knew he was ready. He had played competitive baseball from an early age. Raised by a former major league player, he learned firsthand what it would take for him to adjust to the lifestyle of a baseball player. By age seventeen he had already been living on his own, traveling across the country, and competing against elite players.

His father, Brian, an important figure in developing Brandon's talent, provided his son the opportunities as well as the emotional support he needed to succeed. According to Brian, "When you're drafted as high as he was drafted, it's very difficult to say no if that's what you really want to do. Getting that experience early is hopefully going to jump start you along your path to the big leagues."

There was no doubt in Brandon's mind that baseball was what he wanted to do. Yet he fully comprehended the sacrifice he was making when he chose to bypass college: "I looked at what it would take to go to college in the off-season, and it's going to take me ten years to get my degree. That's a tough pill to swallow, but baseball is my job."

Adjusting to a minor league lifestyle would be filled with its challenges, as well. He would have to get used to playing baseball full-time rather than after school and on the weekends. In one sense, he would have a lighter schedule than he had in high school, but much greater pressure to perform coupled with much tougher competition. He would be away from home even more than before, separated from his family, his girlfriend, and traveling constantly from city to city.

In Brandon's view, "Getting drafted out of high school is not for everybody. If anyone asked me, I'd tell you to get your college education. Not because I don't think I've made the right decision [getting drafted], but because it's not an easy adjustment to the minor leagues."

In college, Vinny Rottino had a long swing. Playing at a Division III school (the University of Wisconsin LaCrosse), the pitches came in under 90 miles per hour, so he had to wait on the ball. Although his team faced good competition, the game was much slower than the pace at Division I schools. He knew that when he got to the next level he would need to make adjustments.

LaCrosse may not have been Vanderbilt or Clemson, but it was a school that provided Vinny with other opportunities he may not have gotten elsewhere. Attending a medium-sized university (with a student body of approximately 10,000 students), he was able to enjoy smaller class sizes and receive excellent, one-on-one instruction from his professors. In a health class he met Dr. Jack Curtis, a sport psychology consultant with the Milwaukee Brewers at the time. Through this class Curtis introduced Vinny to the importance of mental skills training, and used examples of top athletes he had worked with, including Paul Molitor. Through Curtis's lessons, the idea started forming in Vinny's mind that, even though he wasn't hitting the fastest pitches in college, he could still have a shot at professional baseball.

The team he played on was not competitive as far as college baseball went, but Vinny had great experiences with his teammates and coaches, especially his senior year when George Williams led the team. Williams had played 12 years in pro ball, five of those years in the major leagues with Oakland and San Diego. A native of LaCrosse, Williams coached the team on an interim basis and brought on-the-job experience to players like Vinny who had his sights set on pro ball.

"I felt really fortunate to have somebody with major league experience coaching our team," Vinny says about playing for Williams. "I don't know if I could be as dedicated as he was to our team, especially just coming out of pro ball the year before."

Earning a degree in chemistry, an unusually difficult major for a serious athlete, Vinny was one of a small percentage of professional baseball players who completed his degree before signing with a professional team. Like most athletes, he faced a rigidly structured day, especially during the baseball season in the spring. Winter, between November and February, was when the team had off from baseball activities, but naturally players were still obligated to train and stay in shape.

Although some players struggled to make grades while keeping their head in the game, for a surprising number of student-athletes, the tighter schedule enhanced their focus and made them work harder. This was the case for Vinny, who earned Academic All-America honors his junior and senior years, and was "studying constantly" to maintain a high GPA. Because of the heavy workload, he learned to set goals and use his goals as motivation for staying on track. His goal of becoming a professional baseball player helped him through his Sunday nights when he had to finish his homework for the coming week. He was busy but "I wouldn't change a thing about how I spent my time in college."

Not many Division III players are success stories, and that very nearly was the case for Vinny when he didn't get drafted after college. Players who get selected from Division III schools (a mere 20 percent of the total number drafted) are standout players for one reason or another. They may play in warmer climates where they can clock more playing time. Their college may be closer in proximity to heavily scouted Division I schools so they have a greater chance of being seen. Whatever the circumstances, Vinny had to accept the hard reality of being overlooked early in his baseball career.

For some reason, being overlooked didn't deter Vinny. He knew he was a good player and even though the odds were against him, he wanted to give it one more shot at a tryout camp. His determination won him a spot with the Brewers. At the same time, he had no regrets about where he chose to go to college: "I've learned to realize that there's a reason for everything that happens in life. I am exactly where I'm supposed to be. I'm trusting God's plan and that takes the pressure off."

Transitioning from high school to adulthood is a challenging time in life. Unlike some young people during that time, baseball players at least have a clear goal—getting to the big leagues. The steps they need to take to reach that goal, however, may be less defined. In their eagerness to play, those who get drafted out of high school may be ready to dive into a professional career. Wiser influences in their life (a parent or an agent, for instance) may urge them to consider college first. At the same time, being a college athlete comes with its set of challenges, too. A high percentage of college baseball players with elite talent do not finish their degrees before signing to play with a professional team. Likewise, balancing two full-time jobs—baseball and school—requires more hard work and dedication than playing in high school. Neither path—the draft or college—is simple or easy. Ultimately each player must decide which path will fit best with his situation.

Most people agree that if a player gets a high draft selection out of high school that is accompanied by a $1-million-plus signing bonus, he should go into pro ball. This decision makes sense not only from a financial standpoint, but also from a professional standpoint. According to Brian Snyder, "A lot people think it's all about the financial aspect and that's not it. The money's more symbolic if anything. More important is the opportunity you're given through that contract. That team has invested a lot of money in you, so they're going to give you every opportunity of succeeding."

Mike Montana, an agent with Millenium Sports Management out of Cincinnati, says that he tells clients that they have to be offered "life changing money" in order to turn down college. "With that advice, we realize that the definition of life changing money is different for everybody, so we never advise on a specific dollar amount."

One of Montana's clients, Patrick Arnold, took a 15th round draft from the Nationals out of high school, but Montana considers Patrick to be an exception, saying "Patrick is very ambitious—he's started his own baseball academy which he runs in the offseason, he's been through a lot."

His senior year, Patrick received a scholarship to play at North Carolina State, but he knew he was ready to play professional baseball. He knew that he had a solid mental game and that he would be able to take care of himself even in the challenging environment of a minor league lifestyle. "When you go through what I've been through—dealing with cancer from an early age—I honestly don't think there's anything I couldn't handle now," Patrick says.

Both Patrick and his agent agree, though, that most eighteen-year-olds need a few more years of maturing before they're ready to become professional baseball players. As Patrick comments, "Once you sign a contract, you become an adult. You can't have your party years. In college you might be able to mess up a little bit. But in pro ball, everybody looks at what you're doing. If there's one thing you slip up on, everybody knows about it. It's a cut-throat business."

Taking the draft out of high school can be a risk, too. Although major league contracts include compensation for college tuition, many players after they finish their baseball careers do not go back to earn a degree. Some earn credits while playing baseball, but this requires a certain amount of initiative because the baseball season and the college calendar do not correlate well. Likewise, the majority of the players in the minor leagues never see major league playing time. So if they've started their baseball career at age eighteen then end their career in their mid-to-late-twenties, they are left financially strained, jobless, and without a college degree. Statistics show that starting a degree later in life, especially when a person's responsibilities increase with a wife and children, is much more challenging than earning a degree out of high school.

Because of these risks, some people would criticize baseball players for forfeiting their opportunity to earn a college degree before pursuing a baseball career. This may be a valid argument, but in the cases of highly talented athletes, college may be beside the point.

This was true for Scott Sanderson, an eighteen-year major league pitcher who currently works as an agent representing elite clients such as Josh Beckett and Josh Hamilton. Although starting his business degree at Vanderbilt University, Sanderson was drafted his junior year in the third round by the Montreal Expos in 1977. He appeared in his first major league game just a year later. Today, he admits that his baseball career is his college degree saying, "I've earned a Ph.D. in baseball." Since retiring, he has considered returning to college to finish his degree, but realizes that over the years, the experiences he gained through the game, as well as the connections he made, were more valuable than a diploma.

Sanderson's career proves that, contrary to popular belief, not everybody has to go to college. In fact, some people best prepare for their future through working hard and gaining experience. This is especially true in the trades, jobs that require manual labor, but also can be the case for people with creative gifts. This does not mean college is useless to these people—anyone exposed to good teaching, a diverse community, and unique social opportunities will benefit from these experiences—but it may not be necessary for them to establish their career.

Baseball is the type of profession where a person gets better through hard work and experience. There are many reasons to believe college can prepare a player for the game, as well, but, in the words of Vinny Rottino, "You get better at baseball by playing more baseball." This means more time on the field, more batting practice, and more game situations.

Beginning a career in baseball at age eighteen, however, may not be the best environment in which a young player can develop. Jim Murphy, Olympic baseball coach and author of *Inner Excellence*, states, "The general idea in pro baseball is let them play, the cream will rise to the top. It's just a numbers game—if we get enough numbers through our system we'll get somebody to work out." As a performance coach, Murphy believes in the importance of developing each player as an individual, rather than learning through experience, the model commonly found in minor league baseball. In his view, college is almost always the best option for aspiring ballplayers. "The instruction at a good university is as good as, if not better than, pro ball," Murphy says.

Ritch Price, baseball coach at the University of Kansas, agrees that college coaches, unlike many minor league coaches, are trained to teach and develop players. Likewise, in college, coaches emphasize teamwork, whereas in pro ball players need to focus on individual improvement in order to advance to the next level. Price, who has coached Division I baseball at Kansas since the 2003 season, successfully led his team in 2006 to its first conference title in nearly fifty years.

Morgan Ensberg, former major league third baseman for the Houston

Astros, never allowed his dream of becoming a professional athlete to interfere with what he felt was his top priority: getting a good education.

"My parents always said to me, the reality is, education is what everybody does. You go to school, you graduate, you get a job, that's what you do," Morgan says. "This pie in the sky idea of playing sports as a career is just silly. They never discouraged me from playing baseball, but they just made it realistic. Based on percentages, it was highly unlikely I'd make it to professional baseball."

Although he did get drafted his senior year of high school (in the 61st round — a round that no longer exists), Morgan opted to play at USC instead (where Justin Lehr was his teammate). He felt that because he wasn't so focused on performing for scouts or "getting that next hit," he was able to play for fun. He also excelled academically, which earned him a scholarship at USC and a place on the team as a walk-on.

Morgan also knew that as an eighteen-year-old, he wasn't mature enough to go across country and do the grind of professional baseball. "There's no way I could have lived in an apartment with three other guys in Kissimmee, Florida, and played 140 games in 95 degree weather," he says.

Other players agree that their decision to play college ball allowed them opportunities for growth and development that prepared them for their future careers.

According to Adam Pettyjohn, "College helped me grow both mentally and physically. Everybody's different, but I tend to think it's so much more beneficial to go to college. Those are some of the best years of a person's life." Pettyjohn also feels that going to college gives a person a healthy perspective outside of baseball, which could help a person make the transition to a different career after he's out of the game. "For some guys, baseball has been everything in their life since the time they could throw a baseball. When you go to college, though, you gain other valuable experiences and build really important friendships. You learn to work with different types of people."

Playing a sport in college comes with its own set of challenges, though, which can divert a player's focus from his number one priority: developing into a better athlete. One of the leading concerns that college athletes face today is preserving their foremost status as a student during an athletic experience that demands large amounts of time from their schedule. Second, athletes in today's commercialized college sports environment struggle against the pressures placed on them to win and be the top players. The media, especially in the last twenty years, has pursued the coverage of amateur sports. At one point, mostly college basketball and football games were the norm; today, many more amateur games are televised, including college baseball, the Little League World Series, and even high school games in many areas.

Undoubtedly, this trend has many positive effects. For instance, the more media coverage on an event, the more publicity and promotion the host institution receives. This is especially beneficial for non-profit universities and schools who rely heavily on tuition dollars and charitable donations to maintain their budgets. Likewise, athletes, when they know their game is being televised, are that much more motivated to train hard. Media promotion generates school spirit and an exciting, positive environment that many students and alumni enjoy. This further promotes the school so that more and more people wish to enroll, and more and more alumni are inclined to lend financial support. In many ways, television is the best thing that ever happened to schools and universities.

Once the media enters, however, it is inevitable that commercialization—advertisement, naming rights, and corporate sponsorship—is close to follow. In one sense, commercialization, like the media, provides universities with the resources they need to create better programs. For instance, the University of Kansas signed one of the top uniform deals with Adidas. As a result, Adidas pays the athletic department $4 million each year so that Kansas athletes will wear jerseys with the Adidas logo. This means that students who play sports at Kansas don't pay for any of their apparel—uniforms, bats, and gloves. Naturally, the sponsorship becomes a major selling point, as well, when coach Price and others recruit future athletes.

Still, businesses (money-making institutions at the heart of commercialism) are interested foremost in promoting their brand, not so much whether a college athlete is provided with a positive student-athlete experience. In the business world, the process is simple—he who sells the most product "wins." Indirectly, businesses who sponsor college sports project this mentality on college teams. In Kansas's Adidas sponsorship, coach Price agrees that Adidas is "paying [us] to win." Without a doubt, winning college teams generate the strongest fan base, the most money for the university, the largest enrollment, and the most generous alumni donations. So on some college campuses, the message can be crystal clear: our teams need to be winning teams.

Is there anything wrong with college athletic departments striving to put together winning teams? Obviously, if winning wasn't an important aspect of the game, everyone could save a lot of money on scoreboards. Yet, in a college environment, or any amateur environment for that matter, teams are responsible foremost for developing players. And one of the biggest hindrances to a developing player's confidence is when he becomes preoccupied with results—either his individual statistics or the team's wins.

In order for college athletes to contend with the commercial environment of today's game, it is important for them to develop small, tangible, process-oriented goals. Media messages—"they need to win this one" or "he needs to step up his game"—can create anxiety in a player because he realizes that he needs to meet a certain expectation in order to be successful. Often, players not only hear these messages from the media, but from within their own clubhouses, from coaches who likewise feel the pressure to win and produce results. The reputation of the university, maybe even the coach's job (worth big money in many cases), could be at stake.

What many players lose sight of is that they do not have immediate control over whether their team wins or whether they get a hit in a particular game. So focusing on the end result only generates tension, anxiety, and frustration. Players who have spent their lives getting playing time, hitting the winning home run, or pitching the no-hitter can become utterly deflated when they're forced to sit or they cannot perform up to their expectations. These frustrations can derail player careers unless they take the time to define their goals in such a way that they will continue to develop as players. Ultimately, a developing player, someone who consistently gets better each and every day, has the strongest possibility of getting to professional ball and eventually the major leagues.

Another significant challenge that college athletes face is being good students as well as good athletes. This balance can be difficult for athletes to strike, particularly if they are working under a coach who demands a great deal of time. Especially at Division I schools with deeply rooted, highly-competitive athletic cultures, athletes can feel a great deal of pressure to put all of their energy into performing on the field and have very little left for the classroom. According to an NCAA survey, Division I football players reported spending an average of 44.8 hours a week practicing, playing, or training for their sport.[1] Again, athletes may feel pressure from coaches to commit to these hours; sometimes, however, athletes may choose this schedule of their own volition because they believe their athletic performance, not their college degree, is the key to their future.

Robert Kustra, president of Boise State University, understands the complex situation that Division I schools face today as they try to keep student athletes from "turning pro." "We're a university that happens to have an athletic program attached to it, and not the other way around," says Kustra. "It's important to make this distinction, to show the primacy of the academic atmosphere, especially in a Division I program."

Often times it's not the coaches but the communities that treat college athletes like professionals. As Kustra comments, "Turn the radio on in any sports community and you'll hear people criticizing players' performances. By about the third caller I feel like saying, 'Excuse me, you do understand these are student athletes. We can't just jettison them from the program because they didn't perform—this kid happens to be majoring in business and he needs his scholarship in order to earn his degree.'"

In order for the primacy of academics to be protected, universities and their athletic departments must commit to upholding this standard. Unfortunately, in large part due to media "hype" surrounding athletics, many universities have not held to these standards. Although a university's admission requirements are the same for all students, reports consistently show that schools in major athletic conferences routinely allow special admits, or students who don't meet "standard or normal entrance requirements."[2] In these cases, people hear the message that if someone is an athlete, he is eligible for special privileges. This message is deceptive, mainly because most athletes' special privileges end when their athletic careers end. The realities of life—bills, a competitive job market, and family responsibilities—set in rapidly once the illusion of privilege disappears.

For some people, privileges are the reality, particularly for athletes who do play beyond college and establish a successful professional career. Nevertheless, the message of "you're an athlete, we'll cut you some slack" still deceives those who seem to be deserving of such attention and praise.

Brandon Snyder, who was pursued by teams and agents years before he turned eighteen, understood the meaning of special treatment. He describes these as "good problems" he had to deal with before he became a professional player—missing school to have lunch with agents, phone calls with teams, and visits from college recruiters. Being pursued may have been a lot of work, but it was nice to be wanted by so many people. It was a nice position to be in.

At the same time, Brandon realizes how this sort of special treatment can really sidetrack some people. He's played with some guys who have all the talent in the world, but because of "who they are" they may not get in their work like they should. From Brandon's experience, those people don't go very far: "Some guys feel like they're owed something because of their draft picks. That really hinders a lot of people because they give themselves the benefit of the doubt. I've always felt like I've had to work at it to prove myself. Nothing's guaranteed in this game, not even the next day."

Other factors that helped Brandon to keep his head through all his success were his father and some of the teachers at his school. "I had a lot of teachers who didn't really care that I was going to get drafted. I still had to take their tests, I still had to pass," he says.

According to Morgan Ensberg, there's no reason people should be making "excuses" for athletes when they struggle to maintain an eligible GPA. "People have completely fallen back on the idea that somehow these athletes need to be treated differently. Yes, you'll miss some class, but outside of that they shouldn't be getting many breaks," he says.

The media is filled with numerous examples of athletics trumping academics in universities—and yet, many universities do have effective systems in place in order to preserve the academic integrity of athletes. For instance, at the University of Kansas, Kyle Murphy, drafted by the Texas Rangers in 2007, was able to maintain good grades while playing in the Big 12 Conference, largely due to coach Price's emphasis on academics. Kyle says, "Coach Price built a trust with his players that if you had to miss or leave practice early for a tutor appointment or class, you would never be frowned upon or have to sacrifice playing time."

In Price's estimation, each division is set up to meet a different need of student-athletes. At the Division III level, the focus is on academics. Many Division III schools require 1200 to 1300 SAT scores and 3.8 to 3.9 GPAs just to be admitted. Division II has a broader spectrum, including schools like the University of San Diego, a school where graduates can get accepted into most graduate programs across the country because of the university's academic reputation. On the reverse side of Division II, a school like Chico State (California State University) has one of the finest baseball programs in America, but does not have the same academic standards as San Diego.

Naturally, Division I schools are focused on producing winning teams. However, even with all of the time, effort, and resources it takes to create a winning college team, it is possible to maintain solid academics at the same time. According to Price, "The school needs to make an unbelievable commitment to be good in both areas."

In the case of the University of Kansas, the athletic department spent over $1 million in 2009 on academic tutors, and they employ eighteen academic counselors. As for Price's baseball team, his players' GPAs are consistently higher during the spring (in season) than in the fall; likewise, every player but one senior (he transferred to Stanford) graduated, including those who got drafted. Perhaps one of the reasons for Kansas' excellent graduation rate is because it is one of the few universities that offers a fifth-year scholarship. According to Price, "Kyle was an example of a senior draft who started playing in the minor leagues, but still took classes his fifth year in order to finish his degree."

Price is an example of a Division I coach who is devoted to the academic excellence of his players. Many people, including university presidents, believe a university's coaches and athletic director largely determine the academic success of their teams. Price and his assistant coaches recruit players who are also good students. They look for players who have 3.0 GPAs and 1000 SATs, most of whom are likely to graduate.

Kustra, president of Boise State University, gives credit to his athletic director of twenty-nine years for enforcing academic excellence. One of his methods includes roaming the halls with a clipboard to check that his athletes are attending classes. Likewise, Kustra feels confident his coaches will maintain order and discipline when necessary. For example, in 2007 one of the university's first-string football players was sent home two days before the Fiesta Bowl for breaking a 2:00 A.M. curfew. Because his athletic director and coaches are committed to the educational mission of the university, he can feel confident the athletic programs will complement, rather than undermine, the primacy of academics.

Still, no matter what measures coaches and universities may take, the fact remains that sometimes academics and athletics simply are not always an easy combination. For instance, critics argue that college athletics limit students in their choice of majors because their athletic schedule dictates which types of classes they can schedule. Likewise, an athlete, whose sport essentially amounts to a full-time job, must choose a major that is manageable (not "too hard" many would argue) so that he can accommodate his athletic schedule.

Morgan Ensberg did not find this to be the case when he played at USC, saying, "Maybe something like engineering or pre-med may have been too demanding, but really athletes were free to choose any major."

Still, research shows athletes, particularly at Division I colleges, tend to cluster in certain majors, frequently in communications or the social sciences.[3] Typically these majors are less academically demanding than, for instance, the hard sciences; yet, there may be another reason athletes cluster in certain majors, and the reason is not academic.

"If I chose to pursue a major in sociology I would be eligible to play my junior year," explains Kyle Murphy. Kyle wasn't particularly interested in sociology, but he was a transfer student at the University of Kansas, and needed to fulfill a certain number of credits by his junior year in order to be eligible to compete on the baseball team. The majority of the credits he had earned at the junior college fulfilled requirements in a sociology or psychology major, so he chose sociology.

For college athletes who do go on to play pro ball, completing their college degree is the exception rather than the norm. This is especially the case in baseball primarily because baseball is the professional sport that drafts the highest percentage of college students each year.[4] With its complex minor league system, baseball has many more roster spots to fill than basketball or football. Many people feel that if a player turns pro, he doesn't need to be concerned about graduating; he could always work on his degree in the off-season or once his athletic career comes to a close. Yet, graduation rates, many believe, signify whether a university has done its duty in providing student-athletes a college experience that is consistent with the university's mission. For this reason in 1989 Senator Bill Bradley from New Jersey and Senator Edward Kennedy from Massachusetts proposed a bill that would require schools to report graduation statistics to the federal government.[5] From this bill, the Department of Education developed an assessment called the Federal Graduation Rate (FGR) that measures what percentage of college athletes graduate within six years from their college or university. The NCAA, displeased with the federal government's assessment method, developed its own assessment known as the Graduation Success Rate (GSR). The GSR posts higher graduation rates than the FGR because it does not penalize an institution for "failing" to graduate an athlete when the athlete signs a professional contract or transfers to a different school; the FGR, on the other hand, includes transfers and draftees in the same category as dropouts. These measures, although imperfect assessments of a complex educational landscape, provide athletes with at least some picture of whether the school they are attending will actually help them to earn a degree.

According to Ben Miller, a researcher at Education Sector, a non-profit think tank located in Washington, D.C., "Many athletes choose a school because they are looking for good competition and good coaching, but others look at it as an opportunity to get a good education and actually graduate. The vast majority of baseball players aren't going to turn professional, so getting a good education is important."

Regardless of the low graduation rate, baseball players enter college with and maintain grade point averages that are significantly higher than other high-profile athletes in sports like basketball and football.[6] Academic success for a baseball player does not come without great sacrifice, however. Baseball is the sport that has the longest season—60 games on average, which is twice as much as the basketball season, and about five times as long as the football season. This means baseball players are prone to miss more class and travel more frequently than other student-athletes.

But are athletes really looking to receive a well-rounded education in college? Should so many people be concerned about their educational rights if many athletes care the most about what they love the most—their sport?

A well-rounded education is not limited to academics, but entails emotional and physical growth, social experiences, and exposure to different cultures and ideas. All of these factors challenge young people to move out of their comfort zones, explore their talents, and relate to diverse people. This sort of experience—the well-rounded education—is extremely valuable in today's society, and many people, including athletes, treasure the opportunity. According to J.R. Murphy, by giving up the opportunity to play at the University of Miami, he gave up "four years of fun, playing in college, time with friends." Adam Pettyjohn agrees that "those experiences are invaluable, the friends you make are important. It helps you mentally as well as physically."

An athlete's educational experience is an issue worth fighting for, and many voices have been raised over the years in defense of student-athletes' rights. In order to control what may be an overzealous coach's desire to win, the NCAA limits the amount of contact time coaches can have with their athletes. As far as baseball is concerned, players can miss a significant amount of class time, especially considering the long season and the possibility of rainouts and make-up games. Overall, however, college baseball is much less commercialized than football or basketball, so may be less susceptible to the threat of professionalization. According to Morgan Ensberg, "Baseball in college is much more insulated than other more commercialized sports. In fact, college baseball players get the best of both worlds. They get tons of resources, receive good teaching, play in these cool stadiums, but don't have the same pressures as some of the other big-time sports." When he was at the University of Kansas, Kyle Murphy felt that he had a reasonable schedule throughout the baseball season. Competition did include quite a bit of travel, finishing homework on bus rides and flights, but on a daily basis he would work out in the morning, attend class from 8:00 to 12:00, practice in the afternoon, then spend the evening studying or relaxing. In his mind, being a good baseball player and being a good student was challenging yet achievable.

Every player's situation is different—from turning pro, to signing at a junior college, to taking a four-year scholarship at a Division I school. Each path is filled with challenges. Even the first-round draft pick must make sacrifices, and the star college recruit still has to balance his responsibilities and priorities. No matter what the situation, it is a rite of passage to the next step. Once a player enters the minor leagues, he is no longer insulated from the realities of baseball as a business. His first season of professional baseball is a goal he's been reaching for since he was a child, yet achieving that goal only opens him to more rigors, more hard work, and above all more visions of what he might become should he continue on his path.

Four

The Apprenticeship

Our battered suitcases were piled on the sidewalk again; we had longer ways to go. But no matter, the road is life. — Jack Kerouac

ADAM PETTYJOHN HAD AN intense first three years in baseball, an entire career—promotions, call-up, first major league strikeout—packed into less time than most people need to graduate college. Detroit was a team that needed pitching at the time, and Adam was definitely fitting the profile, posting a 2.50 ERA between low A and high A his first season. In just two more years, he'd be pitching in the major leagues.

"At the start of my career I definitely shot through the system. I got promoted every year," Adam says. "When it was happening, I didn't realize how fast I was progressing towards the big leagues."

Unlike most players, who spend an average of four to five years in the minor leagues, Adam didn't have to languish too long in minor league stadiums with poor field conditions, sketchy locker rooms, and cheap dinner spreads like pizza and Taco Bell.

He also spent his first three years working primarily with Mike Rivera, a catcher whom the Tigers signed as a non-drafted free agent in 1997. With Rivera, Adam was able to develop consistent strategy, especially since both were promoted at a relatively even pace: "Mike is a great defensive catcher. He always wanted to make sure I felt comfortable with what I was throwing. We really developed a strong relationship, and it made it easier for me to get the job done."

In Adam's second season he was promoted mid–May to AA Jacksonville where he had a 4.69 ERA. As he faced tougher competition, he was learning that he needed to throw good pitches, no matter who was batting. With many hitters he had been able to dominate, but he knew that he couldn't rely on the batters being worse than he was for very long. "It's a false sense of security when the hitter sucked just a little more than you did," Adam recalls. "If

I threw a bad pitch, a better batter might have hit it 400 feet. That definitely would have happened with major league hitters."

During his third season, he started at AA then was on the DL for the first two months with a strained lateral muscle. Regardless of the injury, he went to AAA in July and faced much tougher competition. As the batters got better, Adam had to make more adjustments, most of them mental. He felt like he had to have "a little something extra" to get his outs, a common way of thinking for many pitchers seeing big-league-caliber talent for the first time. Eventually, he figured out that he just had to trust his stuff.

"A good pitch in A ball is a good pitch in the big leagues. It's hard to think that way when you're facing some big-name talent, but a strike's a strike. A good pitch can strike out any batter," Adam says.

The next year he found his pace in AAA, holding hitters to a 3.44 ERA through seventeen games. His performance earned him the final promotion he had been waiting for: the call-up to the big leagues.

Adam's first major league appearance was on July 16, 2001, twelve days since he had last pitched in AAA. Because of nearly two weeks of rest, he started feeling fatigued by the sixth inning. Still, the game had some great moments—striking out Ken Griffey, Jr., in the first inning, working with catcher Robert Fick, and pitching in front of 40,000 at brand-new Comerica Park.

After that first start, Adam made fifteen other appearances for the Tigers that season. He also had the chance to be on the team with Jeff Weaver, a teammate of his from college and a familiar face that made the transition to the big leagues smoother.

The whirlwind first three years reached a pinnacle that year. Little did Adam know, it would be another seven years before he'd return to the big leagues after that season.

Justin Lehr was never one to wait around for things to happen—when he saw what he wanted, he went after it. If something wasn't working for him, he'd find a way to fix it. And if there was anything standing in the way of his dream, he'd find a way around it.

When Justin started playing low A for the Oakland A's after his senior year of college, he knew he wasn't Billy Beane's first rounder. He was not the sort of player to fit a prototype anyway. His path to the big leagues would be scrappy, shrewd, at times electric—but never something that fit a description.

His first season in low A he pitched a respectable 5.95 ERA, nothing particularly unheard of since he'd come from a Division I program as a senior. Still, in pro ball Justin learned quickly that he could not have an "all or nothing" attitude. Even if he pitched a scoreless five innings, hitters could have figured him out by the sixth and tag him for four runs. He did some great things, then some bad things. That was the nature of pro ball.

With the high A team the next year, he posted a 13–6 record with a mere 3.19 ERA, a great finish to his first full minor league season. The next year at AA went a lot rougher, however, a year that Justin considers "a complete failure." Although he ended with a respectable 5.45 ERA, the inside numbers choked him: 206 hits and 20 home runs. He took some positive things out of that year, too—he led the team in innings pitched, for instance—but overall he knew he hadn't performed the way he needed to in order to get promoted.

"I now can see that that year was a learning process for me," Justin says. "At that time it was like, 'Wow, I gave up a ton of home runs and a ton of hits.' That was really hard to deal with."

What had worked for him the year before wasn't working for him at a higher level. Like many young pitchers, he went through a period of adjustment, a necessary time but unfortunately a time that slowed his career. As Justin recalls, "I was pretty stubborn and I believed in myself, so I wasn't quick to make changes. But I had to learn how to pitch with the stuff I had."

He got sent to the bullpen the next year in AA, and slowly he started to make adjustments that paid off in his performance. His stubbornness did not fade, though: "The coaches I really listened to gave me some space to learn on my own, and weren't in my face right after I messed up. It's a tough balance communicating with pro athletes—timing is everything. A player's not going to listen to you unless he's ready to listen to you."

In 2002 he put up a solid performance out of the bullpen, pitching half as many innings but slimming his ERA to 4.05. He tried not to let his team's mediocre record affect his attitude, but as a young player it was hard for him to separate the team's performance from his own. According to Justin, "I would see a good starter give up eight runs, and I would start wondering how I was going to do. That's a bad pattern. You start to focus on someone else. I'd see somebody get defeated, then I'd be defeated even before I got to the mound."

Even though he still had confidence in his ability, being a pro player changed the stakes a little. Most players he worked with doubted themselves to some degree. As he prepared for his relief appearances, Justin tried to find that place in his mind where he never doubted. "I was like that when I was young. I would make mistakes but it wouldn't matter so much," he says.

Like many players, he lost the ability to let go of the mistakes so freely, like children, who could go to sleep in anger and wake up without a memory of the night before. The charm of childhood had faded as the richness and complexity of adulthood (and the ability to throw 90 mile-per-hour pitches) materialized.

For the first time, Justin started thinking he needed a little something more. Another obstacle—he'd find another way around it.

When Brandon Snyder was drafted by the Baltimore Orioles, it was a bittersweet experience. Obviously, he was excited about being a first round draft selection, and receiving the opportunity to turn pro out of high school. At the same time, some of the fun had ended—the courtship with college recruiters, professional teams, and agents. It would soon be time for him to pack his bags, leave his home, and get thrown into the deep end of the ocean.

In 2005 baseball's amateur draft was not televised. That day, Brandon took off of school and followed the news feed on the internet with a party of family and friends. They were following each team's pick, anticipating when Brandon might receive a call from his agent in Los Angeles.

Brandon got the call about three picks before the Orioles had to make their selection, when "he told me the Orioles wanted me, here's the offer, will you take it."

At the Snyder house, the party continued after Brandon gave his verbal agreement with the Orioles. Ironically, he still had two weeks of high school to finish even though he was about to become a professional baseball player.

"I still had finals to complete, so it was tough," Brandon recalls. "But I had A's in most of my classes, so I was able to exempt a lot of the exams."

He finished school, elated and celebrating with classmates, teachers, and his community. When the time came for him to start planning for rookie ball that summer, some of the excitement began to fade: "It was strange— you're now going to be a professional athlete, this is what you've always wanted to do. Once I got to it, once the whole process was over, it was a little sad."

Before reporting to Bluefield, West Virginia, he took a week with his girlfriend in Florida, took some time to relax and get mentally prepared for what lay ahead.

The Orioles arranged a day for Brandon to sign his contract at Camden Yards. During that visit, he got to hit on the field with the team. He took ground balls alongside Miguel Tejada and answered questions from reporters. For the first time he was feeling like he was part of the team.

Rookie ball began in mid–June and was an opportunity for Brandon to get used to playing every day as well as being away from home for the first time. Although supporting himself for the first time, he was still within easy driving distance to his home. Frequently his family could come watch his games, or if the team ever had an off day, he would drive home for a visit.

That season he became familiar with the expectations of professional coaches, and was able to compete against other young talent, much of it from countries like Venezuela, the Dominican Republic, and Mexico. Hitting well (.271 in 44 games), Brandon was promoted at the end of the season to low A Aberdeen where he hit .393. That season he was eighteen years old.

Meanwhile, after a semester of pharmacy school, Vinny Rottino still couldn't get baseball out of his mind. He questioned whether he was chasing a childhood dream, or whether he still could give baseball some serious consideration. He had heard the stories—players who started in independent ball and got noticed, or players who went to tryout camps and got signed. If he was going to be serious about baseball he had to play baseball.

That Christmas, after he finished his last exam, he quit pharmacy school so that he could pursue a baseball career. In January he attended a Brewers tryout camp in Eau Claire, Wisconsin. To his delight, he put on a show for the scouts and was offered a minor league contract. Vinny knew the contract was only a small first step—teams offered hundreds of players contracts each year—but at least he had gotten his foot in the door. As Vinny recalls, "I had a long way to go—I was an older player, came from a DIII school—but I was playing baseball. That meant I had the opportunity to get better."

That winter Vinny trained in Wisconsin to get ready for his first spring training camp. In March he drove to Maryvale, Arizona, a journey that brought him through six different states, over 2,000 miles. At camp he had the opportunity to put on his first Brewers uniform, to hear opening talks from Brewers coaches, and to mingle with all of the talent the Brewers were training for their big league team.

Throughout spring training Vinny played a variety of positions, and because he was not used to professional pitching, he struggled at the plate. For the first time, he was confronted with the vast divide that separated his training at LaCrosse from teammates who had played at Division I colleges, or who were top draft selections.

While he was going through this struggle, he was reunited with Jack Curtis, his professor from LaCrosse, who now had a position as a sport psychology consultant with the Brewers. Vinny took the opportunity to meet with Jack individually because he was looking for whatever edge he could find to improve his game.

Jack worked with Vinny to establish his professional goals, and came up with tangible strategies for him to achieve his goals. Before Vinny had a chance to dismiss his presence on the Brewers roster, Jack told him to write down the year when he thought he would make it to the major leagues. The request took Vinny by surprise. He'd only been in Arizona for a couple weeks, and already he was wondering if pharmacy school still had his number. "Big leagues?" he said to Jack. "I just don't want to get released!" Jack encouraged him to write down the year and to read the goal every day. Vinny wrote down 2006.

At the end of spring training he didn't get released, even though his batting average slumped in the low .200s. The coaches made the decision on Vinny not because of his stats, but because of what they saw in his demeanor. Especially after meeting with Jack, he carried with him to the field a tenacious attitude. He may have struck out a lot, but worked hard and believed that, with time and effort, he would get better. He was a player who could see a broader vision, beyond the here and now, and was able to maintain a belief in that vision even amid challenging circumstances. Not many players had mastered this mindset, especially not young players, and it was difficult to teach. Vinny says, "It took me a while to believe that goal that Dr. Jack had me write down. Still, I read it every day, and gradually it started working into my mind."

When Vinny was assigned to the rookie team that summer, he was taking one more step, albeit small, towards his goal. He didn't have to return to pharmacy school, and he still had a job playing baseball; for the time being, everything was working out just fine.

Getting to pro baseball for the first time can be a great accomplishment. However, the excitement of the accomplishment can become quickly over-shadowed by the uncertainty of the minor league lifestyle. Some players have to leave their country for the first time and adjust to American culture. Others have to adjust to better competition and no longer being the star of their team. Still others have to learn how to take care of themselves—eating right, getting enough sleep, and building new relationships. So many factors besides the game itself can complicate a player's pursuit of his dream.

Many organizations would say that their minor league systems focus on developing players so that they are ready to contribute at the major league level. The way that players are developed varies significantly from rookie ball through AAA, and likewise individual players may be developed differently depending on their physical talent, maturity, and a variety of other factors. Coaches and players would agree that, although young players are developing their mechanical skills and physical stamina, their most significant development is mental and emotional.

Tom Trebelhorn, former Brewers manager who has held a spectrum of coaching and managing positions at the major league and minor league levels, agrees that the biggest factor of player development is emotional development: "Baseball is an emotional and individualistic game. Nobody can help the pitcher throw, nobody can help the hitter hit. Granted, in basketball nobody can shoot a basket for you either, but somebody on your team can set a pick for you. The left fielder can't help the pitcher. It's a game that is rewarded for individual achievement."

For young players the emotional adjustment can create the biggest challenge to their confidence and ultimately their performance. Many of them were all-star athletes in their home communities; in the minor leagues, though, they may appear average at best. Along with the weight of this reality, some players are learning to live on their own for the first time, away from the support of family and friends.

Jim Murphy, who has worked with major league, minor league, and

Olympic athletes, feels that helping players adjust to minor league living conditions is an essential step in helping them develop fully as players. According to Jim, "If players are going to get the most out of their ability, they need help resolving these issues—and these are often issues that have to do with their lives, not the game."

Many organizations do make efforts to create stable environments for their young players by providing rookie players with host families, English classes for foreign players, and financial seminars to help players manage their money. Nevertheless, organizations need to weed out players, especially at the lower levels. Unlike college baseball, professional ball is a business, and the purpose of their minor league system is to train future major league players so they can have a winning team. Likewise, they are trying to accomplish this with as little expense as possible because they need the majority of their dollars to cushion the major league payroll. These factors define the conditions of the minor league lifestyle—the long bus rides, cheap hotels, and mediocre fields.

Mike Moras, a catcher for the Mets AA team, faced the grind of minor league baseball the summer after he graduated with a business degree from the University of New Haven. Even though he now had the opportunity to get paid to play baseball, he quickly learned that pro ball was hardly a glamorous lifestyle. "It's late nights, sleeping during the day, long bus rides. You're not eating very good food," Mike says. He feels that without the support of his family, it would have been hard to have endured the lower levels of the minor leagues. "I feel very fortunate, just having my family in the stands, knowing I can go out for a nice meal once in a while. It's easier to believe in what you're doing when there's people behind you."

Baseball is one of the few pro sports that develops players within a minor league system rather than depending on colleges. Many players consider this an advantage because it gives them more opportunity to learn and improve so those with less talent still have a chance to compete. At the same time, it is a long apprenticeship to endure before players can even hope to approach a major league roster. Baseball is a game filled with many mechanical intricacies, which is the main reason the minor league system is so extensive. Most pitchers don't develop all of their pitches until they've been in the minor leagues for at least a couple years; then it usually takes a couple more years for them to perfect these pitches. As players are working on their hitting, pitching, and defense, organizations provide players with many opportunities to develop, both on and off the field.

Every team relies on player development to provide future talent for the organization. Small-market teams especially, though, must look to their farm system to provide the major league team with talent. Since most players take at least three to four years to develop, teams like the Kansas City Royals,

Cleveland Indians, and Washington Nationals have had to use careful strategy and long-term planning in order to achieve results.

Small-market teams can provide players valuable opportunities that other teams cannot offer. Garrett Jones, for instance, was drafted in 1999 by the Atlanta Braves, then spent the majority of his minor league service (2002–2008) with the Minnesota Twins. In 2008 he put in excellent numbers with the AAA team, but he still didn't get called up in September. By then Jones was a minor league free agent and decided to start exploring other options.

"I wanted to try my luck with another team," Garrett says. "The Twins had Justin Morneau at first, and they had some other younger guys coming up. I was twenty-nine by that time, so I knew that I'd need to give myself a good opportunity in order to make it. The Pirates had more opportunity for me."

The next year Garrett started in AAA with the Pirates, but after his July 1 promotion to Pittsburg, his career took off, in part because the Pirates were in need of some sluggers. Jones put up astonishing numbers, hitting more than twenty home runs as a rookie, even when starting in the month of July (a feat only matched by one other hitter). That year he became a contender for Rookie of the Year (won that year by Chris Coghlan of the Marlins) and secured himself a spot on the 25-man roster for the following season.

Granted, Garrett's timing was a significant key to his success; at the same time, he attributes his success with the Pirates to a shift in his mental game: "I was always really nervous with the Twins, trying too hard, not letting my natural ability play out. When I went to the Pirates, I wanted to get to the big leagues and I knew I could do it. I kept better control of myself mentally, and when I got called up, I was more prepared in my head. Physically, I wasn't any better with the Pirates than I had been with the Twins, but I had better control of my mental game."

He was planning to attend Purdue before he got drafted in the 14th round by the Braves. Looking back, he realizes he wasn't ready to play pro ball at age eighteen and maybe would have benefited from playing in college: "I didn't know what I wanted to study in school, so I figured I would learn a lot more going into pro ball. I did learn a lot, but it took me longer than most guys. It depends on the player, and obviously I'm in a good position now."

Garrett battled with the mental challenges a lot of young players face when they first reach pro ball. This is because young players are not just learning how to play baseball, but they are also learning how to work their first job, relate to other people, and develop character and experience that will distinguish them on the field. Basically, young players are learning how to play baseball and mature at the same time. Organizations that acknowledge both aspects of a player's development (his development in the game as well as in his life) provide players with every opportunity to succeed.

Perhaps not coincidentally, the Pirates who gave Garrett an opportunity as a twenty-nine-year-old rookie have allocated more of their efforts and budget to developing players through their farm system. As a team that has been without a championship since 1992, the Pirates have had to implement careful, long-term strategy for developing a winning team for the future. This has meant trading key big league talent like Freddy Sanchez, Nate McLouth, and Adam LaRoche in 2009 in order to flood their farm system with promising prospects for the future.

Kyle Stark, director of player development for the Pirates, has incorporated a variety of programs that go above and beyond merely coaching a pitcher how to tweak his mechanics: "Our approach to player development takes two main approaches. One, we want to develop these guys as men, both in the game and for after baseball. Two, we're trying to develop all angles of a player—mental, physical, social, etc. This philosophy applies to every level of our minor league system. As you get to the higher levels, the focus becomes more on the mental side, less on the mechanical."

One component of player training in the Pirates system includes Steve Shenbaum's communication training program. Although Shenbaum's techniques are valuable for players at any age or level, he has especially impacted rookie players and foreign players who are experiencing pro ball for the first time. At that age (international signers can be as young as a sixteen-year-old), players can struggle to listen carefully to each other, or to respond slowly and carefully to a question. With practice, they will gain skills communicating with teammates and coaches, as well as the media.

At the same time, many international players do not speak very good English; while these players take English classes to help improve their speaking, Shenbaum works with all players to build cultural awareness so that they can function better as teammates.

"Cliques are going to form among players," says Stark, "based on the language they speak or their culture. There's a strong comfort when somebody speaks your language, an understandable comfort. But we try to help players find some common ground."

In his program, Shenbaum will have two players stand up, and they will have to find five things they have in common besides the Pirates and their age. This gives some of the well-spoken, confident American players a chance to connect with more timid, unsure foreign players. It also gives foreign players a chance to practice their English.

Rather than learning these skills "on the fly" (or not learning them at all), players in the Pirates system are prepared for some of the challenges they will face when they cannot get along with their teammates, have a run-in with a coach, or give a bad interview after a game. Often times a player's ability to communicate and relate, not his playing alone, can contribute to his development and progression to the major leagues.

The reality of baseball's minor league system, however, is that because it needs thousands of players in order to function, many players get stuck being "organizational players," or players who are on the team in order to develop other top prospects. The older a player gets, the more challenging it can be for him to earn a spot on a big league roster, particularly because clubs want to prove themselves right by promoting their younger draft selections. Every player always has a chance, though, even veteran minor leaguers like Garrett Jones or Daniel Nava. In order to secure that chance, players need to endure the minor league lifestyle.

Baseball is a profession that can intersect many other life experiences, particularly marriage. For many players, especially if they are not getting promoted at a steady pace, getting married may change their willingness to stay in baseball. Although countless players establish comfortable lives for their wives and families, pro sports can be hard on families, especially during the early years of a player's career. Many players have no guarantee that they will be with the team another year either. If they do get released, they have no guarantee another team will sign them. Living with such uncertainty makes it hard to plan for the future, especially for someone who may want to get married and start a family.

Justin Lehr, who got married after his senior year of college, was earning the standard $1,050 a month salary of a minor league player. Playing in the Northwest League, they had to pay living expenses in one of the most expensive parts of the country.

"My wife and I always joke that I was paying to play the first couple seasons," Justin says. "There was no chance my salary could cover our budget. If you have a car payment, clubhouse dues, and rent—right there you're broke. Then add a cell phone, moving expenses. You just rack up debt."

Some young players can supplement their salaries with money from their signing bonuses. But generally only the top six rounds get decent money that could lend them some level of security. Justin signed for $20,000, a figure lower than most in the eighth round because he signed as a senior and had less leverage.

What salary he did make as a minor league player only lasted for six months out of the year, too. The other half of the year Justin and his wife had to find some other way of supporting themselves. As Justin recalls, "For two off seasons we lived with my parents and did substitute teaching. We could make about $2,000 a month as teachers."

Justin admits that being young at the time gave him the freedom to explore possibilities, even though the experience came with tremendous sacrifice. "When you're young, you don't care if it's going to ruin your credit score or you have no place to live. Still, it's a huge risk," he says.

Morgan Ensberg, who got married the year of his call up (2000), comments, "Wives go through so much and nobody knows about it. They end up packing up and moving your family when you're off playing baseball. Then if you get traded, they have to find another place to live and start the whole process over again. Baseball certainly rules players' lives, but it also rules their families' lives, too."

Adam Pettyjohn feels fortunate that his wife and son can stay with him during the baseball season: "Many baseball players are separated from their wives and families during the season which is no fun. The long distance thing can be a strain on marriages and families."

Being single presents players with a unique set of challenges, too. For instance, single players do not have a second source of income to help them get through the early years of their career. Likewise, it can be a greater challenge for single players to take care of themselves, physically and emotionally, when they do not have a spouse or family alongside them.

PJ Forbes, who manages the single A Bradenton Marauders for Pittsburg, acknowledges that young players (often single) frequently struggle in their first season of pro ball because they are still learning how to take care of themselves. Many players "run out of gas" come September and face exhaustion by the end of the season.

"When you're young, a lot of times you think you're invincible," Forbes says. "But come September, these guys realize that the work they did in the offseason wasn't enough to sustain them for playing five months straight. Now they're playing every day instead of three or four times a week. Many young guys can't understand what that feels like until they actually do it."

According to Brandon Snyder, it's not just the playing time that wears players down, saying, "The physical part is not the only thing that makes you tired—it's the bus trips, the hours you keep, the sleep deprivation, the way you get your hours of sleep, your diet—it's that stuff that physically wears you out."

Like any paid entertainer, baseball players keep mainly nighttime hours. Even though games can end as early as 10:00 P.M., players may not leave the clubhouse until much later. They may want to go out for dinner, talk the game over with their teammates, and by then return to the hotel after midnight. It may take another hour or two for them to relax and actually get to sleep. That means the next day they rise by ten o'clock at the earliest (more realistically by noon or later). For a seven o'clock start time, players usually arrive at the field no later than three o'clock. So on a typical day, they have about a four-hour window of time to themselves. With that schedule, a player's entire life during the season can become consumed by baseball.

In order to avoid this constant grind, some players make an effort to schedule other activities in their day. When Brandon Snyder found himself getting trapped in the schedule, he would start getting up earlier, go to a movie or spend time at the mall, anything to give him a break from the game.

On travel days, players have other factors to contend with. When traveling by bus, the team may leave immediately following a game and travel through the night to the next city. They might arrive in the early morning, have to get settled at a hotel, sleep, and get to the field by the afternoon.

Ironically, the conditions of travel, not necessarily playing conditions, can lead to players injuring themselves. When Brandon Snyder suffered back spasms one season, he attributed the injury to sitting up straight on a bus for ten hours. "You're sleeping on buses, your legs are not circulating right. Or you're just changing beds so much, not getting a good night's sleep," Brandon recalls.

One saving grace in the minor league routine are the off days that are scheduled during the season. They provide players with more freedom, even opportunities to spend time with family and friends.

Whenever he has an off day, Adam Pettyjohn helps his wife run errands, goes to the park with his son, and enjoys a nice dinner in the evening. As Adam says, "I love making sure we get to spend a lot of time together. That's definitely the best part of the off days. Getting to enjoy my family without baseball."

For somebody like Brandon Snyder, whose teams have been within driving distance of his home, he would take the opportunity to spend time with his family—watch his brothers' high school baseball games, take a fishing trip, or go turkey hunting in the spring. Over the years, he's learned what he can do on an off day so that he'll feel refreshed for the next day; he's also learned what he needs to avoid: "No country music concerts. I've learned that—it's too tiring, too hard to perform well the next day."

Although the lifestyle confines players in certain ways, it also provides players with many freedoms. For instance, unlike other occupations, baseball liberates players from a nine-to-five schedule, without the confines of an office cubicle, an hour lunch, and two weeks of vacation. Granted, the working conditions of baseball are hardly utopian, yet they seem to be far less agitating than the conditions many Americans endure in "regular" jobs. Shows like *The Office* satirize commonplace job conditions that cultivate frustration: boring work, poor communication (or lack of face-to-face communication), lack of teamwork, and lack of pride in a job well done.

In professional sports, on the other hand, players are obviously doing what they love to do. They may still face the frustrations of a difficult manager, coach, or front office staff, but they aren't sitting at a desk, receiving memos and emails about their assignments. Rather, they have daily face-to-face contact with their coworkers. Their progress, likewise, is tangible, evident in the results of a game or the effectiveness of a swing. Everyone who is employed by the team, from players to ticket takers, believes in their "company" to a certain degree. Their passion and loyalty extends beyond merely the Royals or the Yankees—they love something larger, baseball, and this positive emotion generates good energy in the workplace. Obviously, players feel pride in a job well done, whether they've generated a win for the team, put up good defense, or pitched eight strong innings. Baseball players believe in what they are doing every day, even when the season gets long or they're fighting their way out of a slump. The strength of this commitment gives many players satisfaction in their jobs, regardless of the less-than-ideal working conditions.

At the same time, the freedom of a baseball lifestyle challenges baseball players in a different way—it challenges them to make wise decisions in how they spend their free time, and not to get caught up in the hype of being a pro athlete. These challenges, as the media constantly reminds us, can be even more complicated than the "typical" challenges of feeding a family, making the house payments, and finding a fulfilling job. Many athletes—through a combination of media hype, female attention, and the freedoms of their lifestyle—can develop a distorted sense of reality.

When Magic Johnson was diagnosed with HIV in 1991, the media roundly attacked pro athletes for being sexually promiscuous, especially in the age of AIDS when people were supposed to know better. In a November 18 *Sports Illustrated* article from that year, athletes reacted to Johnson's situation with pity and fear—but not necessarily enough to change their ways. Chicago Bulls center Will Perdue was quoted saying, "Right now, it's easy to get caught up in the ordeal. Everyone says, 'I won't let it happen to me.' But the impact will fade. Everybody has an ego, and let's face it, it's difficult to say no to a beautiful woman."[1]

Twenty years later, *Sports Illustrated* still runs stories about fallen icons like Ben Roethlisberger and Tiger Woods whose women-chasing ways damaged their careers, endorsement opportunities, and reputations. When analyzing the consequences of bad behavior, we often fixate on how an athlete's recklessness has tangible consequences, such as a fifty-game suspension without pay, an alcohol-induced injury, or a nightmare paternity suit. Equally as damaging, however, is how an athlete's poor choices can rob him of a rewarding life. Sometimes losing his money can be the best thing that ever happens to an athlete; wealth and fame can cloud a person's perceptions, and lead him to believe that he has reached the ultimate in satisfaction and fulfillment. Self-indulgence, however, does not satisfy, but only creates a craving for more. Likewise, it isolates a person from friends, family, and relationships that provide perspective and a sense of purpose.

Many people make it their goal, legitimately, to achieve a certain degree of wealth and fame, a goal that can be worthwhile and achievable for many athletes. Life is uncomfortable, painful, and mundane; it is understandable that most people long for financial security, luxuries, and excitement. Likewise, society is often indifferent to people's aspirations or desires, and can often deal an unfair hand to people who have worked hard, stayed out of trouble, or sacrificed on others' behalf. Because of these unfair conditions, many people long for respect—people to know their name, praise them, and at the very least recognize their achievements. It is natural for people to desire wealth and fame, and pursuing major league baseball is a legitimate means for accomplishing this goal.

Something happens, though, between the purity of this desire and the reality of achieving it, as if human nature is too weak to achieve wealth and fame without being corrupted. Once a person begins praising himself for his achievements, he can easily lose touch with reality. Like Kurtz in *Heart of Darkness*, he can enter the endeavor with a noble purpose, but once he sees his own greatness, how he can rule others and become great like a god, he can easily lose sight of his path. Kurtz, who went searching for ivory, died in the jungles of Africa; he was a "remarkable man," but once he had grown sick on his lies, didn't have the strength or the inclination to find a way out.

Young athletes, who have experienced fewer consequences perhaps than veteran athletes, are especially vulnerable to off-the-field mistakes. Likewise, they may be adjusting to the "thrill" of playing pro ball and playing in front of larger crowds.

Tom Trebelhorn, who currently manages the short-season A team for the San Francisco Giants, tries to cultivate a balance in his players so that they can have a fun experience, yet develop good character at the same time. He says, "It's hard to explain to these kids that you will have the rest of your life to do whatever you want, but your opportunity to get to the big leagues will not last. I want them to have a good experience—not to take risks that will embarrass them or hurt their career."

Even what might seem like minor incidents—getting into a bar fight, a night in jail because of a DUI—can significantly impact a player's career.

"Maybe you cut your hand," Adam Pettyjohn remarks, "so you can't pitch the next day. Even if you make it back safely to the hotel, you've got to explain what happened." According to Adam, most organizations do a good job keeping incidents out of the newspapers. But that doesn't prevent news from traveling throughout baseball. "You've really got to be careful, keep your nose clean," he says.

Vinny Rottino, likewise, sees organizations keeping reasonable tabs on players: "They treat you like an adult and expect you to be responsible. But they don't want to be embarrassed. They want a classy organization. If you act like a jackass, you're going to get weeded out of the game, unless you've got amazing talent. You better have ridiculous talent if you're going to be a jackass."

Although baseball organizations do support responsible lifestyles, the conditions of professional baseball make many players vulnerable to poor choices. This can be especially true for players who get promoted quickly to the big leagues.

Adam, who personally experienced rapid promotion to major league baseball, understands firsthand how success, and the money that accompanies it, can complicate a player's perspective: "You throw any twenty-three-year-old hundreds of thousands of dollars, cater to him non-stop, give him first class travel accommodations—there's going to be a lot of immature kids out there who are going to screw up."

Ted Power, pitching coach for the Cincinnati Reds AAA affiliate, also sees the conditions of the baseball lifestyle as a hindrance to a young player's growth and maturity: "Baseball is not a business that lends to the maturing of men. As a baseball player you're told when you go to work, whom you're going to be facing. You have a schedule for everything. Then you get to the big leagues and you're even more pampered, you bring your suitcase to the ballpark and you don't see it again until the next city."

In one sense, suitcases and schedules don't matter that much. In fact, "pampered" might be the last word most minor league players would use when describing their lives during the baseball season. Without a doubt, though, the amenities of being an entertainer could eliminate some of the key responsibilities most working adults face: commuting to work, working long hours, buying groceries, paying bills, or doing laundry. Likewise, ballplayers, no matter how lowly or close to elimination, are the center of attention. A club's entire staff, from maintenance crew to coaches, exists in order to facilitate the players. This means they are the center of their universe—a desirable position, yet a position that challenges their ability to develop a balanced perspective on life.

"When things are going well, everyone comes out to see you perform, you're signing autographs—you think you're invincible," says Adam Pettyjohn.

Granted, minor league baseball may seem to fall short of "celebrity" conditions—there's no paparazzi, no red carpet, and no champagne at the hotel—yet the ingredients for this lifestyle, at the very least this mindset, are present even at the minor league level. In fact, virtually anyone can be made to feel like a celebrity—just throw him loads of attention, talk about what he does, watch him and look at him. This is the high school quarterback, the dairy princess, or the esteemed guest speaker at a convention. A celebrity is simply somebody who is widely known in his society, whether that society is as large as the entire nation or as concentrated as a small town in Alabama.

How then could a celebrity lifestyle be more challenging than an ordinary lifestyle? Many would argue this lifestyle seems more worth living, more fulfilling, and more meaningful. Baseball players entertain people, they are positive role models for children, and they are recognized, literally applauded, for their achievements. Indeed, these are the benefits of holding a place of prominence. Yet, the more visible someone is, the more he is being watched. For most celebrities, this can become invasive; they have a public life that many fans feel entitled to enjoy. Many fans, unfortunately, treat athletes like their property rather than people who have jobs to do and personal lives to maintain. Bryan Burwell of the *St. Louis Post-Dispatch* describes how fans "scream at players, they scream at the manager" for the autographs and attention they feel professional athletes owe them.[2]

Many fans turn to sports as a security, a way of expressing intelligence and emotion that they may not be able to express in other aspects of their lives. Their frustrations get taken out on the players, creating an even greater divide between athletes and fans. This divide isn't good either for the fans or the players—fans start to idealize players and players see themselves as "exceptions" to the rest of society. Both steps romanticize human nature, which remains consistent no matter what a person's background, profession, or social status. The more a divide is created, the more fans and players avoid real interactions, real flesh and blood and dirt under the fingernails. This makes it even harder for players to accept failure, to accommodate something less than the ideal, and that is when athletes can act out in frustration or anger.

Morgan Ensberg, who spent his span of time signing autographs, agrees that the divide between fans and ball players exists: "I'm tired of people thinking that baseball players aren't human beings. People look at us and, that four-foot wall that separates the player from the fan, it might as well be the Grand Canyon."

Mark Vermillion, professor of sociology at Wichita State University, likewise sees the isolating effect fans can have on ball players: "Athletes become so separated. Imagine going out to dinner at night and everyone knows who you are, wants to invade your space. You always see people as wanting to take something from you."

When a player feels constantly in demand, he is hearing the message that he is important, more important than people who aren't as in demand. Even if an athlete knows this isn't true (he doesn't see himself as "special" compared to everyone else), he is still absorbing the message. In some ways, an athlete ought to feel set apart from other people—he has earned a place on the field, in the public eye, because of his hard work and years of perseverance. Yet, this way of thinking can become dangerous and misleading, and can grow exponentially as an athlete's celebrity status grows larger and larger.

The media is filled with examples of professional athletes who have broken laws, fallen into drug addiction, committed acts of violence, and lived unfaithfully to their spouses and families. In one sense this is a double standard: the public expects pro athletes to be held to the same standard as "regular" people, yet they draw so much more attention to celebrity mistakes. The people who criticize pro athletes are the same people who contribute to their precarious circumstances, an environment of entitlement and special treatment. Of course, every person is responsible for his own actions. That is why professional athletes, no matter what level of "celebrity" they possess, must be more prepared than the average person to avoid the mistakes that have sabotaged so many careers and reputations.

Like any entertainer, pro athletes spend little time at home during the season, and much time in public places—hotels, restaurants, and stadiums. Any person's relationships with people at home are deep and complex. They also can be the most challenging relationships because they are constant and require maintenance and hard work. Even though they can be the most challenging, they can also provide the deepest fulfillment and intimacy in a person's life. Relationships in public—with coworkers, fans, and the general public—can be (don't have to be) simple and superficial. The public spaces encourage the possibility of superficial interaction. When an athlete leaves a hotel or restaurant, he doesn't need to return; he has no personal connection to the place, unlike places of his private life—a home, for instance—that are laden with memories. What he does in public can be easily left behind, seemingly forgotten.

Likewise, the life of an entertainer is filled with daily opportunities for indulgence. American society testifies clearly that it is easy for people to indulge themselves in times of plenty, harder to see value in restraint when consequences seem far off, even non-existent. For this reason, Joseph Epstein argues, present-day America seems to be caught in what he terms "perpetual adolescence": "With lots of money around, certain kinds of pressure were removed. More and more people nowadays are working, as earlier generations were not, with a safety net of money under them. All options opened, they now swim in what Kierkegaard called 'a sea of possibilities,' and one of these possibilities in America is to refuse to grow up for a longer period than has been permitted any other people in history."[3]

Many people argue that athletes, especially millionaire athletes, epitomize America's tendency to linger in the pleasures of youth, unwilling to assume the responsibilities of adulthood. Their lifestyles—filled with games, expensive toys, and unencumbered relationships—set the tone for a society that is in love with box scores, *Sports Illustrated*, and *ESPN*. But what's so wrong with diverting ourselves with a little bit of fun? We've come a long way since our Puritan ancestors who considered corn-husking a fun party theme. A society that is affluent and stable has the ability to relax, be creative, and enjoy various forms of entertainment.

But too much indulgence can begin to have the effect of a good narcotic: we can lose touch with reality, with the feeling in our limbs, if we are diverting ourselves too much. We see this, sadly, with entertainers and athletes on a regular basis. People who have indulged so much, who have convinced themselves they've earned the rights to indulgence, that they begin making foolish choices. If we always have to feel good then we never learn how to tolerate pain. And pain is a part of life—*real* life that grows out of truth and genuine relationships, not just something that looks good from the outside.

A person who falls victim to this mindset may develop what David Elkind terms the "personal fable," or the idea that his experiences are unique from everyone else's. This sort of thinking, prevalent among teenagers, limits a person's ability to relate meaningfully to others. Likewise, it can lead a person to develop distorted thinking that can hinder his ability to reach his potential. Essentially, a person becomes trapped in his own idea of the world, an idea based on what he thinks, how he feels, and what he perceives. This person has a self-centered approach to life and the need to satisfy his ego will rule him. When he finds himself in challenging situations, he will often take them personally and fail to consider the circumstances objectively. Without an objective perspective, a person can misread a situation and be unable to understand how to effectively deal with that challenge.

A major stumbling block for some ballplayers is their belief that a person's talent is limited by his genetics; players who have less natural ability may feel discouraged when they begin entering the ranks with more talented players. In reality, innate ability is only a portion of a player's potential. A player has much more control over his performance than he may think if he is willing to dedicate time to developing his tools.

Somebody like Vinny Rottino, for instance, barely made the cut at the Brewers tryout camp because he had a lot of work to do on his swing. However, once given the opportunity to compete, Vinny dedicated hours and hours to working on the skills he needed to make it to the next level.

Research shows that high-level performers typically dedicate at least 10 years or 10,000 hours practicing before they reach expert status. That means even players who are small when they are younger, who don't seem to fit the "profile" of an athlete, still can shape themselves into contenders through hours and hours of hard work.

A rigorous routine not only develops a player's technical skills, but also can transform an athlete's physique—he can increase the size of his heart, the number of capillaries supplying blood to the muscles, and the metabolic properties of fast and slow twitch muscles. Ultimately, a disciplined player can defy genetics and develop into the sort of athlete he hopes to be.

Tom Trebelhorn, who has worked with many different types of ballplayers, sees that baseball players (more so than any other athletes) come in all shapes and sizes. People should not automatically assume that bigger is better.

When Trebelhorn managed the Milwaukee Brewers from 1986 to 1991, he employed the services of sport psychology consultant Jack Curtis to work with his ballplayers, not on their ball-handling skills, but instead on their "mind handling" skills. In Trebelhorn's view, the most important mental tool a ballplayer can have is what he calls an "extravagant imagination." According to Trebelhorn, "When you have an imagination, you can see a situation in your mind before it actually occurs on the field. Those are the best players. They're always ready because they pre-play competitive scenarios in their mind."

Essentially, this is a skill that Curtis and other sport psychologists work to cultivate in players—the ability to imagine or use imagery.

Children of all people have the most vivid experience of imagination. At young ages, we understand so much less about the world, our relationships, and the society in which we live; in a sense, this disconnection from reality allows children the freedom to envision whatever experiences meet their fancy. As we mature, however, and understand the foolishness of our childhood visions, many people abandon the practice of using their imagination and instead stick to the here-and-now.

In today's technologically advanced society, even children are becoming robbed of pure opportunities for using their imaginations. Many technology-based forms of entertainment are visually stimulating—video games, the internet, movies and television.

Trebelhorn laments this trend: "For every song there's a music video—you can't even imagine your own dream today. Rather than going out to the playground to play, kids compete indoors, on a video game. There's only so much room to express yourself through a video game that's based on a pre-set program."

Likewise, a technological trend that has hindered athletes' imaginations, Trebelhorn feels, is the replay button. "With imagination you can envision a situation, then when it comes up you're ready. This country now has a replay button. We're really based on this replay thing—'I could have done this.' Well, it's too late by then," he says.

The replay philosophy also has crept into other aspects of everyday life. If we change our mind about our vacation, we can reschedule the plane ticket (albeit for a cost, yet a cost many can afford). Even in our school systems, which seem more and more desperate each year to graduate students, students are given numerous chances to fulfill course requirements if they show even the slightest motivation to finish.

Sport is a vivid area in American life where missed opportunities still have consequences. If a player misses a fly ball, he can't take back the run that scored. Perhaps his team will come back for the win, but there is certainly no guarantee. In sports, it's not good enough for someone to say, "I could have done this." He has to be ready. A similar philosophy is expressed by Sun Tzu in his famous work *The Art of War*: "The art of war teaches us to rely not on the likelihood of the enemy's not coming, but on our own readiness to receive him; not on the chance of his not attacking, but rather on the fact that we have made our position unassailable." Whether the enemy comes or not—whether the next pitch requires action or not—the best will be ready.

One of the best in baseball, who practiced extravagant imagination and constant readiness, was Paul Molitor. Trebelhorn recalls a game when he was managing the Brewers and they were playing in Toronto. At that time, Toronto's stadium had hard, artificial grass laid over concrete, a surface on which the ball reacted very differently from real grass. "Before the game I said to Paulie, 'You know, I think a guy could score from second base on a wild pitch.' He just sort of gave me a wink. Then I'll be darned, during the game the pitch gets by, and here comes Molitor from second base to score. We had talked about it, but I know he had thought about it even before I mentioned it."

The benefit of having an imagination, pre-playing a situation, is when the situation comes up, there's an instantaneous correct reaction. These types of players don't need a second chance—they get it right the first time.

Good athletes will train themselves to use their imaginations, both during competition and in preparation for a game. In some cases, coaches will guide their teams through imagery exercises, describing the moments and experiences the players should visualize in order to prepare for the big game.

This is a technique Jim Murphy used with his women's golf team at the University of British Columbia in preparation for the RCGA Championships in June 2010. As a team, they pre-played competitive situations, not days or weeks before the competition, but for eight months. Murphy's use of imagery is a testament to the fact that imagery is not just a "one and done" technique, but a mental exercise that requires regular practice.

The reason imagery must be repeated is because the mind becomes influenced by memories, whether it be the mundane repetition of a McDonald's commercial, or something more profound, like a game-winning home run. Imagery, then, is forcing the mind to develop memories that, through repetition, will begin to influence an athlete's physical responses during competition.

Many of us understand the power of imagery when we experience a vivid dream. Even though the memories we develop while we are sleeping usually are not real, they can influence us to physically and emotionally react as if those mental images actually happened. In our sleep, we may flinch, talk, or sweat because of what is running through our mind. Sometimes our dreams can even leave us feeling angry, anxious, or joyful, depending on how the dream influenced our emotions.

Athletes can create the same effects as dreams by practicing imagery. To start, players need to evaluate the strengths and weaknesses of their performance. They can reconstruct outstanding performance in order to build confidence. Likewise, when a player struggles with his performance, he can isolate that weakness in his mind, then recreate that experience by envisioning a successful performance. Through visualizing this better performance, he is training his mind to believe in his potential to improve. Once a player's mind believes something, his body will react according to those beliefs.

Because a player only has so many opportunities to compete, imagery provides additional opportunities to be "in the moment" even when he is not competing. Tom Trebelhorn remarks, "Baseball is a game of consistency, being as good as you can be with the talent you have. Somebody who can figure that out—that generally gets guys major league careers. Of course there are the fifty-home-run guys, the twenty-saves guys—those guys are pretty special. But the other 80 percent of the major leagues, it's those guys who can grind it out every day and stay consistent."

The best way to develop consistency is through repetition—either repetitive play or repetitive imagery (or, ideally, both). This is why baseball has been flooded with so many exceptionally gifted Latin players—where they come, from they go to school and they play baseball. Their lives are relatively simple that way. They don't have to take time off for family vacations, hitting lessons, parties and programs. Although children from Latin countries do not enjoy the luxuries of American children (many of them don't even have basic equipment), they have time, and they invest their time into baseball.

Even though American players seem to "have it all" compared to Latin players, they face the unique challenges of living in a wealthy country. For instance, in America we are bombarded with various forms of technology that can not only be distracting, but also condition us to have short attention spans. By playing video games, surfing the web, or even sending a text message, people are enjoying interaction and stimulation without delay. Many aspects of life, however, are much less gratifying, or take longer to master—completing a homework assignment, reading a book, or saving money, for instance. Baseball similarly is a game that requires readiness, but does not provide players with constant action. Without knowing when he will need to act, a baseball player must be ready at every moment with the same amount of energy and preparation.

A player who uses imagery as part of his training routine disciplines himself to be focused on the moment. This technique can be extremely useful during competition because baseball, unlike other sports, affords ample amounts of down time. According to Trebelhorn, this is why baseball is such a mentally demanding game: "You take a guy and put him in the outfield, he's been doing it for two hours, in the twilight, he misses the ball and loses the ball game. He's had a lot of time to think about things, he's had a lot of time doing nothing, and now he's lost the game. That's a difficult thing for young people to handle."

In order to be ready for that moment, disciplined players will never "zone out," but will always be rehearsing mentally what could happen next. The more a player practices imagery off the field, the easier it will be for him to pre-play certain scenarios while on the field.

Another reason consistency can be challenging for young baseball players is because baseball is a game that exhibits player mistakes on an individual basis. For some players, this exposure can be difficult to handle, and something challenging to bounce back from when they have to go out the next day to perform.

Trebelhorn comments: "Our most popular sports today minimize players' mistakes. Watching a football game, how do you know that a missed block led to a defeat? But in baseball, on a 3–2 count with the bases loaded, you strike out, everyone knows whose fault it was. In our game, the shortstop makes an error, you see it on the scoreboard. This game holds you immediately accountable for your actions, and the pace of the game allows for not only immediate interpretation, but also the time for people to interpret and reinterpret events."

In baseball, the down time can be beneficial for players, an opportunity for them to establish a proper mindset. More often than not, though, the time for reflection results in mental anguish. Often the cause for this anguish is when a player fixates on a moment of failure itself so that he is unable to move on to the next day.

"So many players stay attached to yesterday," says Jim Murphy. "When you're losing there's so much attachment to yesterday, and then you carry yesterday into tomorrow. Ultimately, that's going to affect a player's ability to perform."

Many players struggle to understand that they cannot control their success—the only thing they can control is the goals they establish to achieve success. When a player is hampered with failure, though, his mind may linger in that failure, and he will be moved by doubts and fears that will affect his performance.

Murphy comments, "You can have a five-tool player with incredible ability, but if he has some lack of confidence, some fear, it can easily crowd out those five tools."

As a coach, Murphy tries to help players remain unattached to the outcome of their performance, a skill he feels is seldom taught in pro ball. "Generally, the way most people deal with failure is to go back out there and make them deal with failure again," he says.

Justin Lehr found this to be the case with most teams he worked with: "People don't really want to address that using your mind is as important as it is. They'll say, 'Yeah, you mentally lost it,' but they're not giving you the mental tools to help you."

This can make it difficult for someone to bounce back from failure, especially if they're focusing on the part of their game that isn't the problem.

"You can see it in somebody's body language," says Vinny Rottino, "when they have doubts. They're second guessing a lot, tinkering with their mechanics during the game when that's not the place to do that."

When a player lacks confidence, the battle begins in his mind, usually as the result of a bad performance or a chain of bad performances. A person's mind can be his biggest enemy—but it can also be his strongest tool. The key is for a player to locate the irrational thoughts he is expressing in his mind, capture those thoughts, then reframe them into positive affirmations.

For instance, one of the most common patterns a player can fall into is noticing the negative details of a situation rather than focusing on the positive. When players filter their experiences this way, they tend to "awfulize" an event, pulling it out of context and usually magnifying its significance.

This is a battle pitcher Ian Snell has had to face over the years, starting with the Pirates during the 2008 season when he requested to be sent down to the minor leagues. His motive? He wanted to be removed from the negative reactions he was experiencing from the fans. At that point, Snell found it tremendously challenging to think rationally about his performance and the way others viewed him. A recent *Sports Illustrated* article recorded some of the thoughts that would run through his head: "If a player messes up, why does everyone automatically think he's a bad person? Do parents even want me to say hi to their kids and give them high fives? Why am I always being singled out?"[4]

In order to counteract this way of thinking, a player ought to isolate the negative thought and turn it into a positive affirmation. Rather than, "Don't strike out" (focusing on the negative) he should focus on what he *can* do: "Watch the ball release from the pitcher's hand." By filtering thoughts in a positive framework, a player is able to locate elements he can control in his performance and avoid languishing in feelings of self-defeat and frustration.

Many players become anxious about their performance because they are focused on results, especially the importance of winning. Although winning is important and can be a worthwhile goal, it should not be someone's gauge for success. "Somebody could beat you when he's really having an off day," says Jim Murphy. "Or you could beat him and only have given 50 percent effort. Winning is never a helpful way to measure your success as an athlete."

If a player is constantly enslaved by the obligation to win, this way of thinking will negatively influence his feelings about himself, his performance, and the game. As a result, this tension will manifest itself physically in a player—it will increase muscle tension, blood flow, and hormone production. When a player is not able to control his mind, he will not be able to control his body, and this can be a serious stumbling block for an athlete who is called on to perform at any given moment. Rather than focusing on winning, a player ought to focus on what he can control: controlling his mind and the steps he needs to take in order to be successful.

Although this philosophy is important, baseball players feel the pressure to be realistic, as well; if they aren't producing runs or getting strikeouts, they may get cut.

PJ Forbes, when he works with new draftees, sees this as one of the greatest obstacles young players face: "We're trying to condition them to be team players. But it's hard for them to understand that being a team player doesn't translate into numbers, that the successes of a team are more important than a batting average."

A lot of young people still can't understand that they have very little control over whether they will make it to the majors. For the most part, when a player tries to direct his career or create opportunities, he is wasting needless energy.

As Morgan Ensberg comments, "You have to play well at the right time, and you have to hope that the right person sees you at the right time." When Ensberg got drafted by the Astros out of USC, he was told that the scout was there to see a player on the opposing team, Arizona State. It was a three-game series at USC, and Morgan happened to play really well that series. "I feel fortunate the Astros picked me to play, but I realize that so much of it was timing. You really have no control over timing," he says.

Some players are more natural than others about focusing on the team, less panicky about putting up good numbers. They can have a broader vision of the game, a realization that the situation will shake itself out.

When Vinny Rottino worked with Yovanni Gallardo in the minor leagues he knew Gallardo was a player with a natural disposition for performance. "He's just a cool, calm guy who just naturally doesn't get shaken. When you see that, you realize what a blessing it is," Vinny says. In fact, after Gallardo found out that he was getting called up to the big leagues in 2007, he lay down and went to sleep on the bus. Something in his demeanor allows him to handle his energy.

Trebelhorn describes this as an ability to react to different stimuli. "Every situation in the game presents a certain stimulus. Players have to learn how to handle the excitement the stimulus creates, or else it could interfere with their performance." Trebelhorn agrees that some players simply have this gift; the other 90 percent of players, however, have to fine-tune this skill.

If a player does not know how to control his level of excitement, he can never know what to expect out of his performance on a day-to-day basis. During one game, he may go out flat; during another, he might be too jacked up. Still another day, he might achieve the perfect level of arousal and find the zone. In order to achieve mastery over his energy level, an athlete first needs to understand how the mind and body interact, and then how to apply either energizing or relaxation techniques to regulate his mind and body.

When anxious or too "amped up," an athlete will need to use relaxation techniques to bring down his energy level, and the key to regulating anxiety is learning how to use breathing during those moments. When a person becomes anxious, his muscles tense up. When one set of muscles tenses, the adjoining pair of muscles sets up a counter tension in order to hold the segment of the body in place. This "double pull," a result of over arousal, interferes with an athlete's performance because it prevents appropriately coordinated movement. Too much tension causes a person to overthrow, swing too fast, or misjudge a fly ball. In order to relax contracted muscles, a person must supply more oxygen to his blood through breathing. This will allow an athlete greater control over his muscles and ultimately his coordination as he performs. Proper breathing takes training but with practice, an athlete should be able to relax in any environment under any condition.

Developing a winning mindset takes time and practice, the same way it takes years and years to perfect a pitch or a swing. At the same time, a player's early years in the minor leagues can be a sink-or-swim period in his baseball career. Organizations are looking to weed out players who don't have the talent or the mindset to move through the ranks of the system. Because of the difficult conditions, it can be a time when a player can struggle with his perspective. Abandoning minor league baseball for a steady, more lucrative career may look more and more appealing, especially for players who have endured the system for multiple years.

Many players fight it out, though, because they believe they still have a chance. They are confidently working towards something, even though they have no promises, sometimes not even a general idea of what their future might hold. With perseverance, these players can get over the hurdle of low A teams where the game is still choppy and somewhat immature. More serious business ensues in AA and AAA, both levels at which players regularly get called up to the major leagues. Although the bus trips, locker rooms, and hotels still leave much to be desired, the game flows more smoothly, more like the game ought to look. And moving up—rather than out—is still the direction any player hopes to take. It is still one step closer to his goal.

FIVE

AAA

It is what we make out of what we have, not what we are given, that separates one person from another. —Nelson Mandela

The year when everything seemed to be going right for Adam Pettyjohn was also the year that his life changed dramatically.

While he was experiencing the elation of his career launching, Adam was suffering from colitis, an inflammation of the lining of his colon. Because he was treating it that season with medication, the symptoms (abdominal pain, bloody stool) were less severe. By July, he had run out of medication but opted to stay away from the doctor, who most likely would expect him to undergo another painful, uncomfortable colonoscopy procedure.

In the offseason, though, the medicine began to wear off, and the symptoms were returning, stronger than before. Still, Adam was planning his wedding with his future wife Dee, they were looking for a house, and he continued training as usual. With those distractions, he was able to fight through the symptoms: On their honeymoon in January, however, Adam's wife noticed the bloody toilet bowl. He had been having a bad flare-up, and could no longer hide the symptoms: "My wife said to me, 'I'm not losing a husband because you don't want to go back to the doctor.'"

This time Adam went to a different doctor where they lived in California; the diagnosis was more severe. The doctor put Adam on medication again, hoping to find the right combination so that his body would begin to heal.

By then Adam was losing weight and in the bathroom constantly. He was supposed to report to spring training in February, but he had long since abandoned his workouts. At times he struggled to stand, continued to lose weight, and was losing his voice. His body was not tolerating any food or drink, so he was dehydrated, malnourished, and losing blood. His doctor still hoped to rectify the situation through medication, looking at surgery as a more risky, final resort. Adam continued to experience severe abdominal pain, to the point that he passed out four to five times, and was admitted to the hospital on more than one occasion.

In March, the Tigers encouraged Adam to undergo surgery in Detroit with the team's surgeon, but Adam knew there wasn't a chance he could stand in line at an airport or even sit on a commercial flight. The team arranged for him to fly on a charter, transported him by ambulance to the airport, and had him on a gurney with nurses available throughout the flight. The doctor on call in Detroit told Adam's wife there was a 50 percent chance he wouldn't survive the flight. At that point, his 200-pound frame had dropped to 140 pounds.

The surgery took place on March 17 and took seven hours. The surgeon, Dr. John Eggenberger, removed Adam's entire colon, an organ that snakes throughout the abdominal cavity. He said it was the worst colon he had ever seen, "like a rotten piece of meat." One of the nurses said that when they opened Adam's body, they could see that his organs were days away from shutting down because he had been so depleted of blood and nutrients.

To Dr. Eggenberger's delight, Adam awoke in recovery without any complications. Immediately, he felt better, even though he had a 10-inch incision down his abdomen.

When his wife came to see him, Adam spoke to her for the first time in over a month. Before then, he had only been able to whisper, do thumbs up, or hand shakes. He was cracking jokes again, too, and immediately regaining his strength. Although his doctor estimated he would be hospitalized for 7 to 10 days, Adam left the hospital in four. According to Adam, "It's a miracle that I'm alive. I realize that every day. And it's even more of a miracle that I was able to get back into baseball."

At first when he left Detroit to return home, the only thing on his mind was gaining weight. "The doctor told me not to worry about fat content—if it sounds good, eat it. So we ate all the ice cream and cake, snacks, everything that sounded good," Adam says.

Meanwhile, he worked with a strength coach to gain back his muscle. Because Adam had been immobile for so long, he started with five-pound weights, and over the course of two to three months worked up to 25-pound weights. It took him equally as long to begin running or biking because he lacked the strength in his legs.

His goal the entire time was to return to baseball, even though he went through periods of doubt, especially considering the trauma his body had experienced. But he had encouragement along the way. "I'm relatively self-motivated, so I met the challenge to come back and play. But my wife helped me out so much, too, constantly telling me I was looking better, getting more toned. Some local coaches saw me and told me they thought I still had a chance to make it back to the major leagues. They weren't sugar coating it, but it really helped me stay focused."

Adam never took pity on himself either, even when he was in the worst of conditions. "It can always be worse. When I was in the hospital, I was surrounded by people who had cancer, who were on their death beds. I had no reason at all to feel sorry for myself," he says.

Even with that attitude, he had a long hill to climb if he was going to get his name back on the big league roster. Adam knew better than anyone that he had no guarantees—about his health or his future.

Similarly, Justin Lehr's career took a major turn during his final season in AA. In his case, the change was not incidental, however; Justin was doing the driving, and through his careful planning, he steered his career in just two short years to the big leagues.

He hadn't planned on making any drastic changes. In 2002, recently out of college, he was assigned to the bullpen with pitches that topped at 90 miles per hour. In the bullpen, Justin felt like he had fewer opportunities than when he was a starting pitcher: "If you're a starter, they can always use you in the bullpen, but it usually doesn't work the other way around. From the bullpen, you won't get assigned a start." He wasn't a hard thrower, either, another signature distinction of most relievers, especially closers.

That same year, just after Ken Caminiti retired from the Atlanta Braves, *Sports Illustrated* released Tom Verducci's feature highlighting Caminiti's comments that exposed the "real" game of baseball. Caminiti admitted, "It's no secret what's going on in baseball. At least half the guys are using steroids."[1]

Although Justin knew steroids were present in the game, he was still oblivious to their prevalence and how much they were impacting players' games, especially pitchers. To Justin (and to many players), Caminiti's words came as sage advice from a major league MVP, three-time All-Star and Gold Glove Award winner.

"If a young player were to ask me what to do," Caminiti stated, "I'm not going to tell him it's bad. Look at all the money in the game: You have a chance to set your family up, to get your daughter into a better school.... So I can't say, 'Don't do it,' not when the guy next to you is as big as a house and he's going to take your job and make the money."

At that point, Justin started talking to other players on his team about steroids and discovered that Caminiti's comments were accurate.

"Most guys were open about what they were using," Justin commented. "Then I started looking at who was getting promoted, guys who had been hitting ten home runs were now hitting thirty home runs in the big leagues. Or pitchers who threw 88 were now up to 97. You just can't make those changes on your own without some sort of enhancement."

Justin hated the idea of steroids in the game, because they provided an unfair advantage to players who cheated, meanwhile almost certainly eliminating players who stayed clean. The only players who could stay clean and still have a chance at the big leagues were players with extraordinary talent, an extremely narrow population. Justin doubted he had enough talent to overcome what was going on in the game.

"I knew I had big league talent, but I wasn't good enough to compete with players who were juicing," Justin says. "That's what I hated about steroids the most—it took away opportunity from players like me who had to work at their game, but still had all the potential to make it."

In 2002, major league baseball had testing for steroids, but their program did not suspend players or expose their names on a first offense. As a result, many players were willing to play the system in order to compete and win jobs. If they had gotten caught once, they may have rethought their program in order to avoid getting caught a second time, which meant suspension and exposure. With this system, though, many players were able to juice and avoid exposure for up to three years.

Justin says, "At that time, I felt the majority of players who were passing me by, making it to the big leagues, were probably using."

When many people think about steroid users, they envision players like Jose Canseco, the catalyst of the steroid era, with bulging muscles, baseball bats looking like sticks in their grip. Pitchers didn't have a chance against such power.

Many steroid users, however, were less concerned about developing an Arnold Schwarzeneger look, more interested in getting more pop in their swing, a little more edge on their fastball. Likewise, many post–Canseco steroid users felt they cheated out of necessity, because of a trend that Canseco and others had set in place, and a trend that major league baseball had done little to curb at that point.

Ironically, steroids (what many consider to be dangerous and harmful) empowered many players to develop entirely new attitudes about their games. In order to get the most benefit out of steroids, they needed to follow rigorous lifting routines and adopt nutritious, protein-rich diets.

Justin was one such player who, mid-season, lifted hard in the gym. He also was more careful with his diet, fueling his energy with nutritious foods, cutting back on alcohol, and sleeping more regularly. Ultimately he made the decisions he needed to in order to stay in the game.

Justin came to spring training in 2003 with a completely different perspective on the game and his future in baseball: "I knew I had to think differently about how gaining strength, getting into the best possible condition, would enhance my ability going into the season."

That spring, he also brought a fastball that was clocking 95, a change that turned heads immediately. Likewise, he was leaner and fitter, powered by a self-discipline that was admirable. The club assigned him to AAA that year where he only continued to improve, reaching a 98 miles per hour fastball by the end of 2003. He kept his ERA at a mere 3.72 that season, as well. Says Justin, "I kept at my routines and did everything I could to stay in the game. Many players were washing out—those who couldn't compete with the power that was in the game—but I did what I could to keep up."

When you love something so much, and spend your entire life pursuing it, the thought of losing it can be devastating. Many players, Justin included, would fight to the death for the opportunity to play baseball. They are competitors, those who continue fighting even when it gets ugly, even when lines get crossed. Baseball is programmed into their system. Somewhere along the line, they must have made a connection with the game; somewhere in their past, they must have discovered that baseball was something truly worth fighting for.

"There were players who took the high road and refused to take steroids, but they were the players who washed out pretty quickly," Justin recalls. "It made me doubt what my future would be and how long I would be able to make it in a dirty game."

During his second pro season (2006), Brandon Snyder played half the season in Aberdeen, the other half with the class A team in Delmarva. Regardless of his steady promotion, he was not hitting well. He knew something wasn't right, as "my shoulder just didn't feel right, and I knew it was affecting my swing."

Then, after a particularly painful game, Brandon had a doctor examine him, only to discover his shoulder was loosening out of the socket. The doctor adjusted his shoulder and assigned him a rehab program, yet sent him out to continue playing the season. Although his shoulder felt somewhat better, Brandon still didn't have his swing back. Towards the end of the season, during a swing he made during a game, his shoulder tore completely from the socket. This time not only was his shoulder loose, but he also had torn the labrum that attached the bone into the joint. It was inevitable that he needed to have surgery.

The injury relieved his mind somewhat about his poor hitting that season, yet he feared his condition might permanently impact his baseball career. According to Brandon, "This was basically the same injury that ended Bo Jackson's career, although his was a hip socket. He never regained his speed or agility after his hip surgery."

In Brandon's case, he was concerned about his hitting and, as a catcher, his throwing. The team sent him home early that season and he had the surgery in October. Doctors estimated his recovery would take six months, the duration of the offseason, and that he should be able to return for spring training in March.

Meanwhile, Brandon struggled to cope with the disappointing turn of events: "My goal had been to get to the major leagues by age twenty-one. But with the injury that just wasn't going to happen. I wasn't really sure what was going to happen when I got back to camp in March."

The team assigned him to Delmarva again so that he could regain his strength, and likewise moved him from catcher to first base to alleviate wear and tear on his shoulder. Early in the season, when he was still gaining back his strength, he dealt with some frustrations: "One of the coaches wanted me to change all of these things with my swing. He was trying to fix my mechanics but really I was just getting the strength back in my shoulder. I didn't appreciate how drastic the changes were."

Eventually he found his stride again and returned to his regular hitting form. Likewise, he began accepting some of the changes that were happening in his career. His timeline had been altered, and his numbers the year before hadn't looked good because of the injury. Still, he tried to change his attitude. Rather than seeing his situation as a hurdle, he saw it as a stepping stone, just another circumstance that would contribute to the landscape of his career.

Through his first season of pro ball, Vinny Rottino started hitting much better, mainly because he had the chance to put into practice the hitting instruction the coaches gave him. Although he was playing with the eighteen- and nineteen-year-olds at rookie ball (Latin players and high school draftees), he did not consider himself better than they were, and knew he had just as much to learn. Whenever he could, he would take extra ground balls, and extra at-bats. Through the coaches, he was learning the skills he needed to be successful.

"Baseball's great that way," Vinny says. "You can get stronger. You can take a million ground balls, and at some point something is going to click in there to soften up your hands."

The following year when he was twenty-four, Vinny got promoted to the single A Beloit Snappers, a team close to home with travel extending to cities in Illinois, Iowa, and Michigan. His manager, Don Money, played him every game, even though he was an undrafted player. With that opportunity, Vinny managed to hit 17 home runs and set a franchise record for RBIs with 124. He was also named the Brewers minor league player of the year for his performance.

What he may not have immediately contributed with numbers, Vinny easily made up in his passion for the game and his support for his teammates.

Baseball for Vinny was a very tangible experience. When he worked at his game he could see the results, and when he showed results, he got promoted. There was something extremely satisfying in working really hard and then receiving rewards based on his efforts. He appreciated the fairness of the game, saying, "That's how it was when we were growing up as kids—

my dad instilled in us a good work ethic, taught us at a young age that if we worked hard we could get what we wanted. No excuses—just get 'er done."

In 2005 he was promoted to AA Huntsville, then to AAA Nashville towards the end of the season. The next year, just three years into his career, he played full time in AAA. All the while, he continued to command the field defensively, as well as maintain a batting average in the .300s. As a full-time player, he was seeing more pitches, learning how to work through more situations, and "got better at making adjustments, figuring out what I needed to do to be successful."

Instead of resisting what felt uncomfortable (changing a swing or trying a different position), he embraced the unknown. To him, the discomfort would be worth it if he could learn how to become a better baseball player. So Vinny was the player who wanted to pinch-hit in the ninth inning with the bases loaded. He wanted to learn how to handle those situations and put into practice the mental skills he'd been developing.

"It's just a matter of having the correct thinking," Vinny explains. "If you find yourself in a high-pressure situation, what are your thoughts? Are they, 'I hope I don't strike out and look embarrassed' or are they, 'I'm going to get this job done no matter what.' It's not that you don't have adrenaline running in that situation—but you're just having the right kinds of thoughts. Your brain is extremely powerful. If you doubt your ability and you're super nervous, chances are you aren't going to give yourself as much of an opportunity to succeed in that situation."

By embracing uncomfortable situations and making adjustments, Vinny was preparing himself to be a major league baseball player. In preparation for games, he would visualize himself at the plate, catching a fly ball, making a throw to first—and he would visualize himself succeeding.

Throughout the 2006 season he hit .314 with 7 home runs and 42 RBIs in 117 games. Meanwhile, he'd been hearing talk that, as he predicted, September might be a big month for him that year.

If a player can stick around until he gets to AAA, it's a good sign he's not finished. However, getting there isn't enough—the caliber of talent changes dramatically at the high end of the minor league system. In fact, many AAA players have seen big league time. Some already are big league players on rehab assignments, comfortable with playing in front of 40,000 people against big-name hitters and pitchers. Much of the talent at AAA is major league ready—but there are only 25 spots on a team's active roster, 15 more spots on the 40-man roster. Obviously, talent alone cannot guarantee a player a shot at the big leagues; players who hope to get a chance must prepare in a variety of other ways.

At the same time, the longer a player is in baseball, the greater likelihood that something significant might start standing in his way, such as an injury or the politics of the game. Coaches and managers bring to the game impressive credentials and have the ability to imprint on a player vital skills and strategies that he can take into the rest of his career. Like players, though, coaches and managers are looking to advance their careers, which sometimes can complicate their relationships with players. Players who have seen many different leadership styles can begin to recognize what sort of leader can motivate and inspire players to win. While they are competing against teammates for a job, players likewise need to learn how to connect with teammates to achieve a positive, winning mindset.

For players at this level, an injury can be a major show-stopper, especially if the injury is severe. Because baseball is filled with examples of people who have prevailed over their injuries, it can be easy to assume such a feat is ordinary. In reality, athletes who face injury often suffer a powerful blow to their identities because baseball defines so much of their lives. Other artists have faced similar struggles, and dealt with their injuries in varying ways. Ernest Hemingway, after an airplane crash, suffered memory loss and became depressed because it impeded his ability to write. Christopher Reeve, the actor who played Superman, became completely paralyzed when he was thrown from his horse. Even though he could no longer walk (let alone fly), he spent countless hours performing painful rehab so that he could regain some movement in his limbs. Then there is the all-too-familiar baseball story of Josh Hamilton's drug addiction, a scary descent to near annihilation that was set in motion, to a certain degree, by a back injury he had sustained because of a car accident.

So why is it that injuries have the potential in some cases to pull even the best people to dangerous, low places? Hamilton discusses what the injury did to him in his memoir, *Beyond Belief*:

> To that point in my life I'd never been alone. To that point in my life, I'd never been without baseball. To that point in my life, I'd never been without my parents.
>
> I could sense the doubts from the team about my back, and I began to wonder, too. The pain was there, it was real, but nobody could find anything wrong with me. Doubt started to work its way into my mind, too. Was I imagining it? Did I really want to play baseball?
>
> My mind started to mess with me. My back hurt, but was it real? Were the doctors and coaches who looked at me sideways right?
>
> So maybe it was inevitable that I would find a place outside baseball to hang out.[2]

That place Hamilton found was a tattoo parlor and a group of friends who eventually helped him score drugs. What he described, and what many athletes face when they suffer injuries, was a battle in his mind, similar to the mental battles that pitchers face while on the mound or hitters face in the batter's box. The difference in the case of an injury, however, is that it can make an athlete extremely vulnerable to negative thinking and negative behavior, much more so than in a game situation.

With injuries, athletes may need to tolerate consistent pain, which easily can lower a person's resolve. Because of his inability to compete, an injury may cause an athlete to question his career and wonder (as Hamilton describes) whether others are questioning his career, as well. Most importantly, an injury forces an athlete to abandon, sometimes for an unknown amount of time, his dream. Separation from the game can be as painful as experiencing death, and the time a player spends away from baseball is a type of grieving process. Without a careful support system in place, it could be easy for someone to seek relief and consolation in drugs, alcohol, or other destructive behaviors.

For somebody like Adam Pettyjohn, even though he felt relief that he was still alive, he couldn't help wondering why his career had taken such a devastating turn. That was never the way it was supposed to be, and it was hard to accept that he had gone from major league pitcher to something unknown, maybe not even a baseball player anymore. Still, Adam managed to focus on the work in front of him, one day at a time, without dwelling on his concerns for his future.

"At the end of the day, baseball is a game, it's a privilege we've been given to play, but when it's done it's done," Adam believes. "God will open another door if He closes this one this year or next year."

His wife helped him focus on the positive, as well, never expressing doubt or concern. She continued reminding him that he was healed, and that maybe today was going to be the day his body would start turning.

Keeping a positive attitude can be challenging, though, when a player feels like everything is against him. The more he reflects, the more he realizes that the majority of his life may have been for naught if at the end of the day he won't be able to compete again.

Scott Mathieson, a pitcher in the Phillies system, struggled with these feelings, especially after undergoing his second Tommy John surgery in 2008. Scott's first surgery came in September 2006, after making nine appearances with the Phillies that year, his first major league season, before he "threw a pitch and pretty much the ligament tore off the bone," as Scott recollects the injury.

At that point, Scott planned to return within a year like most Tommy John patients. He made seven rehab appearances at the end of the 2007 season, but he felt like he could hardly throw and was still in pain. Whenever he threw he heard a "pop," which led doctors to believe he had a dislocated nerve. That September, he had a second surgery to remove the nerve and spent the majority of the offseason continuing to rehab. When he tried to throw that February in spring training, his elbow still didn't feel right. His surgeon, Dr. Lew Yocum, recommended Scott see a second surgeon, Dr. Michael Ciccotti, to get a second opinion. Scott opted to have Dr. Ciccotti perform exploratory surgery, at which time the doctor realized the tendon was not attaching properly to the bone. In order for Scott to fully recover, he needed to have a second Tommy John surgery. "The doctor told me there was only a 10 percent chance I'd be able to throw again after the second surgery. Obviously, I didn't find that very reassuring," Scott recalls.

With the first Tommy John surgery, Scott felt confident he could return to baseball, especially because he was still so young (only twenty-three when he had his first surgery). After his second Tommy John surgery, however, he started getting worried: "I got drafted out of high school so I didn't have a college degree. At that time I started going online and looking at schools. I had to start thinking about what else I was going to do."

After the pain of a second surgery, he had to endure an entire year again of rehabbing, but this time with much less certainty that the rehab was worth anything. During the offseason, the rehab went well for the most part and Scott felt like he was making progress. When spring training came, however, it got tougher.

After a day at the field, he would return home around 5:00 P.M. and many times would go straight to bed, staying there until the next morning. It was tough again when guys started leaving for the season and he had to stay in Florida, where it was starting to get miserably hot and he had to perform a monotonous routine day after day.

"That was the hardest thing, just staying motivated," Scott says. "It helped that I was doing rehab with some other guys who were unfortunately on the DL like me. My family helped, too, my dad and my wife. They would tell me that I would have regrets if I quit. They didn't want me to be looking back when I was forty asking, 'What if I stuck it out?'"

Scott made it through all of 2008, from rehab to a throwing routine to eventually returning to the mound. He was eager to pitch his first spring training game the following spring. The three innings he pitched went well; however, the way it made his elbow feel devastated him: "I'd come home and my arm was still hurting. I didn't know what to do. After that first game, within an hour I couldn't move my arm, I couldn't touch my shoulder. I'd lost all range of motion. That was probably my lowest point, when I really thought I wasn't going to play again."

He continued pitching, though, and he continued feeling pain after each outing. "I lived forty minutes from the field, and so many mornings I would start driving and wondered if I should just not go," Scott says.

As he started stringing together outings, though, the pain seemed to lessen. At first he pitched week-by-week, then after five days rest, then four days. Eventually, he got to the point where he could pitch competitively again and not have any problems: "Every once in a while I still have some stiffness. I still wonder if the next pitch is going to be *the* pitch again. But I'm not thinking as much about my elbow anymore, which is good."

In 2009 he pitched at rookie ball, went to high A, and finished at AA. After one particularly bad outing, he realized that he was reflecting more on his performance than he was on how his elbow felt. He knew that was a good sign. Finally, during the 2010 season, Mathieson made his first return to the major leagues since 2006.

Perhaps one of the most challenging parts of dealing with injury is when a player makes a comeback, knowing that he is bound to face adversity and failure.

When Adam Pettyjohn did return to the mound in 2003, he knew that he wasn't going to be at his best: "Right away I knew it was going to be a challenge. Many times I was over-met. I didn't have the strength to compete with those hitters and I didn't have the velocity to compensate for the mistakes I made."

Scott Mathieson feels that going through his surgeries has made him stronger mentally because he had to work again at building up his confidence. As Scott explains, "I had to be willing to go out there and fail before I was going to get better again. Every time I go out there I gain a little more of my confidence back."

Other players like Brandon Snyder experience nagging injuries that don't sideline their careers, but can easily set them back or create frustration. Especially for young people who generally have been healthy and successful all their lives, injuries can place a heavy burden on their shoulders.

"You grow up really quickly when you realize things aren't always going to go your way," Brandon says. "That's really tough when you try to do certain things but your body just won't allow it. For me, I needed to keep the dream alive—that's what kept me motivated. Everybody's going to be different. You have to be a person who understands his journey and goes about it in the correct way. That's a tough challenge—something players face on a daily basis—but it's even tougher when you're dealing with an injury."

Those people who struggle or face obstacles, it could be said, understand the game better than anyone. They're also profoundly aware that their time is limited, and that they need to make the most out of each and every day.

"I've really matured as a pitcher," says Scott Mathieson. "Because I've had to watch so much and deal with an emotional rollercoaster, I'm able to control my emotions much better. I can relax on the mound, not stress out if I give up a solo home run or a double. Of course, that's something I'm still trying to learn, too, but I've really matured that way since my surgeries."

Tanner Scheppers, the Rangers first-round draft selection in 2009, questioned when he was at Fresno State whether he'd actually have a baseball career after he tore his rotator cuff in his junior year. The year Tanner had to watch his team from the sidelines was the year Fresno State won the College World Series, as well.

"That was the hardest thing I've ever done in my life," says Tanner. "I was thinking about the injury all the time, just hoping and praying everything was going to be okay."

Not only did Tanner recover from the injury, but he also played in the Arizona Fall League after the Rangers drafted him in 2009, putting up an impressive performance, peppered with a fastball reaching 98 miles per hour.

Still, anytime someone is injured, he has no guarantees. Even though he puts the work in to get stronger and compensate for what's been lost, his career will be marked by a perpetual weakness he must learn how to handle. This can be frightening and diminishing to a player; at the same time, though, if he believes that each part of his journey has a purpose (even the parts that aren't so nice), he doesn't need to be afraid of the next day. He doesn't need to fear "that pitch" that will blow his arm out for good. If a player thought that way, there would be so many things to fear — getting hit by a pitch, colliding with an outfield wall, or a rough play at the plate. The best thing any player can do is deal with what he's got.

The larger somebody's health concerns, the more problems that could hamper him in the future. Adam Pettyjohn, regardless of his life-threatening experience, has not suffered an injury since that time, a factor that has allowed him to continue to make progress in the game. For somebody like Josh Hamilton who almost single-handedly destroyed his body with cocaine, his baseball future remains uncertain. Although his comeback to baseball has been epic (consider his show at the Home Run Derby in 2008), he represents the epitome of strength contained in what is now a weakened body.

As Jose Vazquez, the strength and conditioning coach of the Texas Rangers, explains, "[Josh's] body is not as resilient as a normal person's. He has brute strength and serious talent, but his ability to heal and his immune system is not there, like it is for a lot of people.... He's such a great story ... he has a great message, but the consequences are still there to be seen."[3]

Likewise, Josh has the daily nemesis of his drug addiction to contend with, a nemesis that caused him to relapse in January 2009, a weakness he will struggle with for the rest of his life. He writes, "I am an addict. That didn't change when I made it to the big leagues. And because I am an addict, I have to go about my business differently."[4]

That means he has to be drug tested on a regular basis. He travels with Rangers coach Johnny Narron so that he can be held accountable in restaurants, and hotels, at moments when he might be at his weakest.

Josh of all people understands the extent of his weakness. He is the sort of person who located his weakness and, rather than resenting it or denying it, included his weakness in his career. It's now part of his program. It's part of his 32-home-run season in 2008, part of his injury-laden 2009, and part of his league-leading batting average in 2010. In Josh's case, his faith has helped him accept his life, for all of its losses and all of its victories: "None of this would have been possible without my relationship with Christ.... I recognized my failings and, most important, my inability to heal myself."[5]

Being tested in our weaknesses shows the great paradox of what it means to be human. Even though logic would tell you some people would not be able to heal from cancer, somehow people are able to do it. Weaknesses can be a benefit to people, a greater challenge to see beyond their faults or frailties, and believe it is still possible to accomplish great things. People do not like to consider their weaknesses, and we often do what we can to hide them or ignore them. When we use our weaknesses to become strong, though, then we are embracing all of who we are, our entire condition, rather than merely who we would like to be.

Every athlete wants to avoid injury, and yet in so many cases, setbacks like injuries deepen a person's character and can give him a renewed, well-balanced perspective on his athletic career. Few people are emotionally equipped to handle life's setbacks gracefully, but athletes particularly—hardwired to compete, suffer through pain, and get better, stronger, faster—may find an injury particularly deflating to their psyche.

"It's hard when you're limited in what activities you can perform," says Justin Lehr, who would be faced with Tommy John surgery later in his career. "You're so used to always giving it all you've got. You're never really sure if what you're doing is enough, because it's so much less than what you're used to doing."

An injured athlete is trapped in a paradox: in order to continue being competitive in the future, he needs to take it easy, let down, and assume the half-time training patterns he's always associated with lazy, undisciplined athletes. He never wants to be that person—yet his injury is forcing him into that lifestyle.

It is important for the injured athlete to recognize that he is miles away from the lazy, unmotivated athlete. Even though his body may be less capable, he can still maintain a champion's mind. He can believe that the "work" of cutting down his baseball activities is necessary for a season, just as the work of rebuilding muscle will be the work of a different season. At the same time, a champion believes in what he cannot see—that even though his ankle or his arm may be wrapped and swollen for the time being, he still has plenty of strikes to throw and home runs to hit once he's up and running again.

For many people, it can be extremely challenging to believe in what they cannot see, especially if what they hope for seems like a distant dream—so distant that they cannot even attempt to look at it with the naked eye. This is why many athletes who incur an injury battle with depression, anger, and fear. Many athletes will ignore symptoms of injury for as long as possible because they are aware of the tremendous emotional battle athletes face when they have to go down for surgery.

This was the case with Diamondbacks pitcher Ian Kennedy, who started noticing numbness in his pitching hand at the beginning of the 2009 season while pitching for the Yankees' AAA team. "After four starts I knew it wasn't going well," says Ian. "My hand was cold—I finally had to say something."

Five days later, Ian was diagnosed with an aneurism in his right shoulder, perhaps caused from the constant motion of pitching. Blood clots were forming in his shoulder, breaking off, and settling in his hand, thus causing the numbness. "If I wouldn't have had the surgery, I probably never would have pitched again," Ian says.

As it was, he was out for the majority of the 2009 season, but was able to return for a couple of rehab innings at single A, then AAA. In September, his manager asked him if he was ready to pitch in the big leagues. Of course Ian assented, yet not without his reservations: "I had worked my way up to my original speed and my arm felt good, but I still had my doubts."

He ended up entering during the eighth inning for the Yankees as the set-up man for closer Mariano Rivera. "I was a little excited with the first two batters, but I calmed down," Ian recalls. "I got the job done."

What could have been a rough road for Ian became an opportunity for him to prove to his team that he planned to return to the game better and stronger. It is this sort of attitude—a desire to find positive meaning in injury rather than seeing it as destructive and debilitating—that allows injured athletes to emerge from their recovery with strong bodies and confident minds.

Research shows that athletes who have practiced imagery during periods of rehabilitation not only speed their recovery, but also cultivate a confident attitude.

For somebody like Brandon Snyder, sitting on the bench can be some of the most trying times of a baseball player's career. He knows that in order to keep his head in the game, he needs to stay with his team just as if he himself were on the field. As Brandon explains, "You have to be a student of the game during those times, or else you can easily lose heart."

This includes stimulating muscle memory through practicing imagery on a daily basis. Even though an injured athlete may not be physically stimulating his muscles, through visualizing different competitive situations, he will literally be practicing the same motions in his head. If done consistently and properly, imagery can keep an injured athlete fresh and ready for competition as soon as his body catches up.

Injured athletes are subject to developing irrational forms of thinking that can hinder their recovery, as well. For instance, an athlete could fall into apathy and depression simply because he feels that without the ideal conditions in place (i.e., he is not injured and can perform to the best of his ability), he no longer can reach his goals. For injured athletes, their goals may be delayed but in many cases they are still achievable over time.

At the same time, many injured athletes may be tempted to find and use recreational drugs. Not only do they hope to alleviate pain, but many also are preoccupied with the pressure to keep their spot with the team regardless of their injury. They do not want to be perceived as weak or a malingerer, so they may go beyond what the doctor orders to numb the pain and gain the courage to get back onto the field.

Although an athlete may consider his drug use temporary or experimental, one-time experimentation can lead to an unintentional pattern. What begins as a need to soothe physical pain may lead to a desire to cope with the mental anguish that many athletes face as they strive for peak performance. When an athlete, particularly an injured athlete, cannot achieve a high on the field, he may seek an alternative high through drugs and alcohol, thus cushioning the blow.

Drug abuse easily establishes a destructive cycle in someone's life, making it extremely challenging to break the habit. For instance, athletes who are separated from their families can fall into anxiety, loneliness, and depression. The athlete's family can react the same way to his absence. When he is gone the family dynamic is disrupted, yet at the same time his return can create a disruption, as well. All of these tensions can affect an athlete's performance, only increasing his anxiety even more because he fears for his job. He may turn to drugs for relief and find companionship and belonging among fellow drug users. In some cases, an athlete may want to find acceptance among his teammates and is willing to join their drug habits in order to feel connected.

For many athletes, recreational drug use may begin with an innocent need to "let loose." Athletes can have a lot of down time on the road and may turn to drugs simply to alleviate boredom. In distant cities they have nobody watching them. Drugs become a way for them to fill the void from one game to the next. As an athlete's career progresses, he may feel the burden to put on a show for the public, both on the field and in his private life. In order to maintain his towering on-field persona, he may be more comfortable off the field, more powerful, while under the influence.

Unfortunately, athletes who turn to drugs often do not sort through the many complex emotions they have been experiencing over the years. Drugs become a crutch that robs someone of the opportunity to grow as a person and an athlete. When someone falls into the habit of a substance, he is depriving himself of the opportunity to gain strength through struggle. This is the same strength that will be sorely missed when this person finally faces a physical and emotional breakdown. Until an athlete learns how to replace his drug-induced vitality with something deeper—real emotions, real relationships, real pain, and real pleasure—he will continue being a slave to the cycle of false hope.

Other factors besides injuries can force players to make some very hard decisions in their careers, as well. Players like Justin Lehr, and especially those who played pro ball the decade before him, were influenced by the presence of steroids in the game, an issue that has found more resolution recently yet still complicates baseball. What Justin believed he was seeing in the game, and what many other players recognized, was that steroids significantly changed the landscape of the game, to the point that he felt he no longer was able to compete. Justin believes that if steroids had never been involved in the game, "I probably would have played a little more in the big leagues earlier in my career."

Instead, Justin floundered like many other players in AA, all the while listening to voices like Caminiti's saying that the reason he was being passed up was because he wasn't doing steroids like everyone else. It was an ethical dilemma for players, yet at the same time, major league baseball was failing its players without properly addressing the issue. The game was changing before everyone's eyes, and many players felt that in order to compete, they needed to cheat.

Congress banned steroid use as early as 1988 with the Anti-Drug Abuse Act (replaced with a more strict Anabolic Steroids Control Act in 1990). Major League Baseball reinforced the congressional ban when Commissioner Fay Vincent sent a memo to every major league team in 1991, reiterating that players who used steroids were cheating. Although Major League Baseball clarified that players should not be using steroids, it did not implement a testing system to hold players accountable at that time. It's like parents telling a teenager not to touch the liquor cabinet when they're gone on vacation, then leaving the cabinet unlocked when they're gone and never checking the supply when they return home.

Rules alone rarely influence people to change their behavior—the influence of people is much more powerful. That is why players who were taking steroids didn't stop, and players who started to take steroids continued to increase. When superstars like Jose Canseco and Barry Bonds were juicing, naturally many aspiring players were inclined to follow their lead. A strong conscience might have been a player's only deterrent had he chosen not to partake, but even then players knew that many who had taken the high road ended up looking foolish when they washed out.

As the media started heating up the issue, circulating the candid comments of players like Tony Gwynn and Jason Giambi, the "institutions" (both the federal government and Major League Baseball) felt pressure to continue working on the issue. In 2001, Major League Baseball implemented minor league testing; then through the pressure of Congress, began drug testing at major league spring training camps in 2003, a relatively loose program that barely scratched the surface of the abuse. As more information continued to be leaked to the media, and major steroid provider BALCO (Bay Area Laboratory Co-Operative) went under legal scrutiny, baseball's initial testing program proved wholly inadequate.

Without a doubt, the situation became complicated with the players' union seeking to protect the rights and reputations of players, and the owners wanting baseball to remain "business as usual" in order to continue revenue flow. At the same time, Major League Baseball was being forced to answer to the United States Government because of the collecting pile of evidence revealing players' widespread unethical behavior.

"It was easy to avoid suspension at that time," Justin Lehr comments. "With a first offense, you'd be sent the clinical track—go to drug counseling, be told you'd get tested again in another year."

Players knew that the rules changed every year; if they were careful about doing their homework, they could usually avoid the only punishment that would deter them from using: public exposure.

"Inside baseball people knew what was going on," Lehr asserts. "Basically, teams didn't want players getting caught, they wanted players to be smart. Still, teams liked power bats and power arms. They wanted to win just like everyone else."

The baseball culture finally began changing, however, by 2005 when stricter testing led to the first major league suspension, Alex Sanchez of the Tampa Bay Rays. Rather than the media leaking players' mocking comments about the "integrity" of baseball, Major League Baseball publicly enforced its policies, showing players perhaps for the first time that the game needed to get cleaned up.

Since 2005, baseball's steroid policies have only continued to gain back terrain that had been lost some fifteen years ago. "The game is coming back," says Justin, "but it's taken years to recover. Fans may think differently, but you can't cheat today without getting caught. Unless you're somebody like Manny Ramirez who can still get a job with a fifty-game suspension, you can't do it. You'll mess up your career."

The 2007 Mitchell Report, an investigation spearheaded by former senator George Mitchell to investigate the "real" story of baseball's steroid era, brought to light names of hundreds of players (some prominent players like Roger Clemens and Andy Pettitte) who had juiced under the radar during their heydays. Although most of the Mitchell Report was merely water under the bridge, it introduced the discussion of whether players deserved credit for their achievements (e.g., Barry Bonds' home run record, Roger Clemens' Cy Young Awards) when they had been tainted by steroids. [6]

The question seems to have an easy answer for fans, but can be much more complex for players.

"You look at somebody like A-Rod," says Justin Lehr, "and he had a chance to play past his steroid use. He's still an amazing player. That may have been the case for Canseco or Bonds, too, but they didn't have the chance to play past steroids. We can only look at their records when they were on steroids and question them, even though they were obviously phenomenal athletes without steroids."

Many players feel like they were placed in a complex situation with steroids, a situation that they, like fans, would liked to have avoided.

According to Vinny Rottino, who entered pro baseball at a time when testing was much stricter, "If I was playing during the era when there was no steroids testing, and I was seeing all the guys I was playing with getting to the big leagues, I'd certainly be tempted. I'd be tempted—it's your dream."

Steroids appear to be a quick fix, a simple solution to a very difficult problem. In reality, though, steroids alone will not launch a player's career, not in a game like baseball that is so technically complex.

Even with his 98 miles per hour fastball, Justin knew that there were more forces at work than steroids in his game to help him become a better pitcher: "Once you get up to AAA, you have to learn how to develop your approach. Throwing hard makes no difference if you can't control your pitches or outthink the hitters."

Ted Power sees many talented, powerful young pitchers in Louisville, but more often than not, they still take years to develop their mental approach to the game: "At this level, and certainly by the time they get to the major leagues, there aren't too many hitters that can be overpowered. You have to outmaneuver and outthink them. You need to know what gives you the best results as far as pitch location, and you need to know what works best in certain game situations."

No matter how physically gifted the player, he still has to use his mind to gain an advantage. Although Justin witnessed the benefits of steroids first-hand, he readily admits that mental skills trump physical ability every time, saying, "If you have a strong mental game, that can be a much stronger tool. Absolutely."

Baseball has a way of revealing how unpredictable people can be. Even when players try to develop routines, mastery, and consistency that allow them to put up a steady performance, so many factors could disrupt a player's ability to perform.

In his experience as a pitcher, Adam Pettyjohn finds that pitchers bring their best stuff to a game only 25 percent of the time. Fifty percent of the time they're missing at least one thing: their good breaking ball, their movement, or their control, for instance. Then the other 25 percent of the time, pitchers are trying to do anything just to keep their performance together. They have to make adjustments on that particular day if they have any hopes of competing.

"You reevaluate throughout the course of a game the game plan, based on what you're missing," Adam says. "If I don't have my good breaking ball, then I have to use something else."

Why do players struggle so much to stay consistent?

There are many variables, according to Adam: it could be a travel day, he might not have slept well or eaten well. Maybe he didn't run enough between outings, now it's 90 degrees in Texas and his legs weren't prepared, so he might start feeling it in the fourth inning.

"Even if you do all your running, all your lifting, and you do all the homework, you're still going to have those days that your body doesn't work," Adam explains. "25 percent of the time you may be in the zone; the other 75 percent of the time you have to be prepared to work at it."

A pitcher works at it by staying in the game even when he doesn't have his best stuff. He battles through his innings, making adjustments, and hoping to find his best stuff. According to Adam, "You can use your mind to get into that 25 percent range. You can get there by persisting and fighting."

Sometimes a pitcher can "find" something he didn't have earlier in the game—maybe it's something a pitching coach said, or a great defensive play that boosts his confidence. If he finds it, then he could ride that confidence throughout the rest of the game. "Maybe you never find it again, but at least you battled," Adam says. "If you can know yourself and know your body, you can make those adjustments."

Finding that confidence has nothing to do with taking steroids. In fact, to a certain degree steroids can provide players with a false sense of security when they are learning to compete. In reality, experience, not strength, can help a player play intelligently.

Scott Mathieson comments, "A lot of young pitchers who get in trouble—maybe they walk a hitter on a 3–2 count that could have gone either way—they have a hard time releasing that play. Often, they carry it into the next at bat, and that's when innings start snowballing on you."

Like any pitcher, Justin Lehr can relate to this feeling. He also realizes that through his years of experience, he's learned how to keep competing, even if he's had a rough inning: "When I was with Milwaukee, I gave up four runs in the first inning. It was looking horrible—it could have been my worst outing of the year. But I managed to regroup and was able to stick around until the fifth inning, when my team put up a six spot. At that point I realized we still had a chance of winning. I was definitely still competing, along with the rest of the team. Those are the kind of games that can get away from guys sometimes, especially when things look so bad early on. You learn how to control that once you've gained years of experience."

So even though players find many different devices to improve their game (some legal and some illegal), even the most physically gifted, the most mechanically sound, and the most experienced player carries with him the deficit of human nature—the inclination to get off track. The moment of performance is a moment of testing. At that moment, a player who used some of the best steroids in the game, who worked to build twenty pounds of additional muscle—he still has to face the same moment as the player whose shirt untucks when he runs because he's so skinny. No matter what "extra" a player brings to the game, he still has to set his mind to overcome his own disbelief. A player who develops this mental tool, no matter what his size or training, can slice through the adversity of competition because he knows he will deliver.

Once players reach the AAA level (and certainly by the time they get to the big leagues), they may find it difficult to compete because the game is no longer based on physical talent, but on players' mental games. Learning how to become a player who can control his mind on and off the field takes time for most players to master.

Adam Pettyjohn agrees: "You have to have a shorter memory at AAA. If you play this game a long time, you're going to fail a lot. You learn the most during those times of failures. You learn how to adjust. But if you can't accept those moments as positives, then it will affect you the next time you perform."

This can be difficult to master, especially because most competitors bring strong emotion to their game; they care about how they perform and they love the sport. Emotions allow a person to experience life's moments more intensely. In this sense, emotions can fuel a player's performance, help him to compete beyond what he might usually be capable of doing. For instance, if a player just made an excellent defensive play, when he gets to the plate, he can carry with him the feelings of joy and elation from his defense. With greater intensity, he wants to find his pitch and continue fueling the positive feelings he's found.

At the same time, as many people know from personal experience, emotions can be difficult to control. They can distort a person's reality, especially if the emotions are negative and begin affecting the way that player thinks. Because baseball is a game of confidence, negative emotions can cause a player to quickly veer in the wrong direction. What became one misplay can easily mount into mistake after mistake. If a player battles against negative emotions, however, he can maintain control even when his stress and arousal level skyrocket.

In order to effectively deal with emotions, a person must look deeper than how he feels at a particular moment. He must consider what he believes—what deeply ingrained manifesto would lead him to react in a particular way to a certain experience.

This part of the mind, what psychologists call the subconscious, works like a tide beneath a person's will—a silent, strong force that pulls a person according to its wishes. The Proverbs refers to this part of a person as the "heart," and warns people to guard it because "everything you do flows from it."[7] For some people, the subconscious is filled with wisdom and truth they have cultivated over the years. For others, the subconscious is filled with negative views of self and others and other types of distorted thinking. In everyone's case, the subconscious begins forming at a young age, so one's parents, upbringing, and childhood environment directly influence the beliefs and values a person will hold. Yet, even a person who has emerged from a loving environment still has had harmful experiences that have shaped his internal belief system. Those experiences can range from something as mundane as accidentally breaking a neighbor's window to facing the death of a loved one. Every person—whether rich or poor, nurtured or abandoned, praised or criticized—has different experiences of pain and suffering to deal with, and often times that pain manifests itself in the negative emotions a person feels while functioning later in life.

For many baseball players, their biggest challenge is believing that they are capable of becoming major league players—that they belong on the mound at Fenway Park, or in the outfield at Busch Stadium. No matter how diligently someone trains, regardless of the praise he may receive from coaches and teammates, a player can still struggle in his heart to believe in his own potential. The tide that is pulling inside of him, against his will, takes him in a direction he does not want to go. Fortunately, unlike oceans, people's minds can be moved. It is possible for someone to reshape his beliefs—even the deepest ones that reside in his most distant memories—when he spends time training his mind.

Many times players admit they feel guilty for having negative thoughts during performance. These thoughts can cause a player to feel isolated because few athletes openly admit their doubts and fears, especially during competition. Yet, an athlete should not feel ashamed for being nervous or fearful; rather, there is shame in attempting to dehumanize oneself, to not feel. An athlete who understands his feelings and then restructures his thinking to reflect a positive viewpoint will become a powerful presence on the field, no matter what fears or doubts he may have been facing.

Athletes who hope to alter their subconscious, the seat of their beliefs, can do so by practicing consistent, powerful imagery. As an athlete regularly engages all five senses in images of top performance, gradually his subconscious mind will begin to accept those images as truth.

Some athletes who feel they are holding back during performance may battle against negative and self-defeating messages from within. A more powerful means of changing this inner message, Eye Movement Desensitization and Reprocessing (EMDR) is a technique that athletes can engage in with the aid of a sport psychologist. EMDR allows a fully conscious athlete to reflect on moments of his performance in order to reinforce excellent performance and likewise reconstruct negative experiences. After a sport psychologist conducts an extensive interview with the athlete, he asks the athlete to focus on a particular aspect of his performance, such as throwing his fastball for strikes. At the same time, the athlete gazes at a light bar which allows both sides of his brain to interact, generating a more vivid experience. Through this process, athletes can connect distressing emotions and negative experiences with more positive, realistic information. Once they can recreate a moment of failure or anxiety in a positive light, their mind will accept this new experience as truth.

Because of all the mental battles players will face, some of the best coaches in baseball understand that they need to help their players not only with their physical game, but also with their mental game.

Brett Butler, manager of the Diamondbacks' AAA team in Reno, tries to provide his players a perspective not only on baseball, but also on their lives. Yet he realizes it can be tough to get through to some people, especially players who have found some success and may not "need" the coaching. According to Butler, "People won't listen to you until they know you care for them. It's like a cold drink of water—when you offer it, some will accept it, and some won't."

Butler, who had a successful seventeen-year career in the major leagues, knows from his own experience that it's easier for people to listen to someone when they know he cares about them: "There are two things people want to hear the most: their name and some encouragement. That's what I try to do. I try to tell these young men that playing baseball will only be a short season in their lives, but they will be men—husbands and fathers—for the rest of their lives. It is more important to spend each day working on your character and your integrity; if you pursue that, you will find satisfaction and contentment throughout your life."

Performance coach Jim Murphy sees this component—caring for players—as the key to motivation: "Highly successful managers and coaches are able to motivate players usually based on two main qualities: they are able to genuinely care for their players, and they communicate effectively with their players."

Unfortunately, these qualities can be scarce, not only in baseball but also in other areas of life. In many work places this can be the frustration that employees face—they lack a strong leader who believes in them and defines a reason for them to be there. Many families today lack this quality—children grow up without parents who care about their lives or who never inspire them to pursue what they love. Sometimes these children can find good leadership in a teacher or a coach; many people, though, children or adults, spend a lot of time wandering, sometimes never finding the purpose of their lives.

No matter what a person's circumstances, though, Butler's view is, "It goes back to choice and attitude. You could take a kid who grew up in a supportive family, and he could make the decision to go down the wrong road. Or a kid from an impoverished situation, single family home, latchkey kid, and he could decide, 'I'm not going to be a part of this. I'm going to get out of this.' The responsibility falls on the person."

Butler himself understood the hardships that players face when they are pursuing a big league career. As a young man, he was undersized, a player that most coaches did not consider a prospect for a major league career. Even though the odds were against him, though, this fueled his desire even more to prove people wrong. In his memoir, Butler writes, "For as long as I can remember, I have used negative input for positive motivation."[8]

When he was drafted in the 23rd round by the Braves in 1979, Butler was given a chance at his dream, but a chance that still seemed unlikely. Still, he prepared as if he knew without a doubt that one day he'd be a major league player. It took him just three years to make his major league debut in 1981. Not only did he make it to the big leagues, but he also went on to enjoy a long, fruitful career that included an All-Star season and a career .290 batting average.

Regardless of a person's attitude, strong leadership still has transformative power—it can convert hopelessness into victory, anxiety into confidence, and pain into power. Ultimately, the greatest leaders sacrifice their own needs for the benefit of their players—something that can be very challenging to do in professional sports where jobs are scarce and employers measure success based on performance.

"You can't fire the players," says Justin Lehr. "That's why you see managers, coaches, GMs taking the heat when a team has a losing record."

So it can be difficult for coaches to focus purely on helping players without an underlying motive for achieving "success" through that player.

Jim Murphy comments: "You have to have a lot of confidence to be a good coach because you have to stop comparing yourself to other coaches and start focusing on the players. You have to believe in what you're doing and be willing to face personal sacrifices if it means the players ultimately will benefit."

Players can tell very quickly who are "players" coaches and who are coaches interested in their own careers. Although all coaches can have positive impacts on players, especially if they know the game and have been in the system for a while, coaches whom players can trust will be able to achieve the most powerful results with the team.

"Trust is huge," according to Vinny Rottino. "You can see within five minutes of talking to a coach whether he's a coach for the players, or a front-runner, a coach who's trying to promote his career through the players. You kind of write those guys off right away. You doubt whether they really have your best interests in mind. When you doubt what they're teaching you, that only affects your ability to perform, because baseball is a game of confidence."

Players can have divided opinions about coaches and managers, as well, based on a variety of factors—their age, their position, or the stage of their career.

For instance, Justin Lehr, when he played for Oakland's AAA Sacramento Rivercats, was not alone in finding manager Tony DiFrancesco frustrating, negative, and unapproachable. He also questioned some of what DiFrancesco was teaching him, and ended up finding his own way to make adjustments: "I remember getting called into his office when I was in AA, and being told that my fastball wasn't good enough to throw for strikes, that I needed to pitch it off the plate and throw my off-speed for strikes. That just wasn't the right advice."

Justin admits that age may play a major factor in how a player relates to certain managers, as well: "I was young when I worked with Tony, early in my career when I was still figuring things out. He has a strong personality and I was stubborn, so that definitely was not a good combination. But at the same time, I know I wasn't the only player who struggled to work well with him."

Unlike Justin, Adam Pettyjohn had a completely different experience with Tony DiFrancesco, although his experience came later in his career (2004 and 2006): "I always liked Tony D because he knew the game, and he gave pitchers a chance to work at their game. He didn't pull you the minute you got into trouble—he gave you the chance to develop."

In Adam's first stint with the A's, he had a good first outing, but then went on to have three "horrendous" consecutive outings. "I mean *horrendous*—probably the worst three-start stretch of my career," he says.

Adam pitched fewer than six innings in those three games, and gave up approximately twenty-four runs total. It was taxing on the bullpen and wearing on Adam's confidence, especially since he still wasn't at full strength since his surgery.

Rather than facing a managerial chew-out, Adam found DiFrancesco addressing him professionally in his office: "He just told me he needed to get me on track, I was killing the bullpen. He believed I was a better pitcher than I was showing. It really helped me reevaluate what I was doing, especially because he stuck with me. He didn't point me out in front of the team or throw me under the bus to the media. I really respected him for how he worked with me."

After that talk, Adam was able to get on track and went on to pitch a complete game, eventually a shutout game, and won the playoff game that took the Rivercats into the championship round in 2004. That year, the team took the championship.

Even though Adam valued his time with DiFrancesco, he acknowledges that not every player worked well with the manager: "He was strong-willed, to the point, not a lot of sense of humor. Everything was business-oriented for him, but I liked that. It kept your attention solely focused on the game."

Justin agrees: "He gets results. Sacramento has been a winning team for many years."

Still, it is an important trait that a team feels like their manager is on their side, working for a common goal and for the benefit of the team.

With the Norfolk Tides under manager Gary Allenson, Brandon Snyder found a leader who understood his players and had good timing when communicating.

"Maybe we had a bad game, and we'd expect to get some heat from him," Brandon recalls. "We might be hanging our heads in the locker room when he'd come in and break through the tension with, 'What's wrong with everyone? We got our asses kicked today—let's go get them tomorrow.' That loosens guys up. Now we might get a different talk eventually if we keep losing—but by then we'd need to hear it."

It's important for managers to stay in touch with players on a regular basis, not necessarily because they need to talk strategy or technique, but simply to maintain camaraderie and open lines of communication. If a manager is in touch with his players, he can "read" their strengths and weaknesses, their tendencies and their preferences.

When Jim Murphy interviewed manager Terry Collins for his book *Dugout Wisdom*, Collins expressed that he makes it a point each day to greet his players. He tries to engage at least two or three players in personal conversation, asking about their family or their lives. Although it isn't a manager's place to become "one of the guys" necessarily, his interest in players' lives promotes trust and more meaningful relationships.

Adam Pettyjohn comments, "You know when a manager is watching out for you. He doesn't always have to be going strictly by the rules or what the organization wants. Maybe he gives the team a day off from batting practice when it's been a long road trip. He just has a feel for his players on the team."

When a manager understands his players, he can create a powerful dynamic in the clubhouse and on the field. "You don't want to create robots," says Jim Murphy, "so it's important to let players be themselves within the context of the team. Some of the best teams have the fewest rules, but they respect each other and they show up on time and give 100 percent."

Coach Smokey Garrett, hitting coach for the Louisville Bats, believes that it's his job to know each hitter so that he can train them based on their personality and abilities: "I talk to players about what kind of a hitter he is and where he fits on the team. Are you a hitter who gets on base and scores runs, or are you a hitter who drives in runs. The last thing you need is the little guy to go up there and try to hit home runs. That's not his role. He might hit a home run once in a while, but that's not his trump suit. I'm there to help him find what he needs to do to be the best player *he* can be."

Once a player knows his role, he can become an influential member of the team. When players influence one another, especially with positive characteristics like a desire to win, the team grows into a much more formidable force. Naturally, winning can cultivate a strong team dynamic—everybody's happy when the team is successful—yet a team's "winning culture" should come from within the team, not originate once the scoreboard pronounces it.

Many regard Joe Maddon, the Tampa Bay Rays manager with the winningest record in franchise history, as a model manager, somebody who holds his players' respect, yet is not afraid to speak his mind when necessary.

One key to Maddon's success is his belief in team chemistry, and the important role chemistry plays in fostering strong performance: "I'm a big believer in how people interact within the group. I've often had discussions, arguments with different people who believe winning creates chemistry. My question is always, 'If you haven't won yet, how do you win?' I believe it can be nurtured—in a sense, created—if you really pay attention to it."[9]

Some teams can develop team culture through careful selection of players. This is a luxury usually not available to managers at the minor league level, simply because they rely on scouts and the general manager to make decisions about acquisitions. At the amateur level, however, many coaches regard recruitment as one of the most important components in their team's success.

Raphael Cerrato, head baseball coach at the University of New Haven, feels that "recruiting is one of the most important things we do." From his vantage point, coaches in college baseball can develop closer relationships with players than at the professional level, an aspect of his program that he finds extremely rewarding. "In pro ball, you might be with a guy for a year, then he goes to another level, gets released, or traded," Coach Cerrato explains. "In our program, though, I enjoy recruiting someone at age seventeen, getting to know him for four or five years, then seeing him graduate as a twenty-two-year-old man. It's a privilege to be a part of that process."

In minor league baseball, although players may have many of the same teammates from rookie ball through AA, the dynamic changes at AAA. At AAA, players function much more like major league players, which means getting traded, promoted, or released when the organization sees fit. So how does a team develop chemistry in what could be considered a rather disconnected environment?

According to Brandon Snyder, once players reach AAA, they have developed their individual game so extensively that they know how to work with just about anybody on the team. "If something needs to be communicated, you usually have veteran guys stepping up," Brandon says. "But you're past relying on other players at that point—you get your job done, and that feeds off other players getting their jobs done."

Even as players develop individual careers at the higher levels, baseball still is a team sport. Teams, like any community of people (e.g., families, governments, or workplaces), become exponentially more powerful when they develop internal momentum. The key to finding this momentum is that players understand their roles and genuinely believe in the collective goal of winning.

The challenge many players face at the AAA level, however, is every player hopes to put up numbers so he can get a look from the major league team. Desiring to help the team and desiring to put up good numbers can be a paradox many players face; for some it is a paradox that may be difficult to reconcile.

According to Vinny Rottino, the paradox is actually the solution to any player's career: "You'll be a winning player if in the front of your mind is, 'How can I help this team win?' Your personal goals will actually take care of themselves if you're that kind of player. You will play better defense, you will have better at bats if that is 100 percent your conviction."

In the same way that good coaches need to be sacrificial of their own goals and ambitions, good teammates will sacrifice their desire to "shine" in order to help the team. Even though somebody may know what he wants— a promotion, a call-up—in order to achieve it, he cannot focus on it. Instead, he must focus on the larger perspective of the game, the larger purpose.

"I'm a big believer that I'm here not just to get better at baseball," Vinny comments, "but also to pick other guys up, to encourage those people God has placed in my life."

The more players on a team who have a self-sacrificial attitude, the desire to play 100 percent for the team, the stronger the team will perform.

"That attitude's infectious," says Vinny. "If you're a pitcher who's on the mound to pitch for the guys behind him, guys will dive through a wall for him. They believe, 'This guy's out here for us.' It's rare to find a team where every guy has that focus. But if you have the majority of them, then you're going to be a winning team, and it's fun to play really hard with those guys."

Through this type of mentality, players can develop trust with one another, even over a relatively brief period of time. Especially if the player has been in the game for a while, he may develop a reputation that precedes him, so that players know what to expect of him.

Vinny refers to Jason Kendall as a great pitcher's catcher, because "pitchers know they can trust him; he calls a good game and that takes that pressure off the pitcher's shoulders."

Of all the positions in baseball, the relationship between a pitcher and a catcher may be the most vital. The pitcher has the most control over the game, and in order to throw good pitches, he needs to believe in the pitch he's throwing.

Adam Pettyjohn, who has worked with great defensive catchers including Mike Rivera, Craig Tatum, and Vinny Rottino, feels most confident when he believes in his pitch: "You can throw what might be the wrong pitch for that situation and be totally committed to it and have it work. Or you can throw what might be the right pitch, not be committed, and it gets hit 400 feet. As a pitcher, you've got to decide, because you're the one who has to live with the results."

The more a pitcher trusts his catcher, the more naturally he can rely on the catcher to make the calls. It may take time, however, for a pitcher to believe in a certain catcher, depending on the situations they face together.

Scott Mathieson comments: "If you go out there and throw everything the catcher says, but if you are thinking of a fastball and he wants a breaking ball, you won't throw it with conviction. And if you're not totally decided on something, you're not going to put your best effort into it. You'll try to put your best effort into it, but you're double thinking yourself, even into your windup."

Becoming a successful teammate at the AAA level can take some time, especially when the living conditions of the minor league lifestyle do not change regardless of the major-league-caliber competition. The most successful players realize that for most people, especially in a complex sport like baseball, success takes time. Many players have major league talent, but a much smaller percentage of players can continue to carry that belief month and after month, year after year, as the windows of opportunity shift with major league teams. So many players have always believed all the work and frustrations are worth it if, in the end, it leads to the quintessential moment of the call-up. Even the best can be worn down, though, through injury, disappointment, and unfulfilled promises.

Without a doubt, players who manage to stick with the game see a vision beyond teams, managers, and the teammates they grow to admire and love. They see their first love—baseball—as something much more powerful than solitary moments along the way. Because they love baseball so much, they don't get waylaid, even though sometimes it can be painful to change directions and leave certainty to the wind. This is their journey.

A player's journey, in many ways, comes down to his attitude.

Brett Butler recalls his father's words of advice to him throughout his life: "If you don't believe in yourself, nobody else will."

He has tried to pass the same attitude on to his children. Explains Butler: "My desire for my children is that they have no regrets as they live their lives. Unless you take that chance, your dream may never happen. That doesn't mean you'll get exactly what you want, but you can position yourself in such a way that it could be possible. That way if you don't make it, you can still feel satisfied that you did everything you could. You didn't sell yourself short on something else along the way."

SIX

The Call-Up

Things are sweeter when they're lost. I know—because once I wanted
something and got it. It was the only thing I ever wanted badly ... and
when I got it, it turned to dust in my hands.—F. Scott Fitzgerald

Adam Pettyjohn couldn't help but question whether he'd actually be able
to make a comeback. Detroit released him after 2003 and he got a job with
San Francisco for the following year. Mid-season they traded him to Oakland.
With both teams he was pitching at the AAA level, and many times he knew
he was over-matched—he didn't have the strength to compete with hitters,
he didn't have the velocity to compensate for the mistakes he made. At the
end of the season he had three horrendous outings in a row and he was very
close to quitting.

"My wife kept encouraging me, telling me I still hadn't gotten my true
self back yet," Adam recalls. "It took two years for my body to deteriorate—
it would take at least twice as long to get it back."

In the offseason he didn't get any calls from major league teams, which
didn't help the matter. He was reluctant to listen when his friend Jim Wohlford
encouraged him to go to independent ball. It was no secret that guys who
went to independent ball often never made it back to major league organizations, and Adam didn't want to be another one of those statistics. However,
what his friend told him was true: he needed to do more pitching if he was
going to recover his strength and velocity.

In independent ball, Adam dominated, an experience that helped build
his confidence and gave him more opportunities on the mound. Also, to his
delight, it gave him an opportunity to sign with Seattle in 2006. Again, mid-
season he was traded to Oakland, where he compiled a 4.57 ERA for their
AAA team.

Finally, in 2007 he started to see flashes of his performance returning,
like he had performed in 2000. He could pitch again at 88–89 miles per

113

hour, and he started noticing the change in the hitters' swings. He could freeze-up a hitter again with a good fastball, or throw off a hitter's swing with a curveball. "It was a relief to finally see some of the signs of my return," Adam says. "Except this time I was twenty-eight, no longer fresh out of college. That didn't make my situation any easier."

During the 2008 season, when Adam pitched for Cincinnati's AAA team, he heard talk in the clubhouse and through the media that the Reds might be in need of another starting pitcher. Like most players who hear those conversations, Adam didn't take anything too seriously. He just continued competing, doing what he was doing.

As September neared, Adam's manager Rick Sweet told him he had recommended to the general manager that Adam go to Cincinnati. He couldn't promise anything, though. He had no control over what the team did.

Soon after that conversation, Adam got the call.

"It's amazing, of course, to get that call," Adam explains. "But for me it was the second time—this time I just had a feeling of appreciation, here's what the Lord has given me after all these years."

Immediately he flew to join the team in Milwaukee for two games. It wasn't until the team flew to Arizona that Adam pitched in his first relief appearance; he got another appearance a week later. As the season was coming to a close, Adam wondered what to expect from manager Dusty Baker, who at one time had spoken to him about getting a start.

Finally, his start came on the last day of the 2008 season, an opportunity he embraced, yet a tough assignment nonetheless. "I hadn't thrown more than twenty pitches over the last three weeks, so it was tough to stay sharp," Adam remembers. Because it was the last game, many players were already focused on heading home, especially because the Reds were not in playoff contention that year. The outing was rough for Adam, both physically and mentally, a seemingly insignificant end to a long, insignificant season. Yet for Adam, that start meant so much more: "I made it back. After all that I'd been through, all the doubts I had, I got there."

In 2004, Justin Lehr's dreams were realized when he got promoted to Oakland on June 17 to replace a pitcher on bereavement leave. Over 27 appearances, he posted a 5.24 ERA, and recorded his first major league strikeout against Sammy Sosa.

After that season, the A's traded Justin to the Brewers, and he continued to shine, maintaining a 3.89 ERA throughout his 23 appearances in Milwaukee. Although he had not taken on a regular role with the team yet, he proved that he was able to compete against hitters at the big league level. He was used to facing dominant hitters at the AAA level; very little changed at the major league level as far as the hitters' abilities. If anything, major league hitters had reputations that preceded them, and Justin had to learn to settle down so that he wouldn't be intimidated by names like Albert Pujols and Ken Griffey, Jr.

What came as a surprise to Justin that year, though, was a fear that had been creeping up in his mind: "I was so obsessed with thinking they were going to tap me on the shoulder and send me down. I was a wreck; I couldn't focus on anything. That was the first time I realized, 'This is not right.'"

His ERA proved his paranoia was unfounded; yet, in the back of his mind, Justin knew he had given up something that had allowed him to be successful in the past. It had allowed him to reach the big leagues. What if now, on his own, he couldn't maintain that success?

Finally, as a last resort, Justin turned to the team's employee assistance program and asked for help: "I said I don't know what *kind* of help I need, but I need help." They referred him to a local sport psychology consultant who worked with him for the remainder of the season.

"I didn't know what I was looking for," Justin says. "What's funny is just starting the process, getting some crap off my chest, was totally helpful. And I ended up finishing the year with good numbers."

While he worked with the consultant, Justin began realizing that while he was pitching, his mind would fill with negative thoughts. Generally he was not a negative person, but when he considered game situations, he realized he would think negatively: "I'd be thinking about getting released while I'm trying to make pitches. Then I'd get down on myself for thinking that way, even though I couldn't help it."

Through the course of working on his mental game, Justin learned that the thoughts he was having were normal, something that many players struggled with. It was useless trying to stop the thoughts from coming; those efforts only made him feel more guilty or anxious. Instead, he learned a process to manage those thoughts.

Even though Justin had found an effective, long-term strategy for competing, his numbers dropped in 2006, and at the end of the season, the Brewers released him.

"It was kind of frustrating because at the time I was designated in 2006, that's when the mental skills started taking effect," Justin recalls. "It's taken a long time; I thought it'd be quicker. Still, I stuck with it because I knew I had a lot more potential."

The next season he signed with Seattle and, like Vinny Rottino, worked with Jack Curtis, who now worked with the Mariners. With Jack, Justin discovered that although he had learned to reframe his thoughts and visualize game situations, he still struggled to believe that he was a major league pitcher: "I had to ask myself if I really saw myself as a major league pitcher, or if it was just something I really wanted to do."

There was more work to be done. That spring training, Jack Curtis hypnotized Justin in order to train his subconscious mind to believe that he belonged on the mound.

"You can sit and tell yourself all these things, but your subconscious mind still has control," Jack explains. "It can block the changes you're trying to make within your mind. The longer you've believed something subconsciously, the harder it is to change that belief."

Through hypnosis, Jack helped Justin get past the barrier of his subconscious mind, and establish more deeply his belief that he was a major league pitcher: "Immediately when I left the room, it completely transformed the way I thought about myself," Justin recalls. "I knew that I was going to get this opportunity and I was going to accomplish this."

Even though Justin now believed it, it still took three years for him to earn another opportunity to pitch in the big leagues. "I had so much success in the minor leagues over those three years [2007–2009] that it was almost a joke it took that long."

That season with Seattle (2007), Justin returned to the starting rotation at AAA, a change he also felt would position him better for his return to the major leagues. That became his stipulation for signing with Cincinnati in 2008, as well.

Meanwhile, his numbers during the years leading up to his second major league debut were even better than the years leading to his first debut. He earned minor league all-star accolades in 2008 and 2009, and was named pitcher of the week multiple times those years. At the close of 2009, he was named the International League's most valuable pitcher.

Although he had been forced to contend with the steroids culture as a young pitcher, he had managed to salvage his career throughout those years. Following those years, with Jack Curtis and the aid of sport psychology, he had found something more powerful to enhance his game and bring him once again to the brink of the major leagues—a powerful mind.

"I feel like now that the playing field is fair again, the game is coming back to me," Justin says. "I don't have any regrets about decisions I made then—decisions that gave me the ability to stay in the game during a time when baseball didn't have a level playing field. The game is even now, and because of that, it is even better."

A little over a year after his surgery, Brandon Snyder got promoted to the high A Frederick Ironbirds where he hit .315 on the season. Finally, he was feeling comfortable again, like he was returning to his true form.

That offseason, Brandon made an effort to shed some pounds he had put on when he was recovering from his surgery. After his injury, he went on the "Chipotle diet," so to lose weight he switched to more nutritious eating and worked hard in the gym. In the end he lost close to twenty-five pounds, more than he originally intended, and he felt strong and trim. Ultimately, the weight loss hindered him somewhat towards the end of the 2009, though: "I ran out of gas a couple weeks after the all-star break. It's a learning curve— after that I focused less on running, more on weights and nutritious eating."

In 2009 Brandon was also invited to his first big league spring training in Fort Lauderdale. During that time he got to talk to some of the coaches and they explained to him that they saw him as the Orioles' future first baseman. Although those conversations were exciting, Brandon still knew they weren't going to give him the job—he still had to earn it.

"I know that when they call me up, they don't want to have to send me back down," Brandon says. "They want me to be a determining factor in the success of the Orioles. When I get there, I don't just want to get my foot in the door. I want to bust the door down."

He was one of the last cuts at spring training even though he had played at single A the season before. The team assigned him to start at the AA team in Bowie, where he played half the season batting .343. When he was promoted in June to AAA Norfolk, though, his performance faltered: "All I could think about was getting the call up in September. Instead of going out and just playing, I was trying to prove myself every day."

Brandon noticed how his attitude affected his performance. When he was at AA he would have slumps, but because he was so relaxed the slumps only lasted a couple games. Once he got to AAA, he was much more self-conscious; slumps lasted for weeks instead of days, and he wasn't having fun.

"I learned a lot from that year, and I realized it was a good thing I didn't get called up," Brandon admits. "I wasn't ready—there were still some things I needed to work on."

Brandon would get down on himself for his poor hitting. If he'd return to the dugout with an 0-for-3, he'd be furious. Then one day a teammate spoke to him and said, "The reason you're not going up in September is because of your attitude. The minute something bad happens to you, you fold."

Even though he didn't like to hear it, Brandon knew it was true. By the end of the season, he was worn, frustrated, and ready for some time off to get his head straight. Then the team told him they wanted him to play for the second time in the Arizona Fall League. "At first I really didn't want to go," Brandon recalls. "I was really annoyed with my performance and I didn't want to prolong the season."

His coach explained that they wanted to send him to the fall league so that he could end his season on a positive note. Brandon felt reassured by the team's faith in his abilities; he also was reluctant to contact the front office and tell them he didn't want to go.

The 17 games in October facilitated a major turn-around for Brandon.

He felt more relaxed, enjoyed playing again, and ended with a .354 average. "Playing for the fall league helped me believe I was a major league baseball player," Brandon says. "If I could play with the league's best prospects and still hit over .300, then I could play in the big leagues."

Mentally, he was returning to the place he had always been as a baseball player: "Ever since Little League, I'd just go out and play because it was fun and I was good. I never tried to do well—I just played. Otherwise I'd be putting too much pressure on myself and my instincts would go out the door."

Instead of focusing on the box score, Brandon started evaluating the quality of his at-bats, whether he took his walks, and whether he played good defense. He felt much better walking away from every game knowing he had done something well, even if he'd gone 0-for-4 at the plate.

"Since I was young, I've always worked so hard on my mechanics, and I've gotten very good. But it's been harder, especially since my surgery, to deal with adversity," Brandon comments. "It's easier to work on your swing, it's harder to work on your thoughts and how you process the game."

When we finally get what we've wanted for so long, it can be a cruel moment. It is something we've rehearsed in our heads so many times, so perfectly, somewhat abstractly without the realism of time. Some days it seems entirely possible, even close at hand; other days it is far, far away. When we finally get it, though, it is a little sharp with reality—a great pleasure cheapened with unpredictable emotions, bad weather, or a sore back. What should have been perfect is still good—but we have to reconcile it somewhat with the better version in our head.

Then there is when it is over, when the moment has finally been enjoyed, and we wonder whether there will be another. Could there possibly be another like it?

It is important to move on quickly, before we become trapped in nostalgia, unwilling to find new moments that can bring us momentum again. Maybe nothing can ever be as good as that—but there is still more, and living means rising and falling, and each day finding more.

The team was about to fly from Albuquerque to Nashville when Vinny Rottino got called aside by his manager, Frank Krembliss. Frank told Vinny he wasn't going to Nashville—he was going to Milwaukee. That meant he would be playing in the major leagues.

It wouldn't be the first time Vinny had set foot in Miller Park. When he had played for the Beloit Snappers they faced off against the Appleton Timber Rattlers at Miller Park, at the time under much different circumstances.

When Vinny flew to Milwaukee the next day he wasn't alone. Mitch Stetter also joined him from the Nashville team. Vinny wasn't a strange face in the clubhouse either because he had worked with the same players and coaches at the big league camp earlier that year.

Although he had swung a bat countless times throughout his career, he had never swung a bat in the major leagues. His first opportunity came the first day he arrived. Manager Ned Yost put Vinny in the on-deck circle to hit for the pitcher should Jeff Cirillo get on base. When Cirillo singled, Vinny began his walk to the plate.

The moment was surreal. Suddenly, 40,000 fans were on their feet, not because he was a famous player they paid good money to see. He was a local celebrity, a home-grown talent that fans valued even more. In the seats his parents looked on, his friends with shirts that spelled his name, and his old baseball coach, Jack Schiestle, watching his young prodigy experience one of his greatest moments.

The debut would have been just about perfect if Vinny had gotten on base—but he didn't. Instead, he struck out, swinging on a pitch that was too close to take. The strikeout didn't matter, though. That was just baseball, and Vinny knew it better than anyone. A strikeout, just like a hit, broke him through the barrier, the wall that separated major league from minor league. Now he was finally getting his chance.

As September continued, Vinny grew more comfortable, less star-struck, and held his own at the plate. With a little more experience, he realized he was not overpowered, and he could play fast and hard like everybody else. Major league baseball was not so distant from the competition he'd been facing all season at the AAA level in Nashville.

Still, Vinny's ability was only one of many factors in a complex equation the organization was trying to figure out. The Brewers saw playoff potential in the team's future, and they were trying to purchase, trade, demote, and promote a team that hadn't experienced postseason play in twenty-six years.

During the 2007 season, Vinny shared catching duties with the team's everyday catcher, a role he enjoyed and gained confidence in. In his second September call-up, he felt more comfortable, less pressure, and fought hard during the opportunities he was given.

In one of those opportunities, a game against the San Diego Padres that had extended into the tenth inning, Vinny hit a walk-off single that put the Brewers over .500 on the season for the first time in thirteen years. "That was an amazing moment—it felt really amazing to be able to come through for my team," Vinny says.

Now with a taste for major league competition, Vinny felt revitalized and ready for whatever might be next. There was no turning back.

For baseball players, September can be an exciting month. It is the final month before the postseason, a time when teams that are neck-and-neck begin counting games, wins and losses, in hopes that when the last game is completed, they'll end up on top.

September also is an exciting month for minor league players who have aspirations of getting called up to The Show. It is the time of year when teams expand their rosters to include players that the organization believes may have a future with the major league team. For minor league players, September may be the biggest opportunity of their careers, an achievement they have been fighting for throughout the years. Although to some (including the media) a handful of major league at-bats may seem like an insignificant accomplishment, baseball players who finally reach a major league stadium's sacred ground calculate their appearances, their hits, their moments, with the familiarity and affection of a father doting over his child.

If good baseball is good baseball, though, why does major league baseball matter so much to players?

Certainly the salaries, the prestige, and the first-class treatment of major league baseball appeal to any player. Major league baseball encompasses the best of both worlds—players get to do what they love and they get treated royally while doing it.

There is another reason major league baseball matters so much to players, though; they believe in baseball, not just as a self-serving way of life, but as an enduring experience, something that inspires life and the pursuit of excellence. With each game, baseball is filled with new opportunities as different players contribute their stories to the history of the game. And the history of baseball is complex—decorated with the traditions, records, and cultures that have expressed a way of life for over a hundred years. Through baseball, so many people have spoken into the lives of other people. When players finally make it to the major leagues, they join very prestigious company, both past and present. Like the great players who have gone before them, they now have the opportunity to make a statement, not through words but through actions. They are on a platform where many people are watching expectantly, hoping for brilliance, the greatness that the average person cannot achieve.

The journey does not end when a player gets called up to the big leagues, even though it may appear in all ways as if his ultimate goal has been met. The majority of players who see major league time do so during September, a mere month of the season, with only a handful of at-bats or innings pitched. Although this is no small achievement—it is the major leagues, 45,000 fans, and live television—it is a taste of greatness that introduces an even greater hurdle: how can a player transform a call-up, a blink of the eye, into a major league career?

Where a small percentage of players see major league time, an even smaller percentage become everyday players at that level. Any time an organization decides to promote a minor league player, they are taking a risk. That is because a player's stellar performance in the minor leagues frequently does not transfer to the major leagues, or at least not immediately. The most common setback players face when they get called up is to lose their belief in their ability to compete.

According to Vinny Rottino, "A lot of guys have the talent, but then they get to the big leagues and don't fully believe it. Baseball is such a game of confidence—it's a sport where, if you believe that you belong, then you're going to belong. Really that's the only difference between the major leagues and the minor leagues—your belief that you belong."

Justin Lehr, who worked on his belief that he is a major league pitcher, realizes that developing that belief takes effort and practice: "Most guys would say they have a good mental game. I believed I had a good mental game—but when I got to the big leagues, I realized it wasn't good enough. So I've had to take that next step—to practice affirming in my mind that I belong in the major leagues. I've practiced controlling my mind."

Many players struggle with the mental transition to major league baseball, and unless a team has reason to be patient, a player may lose his opportunity while going through this transition.

According to Tom Trebelhorn, "People who say baseball is a thinking man's sport just mean players have more time to think. That can be really tough for young players. In the big leagues, you better have the ability, the confidence, and a clear conscience all the time, or else you'll be gone."

Bob Tewksbury, a former major league pitcher, found that the biggest challenge when reaching the major leagues was dealing with the level of performance on a regular basis. "There are going to be days when you aren't able to perform," Tewksbury explains. "The guys who can deal with failure better have a tendency to stay in the major leagues longer. The guys who try harder may lose their confidence, and then their performance declines—those are the guys who lose their jobs. It's easy to tie in your confidence with how well you're doing. You've got to be able to understand that there are going to be ups and downs, and it takes a while to get to know that."

Many players, either consciously or subconsciously, carry stress with them throughout their careers, simply because they know they have to perform in order to keep their job.

Morgan Ensberg admits, "Basically for eight years I went to bed scared to death, even during the years I played well. You just don't know if you're going to be there the next day."

Tewksbury can relate to Morgan's frame of mind: "I used to joke with my wife that if I had a good game, we'd eat at a nice steak house, but if I had a bad game, we were eating at McDonald's. That's how it is for a player. If you have a good game, you're there for another day. If you don't have a good game—who knows?"

Performance can be a player's biggest challenge when he reaches the big leagues for this reason. Rather than relaxing and relying on the skills that got him the call up in the first place, he may think he needs to do just a little bit more when he reaches that higher level.

According to Ted Power, pitching coach for the Louisville Bats, "Really, it boils down to guys just trusting their stuff. They've already got the ability to compete; when they get called up, they just need to believe it."

This means they need to become comfortable in the company of celebrity ballplayers who have established names and careers in the annals of baseball.

Brett Butler recalls the first time he got to the big leagues with the Braves and the team played against the Phillies and Brett's idol, Pete Rose: "From the dugout, I watched Pete hitting BP—the next thing I know one of my teammates walks up to Pete, and pretty soon Pete is coming over by me. He asks me if I want to talk hitting, so I started asking questions."

Until that moment, Pete Rose had been a face on TV or a baseball card. Once Brett got used to the fact that he now belonged in Pete Rose's company, he could get back to playing baseball the way he always did. "Once you figure out those guys put their pants on like everybody else, you take them off their pedestal," Butler says. "Those that can do this stay for a long period of time, and those that can't don't stick around for very long. There are few people who can stay in major league baseball or a big corporate environment for a long period of time. It's hard to sustain that belief."

It is not uncommon for players experiencing major league play for the first time to battle with excessive amounts of nervous energy. If a player does not learn to harness this energy into his performance, he is more prone to make mistakes, lose concentration, and lose his opportunity to make an impact on the team. Athletes who understand how to control their energy before and during a game likewise will have much greater control over their performance.

Another reason playing major league baseball is a mental adjustment is because players at that level are savvier and more intelligent, because they have additional tools and years of experience often unavailable in the minor leagues.

When working with pitchers, Ted Power tries to train them not to rely on the speed of their fastball: "Once you reach the major leagues, there are very few hitters a pitcher can overpower. I try to teach pitchers to understand their abilities, which pitches they can locate the best, what works to calm yourself down when the situation gets tight. In the big leagues you have to outmaneuver and outthink hitters. A catcher can help you with that, but ultimately a pitcher is responsible for his performance. This is something pitchers get better at over time."

For many players, getting called up can be like a catch-22—they want to have their shot in the big leagues, but once they get there, they don't get as much playing time as they had been getting in the minor leagues. When they are supposed to be proving to the club that they belong, they may be forced to perform after days of sitting on the bench, when mentally and physically they may have grown a bit rusty.

For this reason, Brett Butler feels it's important that organizations be careful not to call-up players too quickly: "It happens all the time today—you have kids getting called up too fast. They may have all the talent in the world, but they still haven't developed the mental ability to adjust. You look at guys like Don Mattingly, Wade Boggs, Tony Gwynn—they spent years in the minor leagues to develop their roles."

As a result, many players today shuffle up and down between teams.

Ted Power comments, "An organization is trying to help the major league team win, but this can make it difficult for some guys to develop. Today it's very common for players to go up and down, a bit too common."

For many players, though, it takes more than one call-up for them to adjust to the big leagues. Getting sent down can help a player with that adjustment.

Rick Rodriguez, pitching coach for the Sacramento River Cats, comments, "Sometimes players need to get removed from the pressure, have some good outings, gain the confidence back, then get sent back up."

Other factors determine a player's potential opportunity with the big league team. In order for a player to win a regular spot, he must convince the organization that he can contribute. Still, this may not be enough. Organizations are limited by a variety of factors—payroll, positional needs, multi-year contracts, and free agency. Sometimes they only have one shot to get it "right"; this may make an organization less inclined to make risky moves.

But what are "risky" moves from an organizational standpoint? When an organization decides to take on a player who may not have a prototypical career—he's not mentioned in *Baseball America*, didn't attend a Division I college, may have been a double-digit-round draft selection, or (worse) put in some time in independent ball—there is a higher probability he will not be successful. This may be because, as predicted, he comes in with less training or experience than the prototypical player; on the other hand, this may be because organizations have less confidence in that player's potential, so he receives fewer opportunities. Nevertheless, this player may shine through just as brilliantly as the first-round draft pick. Organizations know this but they are often more reluctant to take a risk on players who have not gone through the usual channels that baseball endorses. With these odds, players who aspire to reach major league baseball have very limited opportunity.

Regardless, many players, even those without prototypical careers, want baseball badly, and are willing to fight and work for their dream. As a result, baseball each year is filled with stories of players who seem to be unlikely prospects for major league baseball, yet their determination, and being in the right place at the right time, allow them to prevail and thrive in the big leagues.

Many players find they can work their way into a major league position because baseball's extensive minor league system has given them years to develop their skills.

Vinny Rottino agrees: "A lot of times players may struggle in the minor leagues, but then they figure it out and eventually make it to the big leagues. If the system wasn't so extensive, a lot of these guys may have been weeded out before they had the chance to make it."

Yet, players who have less promise in the eyes of the organization may need to think of additional ways they can get noticed and find opportunities.

Somebody like Adam Pettyjohn has pitched with six different organizations since coming up through the Tigers system. With each team, he found a new opportunity to earn a spot on the major league roster. At the same time, switching teams can create additional challenges.

"You have to go in and prove yourself all over again with the new organization," Adam says. "They don't know you until they see you perform. Plus, every organization has already got their draft picks, so it's a tough situation trying to get promoted over those players."

From a player's perspective, it can be worthwhile to do research on teams and managers.

After returning from his surgery, Adam felt he would have more opportunity with San Francisco and so decided to sign with the team during the 2004 season. By then he was a minor league free agent and had some flexibility choosing where he wanted to go: "It's a player to player situation. For me, I wouldn't want to sign with a team with three lefties in the rotation. Sometimes you may only have one offer; other years you may have some leverage."

A player's agent can help him make good decisions, as well. He's someone who works with teams' general managers, as well as the team's skipper. Based on his knowledge of these people, an agent can advise his client to find a situation where his skills may prove most valuable.

In 2009, Jeff Weaver was an example of a player who positioned himself for success. At the beginning of the season he received no major league offers, so he signed with the Dodgers and started with their AAA team. Due to injuries throughout the course of the season, Jeff got called to Los Angeles to pitch for manager Joe Torre. That year not only did Weaver end up pitching for the Dodgers, but he also ended up pitching for the team in the playoffs.

According to Adam Pettyjohn, Weaver's familiarity with Torre's managing style helped him position himself that year: "A pitcher with not as much major league experience might not have gotten the call from Joe. Joe wants a guy who doesn't have nerves, who's been there and done that."

Justin Lehr throughout his career has actively pursued situations with teams that would allow him opportunities to pitch in the major leagues. In 2007 with the Mariners, he knew that he wouldn't have many opportunities for major league time and so requested his release. When the team wouldn't release him, Justin chose to go on the disabled list for a month.

"I had become their organizational player, not a big league option anymore," Justin explains. "You get caught in that mode of just playing for your paycheck. If that's the point you get to, then it's time to quit. The minor leagues is no life for a guy, especially a guy with a family."

Still, some players have fought it out for years in the minor leagues, sustaining their hopes that eventually they'll get the call from the major league team.

In an article for *ESPN*, Ramona Shelburne covers John Lindsey's career, a veteran minor league player who had been waiting sixteen years for his first call-up. Lindsey's stint in the minors is somewhat exceptional—he holds the records for the most years in the minors without major league time—but he is not alone in the extent to which some players will go in order to achieve their dream.

Some may ask, though, how can he hold out for so long without a single opportunity? At what point does someone decide to throw in the towel?

For someone like Lindsey, he still puts up good numbers, including a .402 batting average at the all-star break in 2010. With those numbers, he still has a chance, even at age thirty-three. The other reason he holds on: "I could tell my kids, 'Your daddy played in the major leagues.'"[1]

Finally, in 2010 the Dodgers gave Lindsey his chance and he recorded his first major league at-bat on September 8.

Players like Lindsey are admirable examples of perseverance, people who believe in their dream even when the years get long, who return to the field each day without bitterness, with the continual belief that every year they are getting better. This mindset allows players to be successful, even when the odds seem to be stacked against them.

For many players, the key to maintaining belief in their goals lies in their focus on the process rather than an obsession with winning. When someone's only goal is to win, he can put himself into a dangerous position. He will perform only so that he will win, which means he could perform below his capability if that is all that is required for him to win. He can also become easily frustrated if he cannot perform well enough to win. However, if a player focuses on becoming excellent (rather than merely a "winner"), he will continue to grow and achieve victories on a regular basis.

When a player focuses on the end result of his performance, he can become easily distracted from focusing on the techniques that will allow him to achieve victory. Obviously every player wants to win, but if he focuses on the process rather than the outcome, he will have greater access to all of his power, skill, and potential.

A player can be most effective, likewise, when he stays focused on the present moment. He may want to think about the end result of a game, a promotion, or a milestone he'd like to reach—but thoughts of the future (or past, for that matter) limit a player's ability to perform and experience harmony in the present moment.

Vinny Rottino remarks, "As long as I have a uniform I belong here. I still trust and believe that I'm exactly where I'm supposed to be. I'm here right now with an opportunity—that's the only way you can do it."

In his pursuit for major league time, Vinny was willing to accept what many would consider a demotion, playing with the Brewers' AA team rather than the AAA team, because he knew he'd have more regular playing time at AA. "The way you get better at baseball is by playing more baseball. I'm willing to do whatever it takes to get out on the field," Vinny says.

A rare percentage of players establish themselves in the major leagues at a young age. Usually these players have exceptional talent, above and beyond what may be typical for somebody their age. These are the players who define the game—Tim Lincecum, Joe Mauer, and Stephen Strasburg—who have the ability to explore unchartered territory in baseball.

More common, though, are players who have to work hard everyday just to get an opportunity. As Tom Trebelhorn comments, "That's probably 80 percent of the major leagues. The talented and gifted are few and far between, but those guys who can grind it out day in and day out, they are more common."

Morgan Ensberg is an example of a player who found his way to the major leagues, but battled each year to get consistent playing time: "I never had the feeling that I was a team's only option. I had three or four years that I hit over twenty home runs, but I was still playing only half the time and never really felt settled. I just didn't feel like this was mine for sure."

Young players especially can struggle with the uncertainty that they belong in the major leagues. When someone is young, his perspective tends to be more focused on immediate experience rather than long-term goals. When someone ages, however, he begins to collect more experiences that prove life is filled with many opportunities. Usually a single, isolated moment, no matter how powerful it may seem at the time, cannot define a player's ability and career.

Yet, baseball poses this paradox: the game values the maturity of veteran players, but prizes the strength and versatility of youth. Baseball runs on a short calendar and players only have a limited window of time in which they can compete. Young players have the potential to contribute more years to an organization. At the same time, veteran players (minor league or major league) have years of knowledge and experience that they bring to their game. This additional mental tool can give veteran players an advantage over emerging prospects, even if talent-wise a younger player may have more potential.

For instance, Justin Lehr admits, "At this point I'm limited physically as far as what I can contribute to a major league team. I don't nearly have the same stuff I had four years ago. The reason I can still compete, though, is because of what I can do with my mind versus my body."

Veteran players have had more practice controlling their emotions and maintaining a consistent disposition throughout a game. Genetically, some people are more predisposed to this than others, yet the experience of age allows many players, predisposed or not, to master this skill.

Tom Trebelhorn sees this emotional battle with the young players he coaches: "They always talk about slowing the game down—I'm still not sure what that means. Really you have to not get too excited mentally and get ahead of yourself. You want to think ahead and pre-play, but you can't get too far ahead. Take it one event at a time." He also acknowledges this is a challenging skill for young people to master. "Let's face it, I didn't know this when I was these guys' age either. I wish I had, but it's just something you learn through experience."

The other skill that can be challenging for young players to master at first is the ability to make adjustments in their game. In order to do this, a player needs to be willing to listen to a coach's suggestions, and determined to find a "solution" to his problem without becoming frustrated. Adjustments usually take time, as well, and require a period of struggle before a player sees positive results.

For instance, Vinny Rottino began working on some adjustments in his swing during his 2008 season, which initially led to a drop in his numbers. The adjustments, however, paid dividends during his 2010 season when he hit .308 on the year: "Sometimes if you get too caught up in the game about mechanical stuff, you're not going to have the results. Once you're in the game you just have to see the ball, hit the ball. You can't start thinking about it—you just have to compete."

Many times call-ups experience success early on, but then slump in their rookie season or the following year. Initially, pitchers have not seen a player fresh out of the minor leagues; however, in time they begin to figure out the player so that he has to make adjustments in order to be successful.

Smokey Garrett saw this happen with his young prospect Jay Bruce when he got called up to the big leagues in 2008. According to Garrett, during Jay's first season he had "a ton of confidence, he was energetic, he believed in himself." Then his second season he struggled a lot more. "All of a sudden doubt set in and he lost his confidence, and all of a sudden he didn't do as well. His natural ability hadn't gone anywhere; somewhere along the line he just lost confidence in his ability."

This is where a young player can benefit from the influence of experienced players and coaches. These are the people who, according to Adam Pettyjohn, "can keep someone level-headed."

Fortunately, baseball is the type of profession where people are willing to invest time in other people in order to help them succeed. Masters of the game are willing to teach their knowledge to younger players because they want to preserve the techniques and traditions of a game that they love and respect. Young players who are willing to listen usually will find an eager teacher in a veteran player.

According to Justin Lehr, this arrangement is most common at the major league level: "Guys are a lot more secure in their jobs. An older reliever might take a younger reliever under his wing because he's not competing against him. He's free to help him." For Justin, Jim Mercir and Chad Bradford were players who mentored him when he was a reliever.

Brandon Snyder during his minor league days got to work alongside veteran players Aubrey Huff and Melvin Moore. Brandon comments, "The best part of pro ball is having older guys to help you get a picture. It's an awesome part of the game."

Because many professional players have received the time and skills of veteran players, they likewise are inclined to pass along what they have learned to younger players, even at the prospect level.

Brandon, for instance, spends time in the offseason speaking at local high schools. He tries to give players good advice not just about baseball, but also about how to make good decisions in life: "It makes a difference that I'm a professional player and can relate to them that way. They can all play, but it's harder for them to understand the mental challenges — knowing themselves, knowing their game, knowing how to act off the field."

Likewise, Vinny, who benefited since his high school days from Jack Schiestle's coaching and instruction, works with Jack in the offseason at his hitting facility in Racine, teaching emerging ballplayers the skills he's learned from his professional experiences.

Blake Pindyck is one player who has been influenced by Vinny's mentorship. He remarks, "Vinny's just a gritty ball player, and he's not stuck up, not afraid to reach out to someone who needs help or encouragement. One season he called me when I was having a tough time, and he just reminded me about having fun and how to take a positive mental approach. That's really had a tremendous impact on my game and my life."

Every player has an example of a coach or ballplayer who has taken the time to teach him, advise him, or encourage him. The impact of this relationship, whether coach-to-player or player-to-player, has powerful and lasting effects. Ultimately, a player who has received the care and concern of a coach naturally responds by offering the same to other players. These are the people who draw the most from the game—those who have been given much and are willing to give much in return.

The call-up is a very important time in a player's career; for the first time, it provides an open door to a player's ultimate goal: joining a team's 25-man roster. Yet a September call-up is not enough. For many players it provides a taste of major league competition, yet it is still a limited opportunity, a narrow timeframe players must use to prove they belong. Working their way into a regular roster spot can be much more complex, especially for players who have had to work hard to prove they can compete at the major league level.

Adam Pettyjohn comments, "When you start to get older in baseball years, an organization may be tempted to go with the twenty-four-year-old prospect. But all you can do is keep proving yourself and hope that a need opens up on top. If not this year, then maybe next year. As long as you keep putting up numbers, you still have a chance."

SEVEN

Winter Ball

I don't like work—no man does—but I like what is in work—the chance to find yourself. Your own reality—for yourself, not for others—what no other man can ever know.—Joseph Conrad

Although Mexico has borders, sometimes they are easy to cross, while at other times, impossible. It depends on who you are.

For Americans, Mexico does everything cheaper—Kahlua, vanilla, hotels, prescriptions. Still close to the wealth and development of America, border cities like Tijuana and Mexicali offer relief from American regulations—taxes, licenses, and the red tape that makes America so civilized.

The border that is so easy for Americans to cross looms like a mountain before many Mexicans; nations generally do not welcome people who come with empty hands and empty pockets.

Yet if the border had been negotiated differently hundreds of years ago, it might have been impossible to distinguish between the arid plains where California stops and Mexico begins. As it is, the same place is divided by years of privilege and years of poverty—one place always trying to escape to the other place, and usually not the other way around.

Except when it comes to baseball. In baseball, Mexicans and Americans are exchanged regularly, evenly, throughout the summer and the winter. Everyone gets a chance, and the best team, no matter which side of the border, wins.

Adam Pettyjohn went to Mexico during the winter of 2007 to play in Mexico's winter league and, as an American player, experienced many of the cultural challenges that Latin players face when they move to the United States: "The most important thing I found was to keep an open mind because no matter how Americanized everything is, it's not America. Some guys that go down there expect it to be like America, but it's not. You have to be willing to gain some new experiences if you're going to have success down there."

Played in minor-league-sized stadiums, sometimes half-empty, sometimes roaring with fans, games in Mexico usually last four hours. Baseball, like many things Mexican, does not rush. Sometimes three or four pitchers take on an inning; rosters frequently change, depending on how well someone is playing. Teams are not shy about releasing players, even after a week's time.

"Because the season is so short, they can't afford to give away a week or two of games," Adam says. "Every game means so much — if you're not producing, especially as a foreign player, they'll ship you out."

When Adam played in Mexico, he had the opportunity to pitch an additional 40 innings; this allowed him to condition his arm for a full season's work, about 200 innings. "It really gives you momentum going into spring training, as long as you're not getting overworked," Adam claims.

Some players, especially big league players, do get overworked by their winter teams and then are in danger of breaking down mid-season. Many major league clubs deter their star players from playing in the winter; yet, to players like Edinson Volquez and Johnny Cueto, it is an honor to play before their people.

When Adam played in Mexico, he played with five other Americans on his team. Although he got to know all of his teammates, and many of them spoke English, he bonded most with his fellow Americans. "We had a great group of guys — but there's just nothing like having another American close by when you're down there," Adam says. "You realize what those guys go through when they leave their countries to play in America."

It's all part of the thrill of crossing borders — you'll always find something new and different on the other side.

Justin Lehr has been around the globe playing baseball — Mexico, Venezuela, Korea, the Dominican Republic, and Puerto Rico. After the 2009 season when he pitched for the Reds, though, he took a break. "It was the first year of my career I hadn't done any winter ball. It's just great baseball but it wears you out," he says.

During Justin's first winter ball experience was played in Puerto Rico, an island similar in climate and landscape to its western neighbor, the Dominican Republic, yet as an American territory, more privileged economically. Like most players, he stayed at an apartment on the beach in San Juan, the capital located on the northern coast of the island. As a rookie minor league player, he earned $5,500 for the season — not quite enough money to put any towards savings, yet plenty to live off of and enjoy a three-month stay in a resort city.

Justin got connected to the Puerto Rican team through his teammate Luis Lopez. He felt fortunate to have gained a spot because, like the other winter leagues, Puerto Rico hoped to lure established, well-known players who could win. Justin loved the competition and he loved the atmosphere the fans brought to the games.

"It's really not something equaled in minor league baseball," says Justin. "These fans are really knowledgeable about the game, and they have a win-at-all-costs mentality. You just don't find that in the minor leagues."

Even with the intense competition, Justin felt he could be a little more laid back during winter ball, simply because he wasn't playing for a promotion, the constant preoccupation players have in the minor leagues. According to Justin, "It's like playing for a paycheck. You don't have to worry about protecting your stats or looking good. You can play to win but you still don't have to feel all that pressure."

Still, like most Americans, he went through periods of cultural adjustment. Although teams had people available to interpret Spanish for the American players, they still had to face day-to-day moments in which they didn't understand what someone was saying. Or they might be misunderstood and create the wrong impression.

People may recognize winter ball players on the street or at a local café. In Puerto Rico and all Caribbean countries, winter ball is their major league season. Fans are passionate about each game, and that energy spills over to the players. As Justin remarks, "You just don't see that kind of enthusiasm in minor league games, or even in major league games sometimes. People really know what's going on."

American players are not completely alone during winter ball, as many American coaches manage or coach winter ball teams. Still, teams tend to play a different style of baseball in the Caribbean, something comparable to what was played in America during the 1970s. "They're not used to having as much offense as American baseball, so it could be the first inning with two guys on, and they might sacrifice the number three hitter to score a run," Justin says.

Learning how to play baseball in different cultures can be an enriching experience. Not only does it expose players to different competition, but it also connects them to different parts of the world. Justin sees his time playing winter ball as an invaluable part of his career: "It's fun being in different cultures—I love it that I got to do things I normally never would have done, got to see all sorts of towns and meet some really great people. People are as similar as they are different—I met some really good people."

It makes sense that where people are the poorest, they will play baseball the hardest. In the Dominican Republic, the people play to find a distraction—from the heat, the hunger—to fill the moments of their simple lives. They play because baseball is something worth fighting for in a land where, any other sort of battle—against AIDS, against poverty—would be in vain. In baseball, boys can win. If they make it to America, they can really win.

Vinny Rottino signed up for winter ball in the Dominican Republic in 2007 because he heard the island had good baseball. Like many players trying to win a roster spot out of spring training, Vinny knew that three additional months of playing could help him prepare even more.

The Dominican Republic is not for everyone, particularly American players unfamiliar with the type of poverty that exists beyond American borders. But like many tourists who travel to seaside resorts like Punta Cana, baseball players belong to the 10 percent of the island's population who take advantage of the tourism industry (the remaining 90 percent service it).

Vinny's team stayed at a resort in La Romana, a city on the southeast coast of the island, and played games in the evenings, when the torrid daytime temperatures cooled pleasantly. Living in the Dominican Republic was a shock at first, but the shock did not last long. As foretold, the Dominican people were fierce about baseball, and Vinny thrived in that environment: "They love it. The stands are packed for every game, they're screaming, banging on noisemakers. They're going nuts."

Dominicans are good at their game not because they have fancy (or decent) equipment, organized leagues, or top notch coaching. They're good because they're devoted heart and soul to the game, and that has been their way of life for over a hundred years. As Vinny recalls, "You see people on the streets with a hat of the team you're playing on. They know what's going on and they care about who's winning."

The problems of the Dominican Republic are complex, deeply rooted in the nation's struggle to establish a national identity, their hatred of things Haitian, and a history of unstable dictators. Any act of kindness, change in a beggar's hand, merely puts a Band-Aid on the internal bleeding of the nation.

Still, kindnesses console. And baseball for Dominicans is one of those kindnesses. Vinny explains: "You've really got to put on a performance down there, or else you'll be gone pretty quickly. Especially for the Dominican players who return to play. They feel a lot of pressure playing back home for their own people."

Vinny knew what it felt like to be a foreigner and got at least a small taste of what some Latin players face when they move to the United States to play.

"It was a culture shock at first," admits Vinny. "I never really got used to the food. It's just different from the food you're used to, so that was a really big adjustment. But I picked up a little Spanish while I was down there and I really enjoyed playing with my teammates."

His team, like most winter ball teams, had a handful of Americans and the rest were Dominicans. Although American players usually blended well with Dominican players, they were still profoundly aware of certain cultural differences. For instance, most Dominican players carried guns in their equipment bags. Many of them lived in cinder-block houses, too, when they weren't playing baseball.

One of Vinny's best friends in baseball, Ozzie Chavez, signed to play baseball at age fifteen. Over the years he's adjusted to playing baseball in the Brewers minor league system, yet he feels the most pressure when he returns home each winter to represent his team, the Azucareros del Este La Romana. "If you make an error in America, nobody sees you," says Chavez. "If you make an error at home, everybody sees you." Vinny agrees that during winter ball, the pressure is on: "Teams are not interested in developing their players. They are only interested in winning. They want players who will come down to the team and perform immediately."

As a nation, the Dominican Republic is not competitive—they fall well below other countries economically, academically, and politically. When it comes to baseball, though, Dominicans are at the top. Playing in their league can be both grueling and rewarding. In Vinny Rottino's mind, the pain is worth the gain: "When you're pitching at Yankee Stadium next year, you'll be able to say to yourself, 'Shoot, I played in the Dominican Republic. I can play anywhere now.'"

Winter ball can provide American players with many different opportunities—the opportunity to make extra money, to play really competitive baseball, and to travel and experience different countries. Perhaps the most important part of winter ball, however, is that it provides players with a bigger picture of baseball—a picture that includes a rich and competitive history in Latin America. Within this history are people who, like Americans, love the game and are willing to make tremendous sacrifices in order to have a chance to make it to the big leagues.

Yet, Latin players are different, as well, working through challenges that are unique to their nations and cultures. Some may have lost family members to gang violence. Others started swinging a stick instead of a bat, and didn't own a pair of shoes until they were ten. Still others acquired only an elementary education, and didn't speak a word of English, didn't really speak Spanish very well, when they first came to America.

These players, now comprising approximately 30 percent of major league baseball (nearly 50 percent of minor league baseball), have important stories to tell. They proclaim an important truth in baseball: some of the greatest players are born out of the most difficult situations. Adversity, rather than luxury, gives someone a reason to fight hard and to find a better life.

Yet, no matter what one's background, baseball remains the same. It is nine structured innings of play in which players work towards a common goal. The reasons people play baseball, however, may differ from person to person; everyone has something slightly different to express on the field, a different set of memories and circumstances to sort through over the course of a season. Still the need for victory is universal. In victory, we can press down the obstacles that burden us; our hope, our belief in the future, is renewed. Winning, of all things, makes us feel alive.

Baseball is the arena where cultures meet. Yet, because baseball has always been called "the American pastime," many Americans do not realize that rich baseball traditions exist outside the United States. When players find the opportunity to play winter ball in Mexico, Puerto Rico, Venezuela, or the Dominican Republic (all part of the Caribbean League), they find slightly different baseball, but just as competitive and just as intense as American baseball. In order to play winter ball, usually a player will find a connection from a coach or another player on the team. In earlier years, before players earned millions of dollars, major league stars would play winter ball regularly in order to supplement their incomes. Today, few major league players risk playing in the offseason, except for players who are native to that particular country.

Vinny Rottino remarks, "Somebody like a Ronnie Belliard plays every season [in the Dominican Republic]. He gets paid well but it's more about him being home with his people."

Marcos Breton, journalist and author of *Home Is Everything: The Latin Baseball Story*, sees this hometown loyalty in Miguel Tejada: "Against his better judgment, against my better judgment, Miguel Tejada has continued to play in the Dominican Republic. He can't resist it—he feels a lot of pressure to play."

Yet, Breton asserts that fewer and fewer big league stars are turning to winter ball these days: "Winter ball now has become the place for the American player who wants to show something so that somebody will notice him, to strengthen his position in the United States. The really successful big league player is not going to risk his livelihood in Mata de Cabo, Venezuela, where people are packing heat in the stands."

If big league players do participate, it's usually towards the second half of the winter season. "Especially in December," says Adam Pettyjohn, "that's when teams are looking for new players. If you're a big league player, those countries are willing to pay you $30,000 to $40,000 a month, tax-free. You can take a couple months off to rest, then go down for a month in December, get in shape, make good money."

No matter what stage of his career, though, the player who chooses to play winter ball will be in good company.

Ozzie Chavez, who now plays in the Phillies system, feels playing winter ball in the Dominican Republic is harder than playing in Lehigh, Pennsylvania: "It's a different level. Here you have single A, double A, triple A. But in Dominica, you only have one level. It's big league level."

For young players, winter ball is great training for the sort of competition they will face when they get called up to their American teams.

Vinny Rottino agrees, saying, "The Dominican league and the Venezuelan league are both very close to big league baseball. Getting to play three months of baseball at that high level will help get a player ready for the big leagues."

Because the competition is so intense, many players find it grueling to play winter ball then launch almost immediately into spring training when they return to the States. "It has to be done in moderation," says Justin Lehr. "You have to learn what your body can handle and how to manage that."

For three different winter ball seasons, Justin's team made it all the way to the Caribbean World Series, which only cut his offseason time even more short: "Three of the last six years I've gone to major league camp with just six days off. It's difficult to recover from that. At the same time, money starts to double and triple for players going to the World Series, so that's hard to resist. It's hard to resist the competition, too. You want to win."

Winter ball also can be a good opportunity for some players who missed parts of the regular season to get in shape, especially if they are coming off of an injury. "You want to look good to your team back home," Adam Pettyjohn comments. "Playing winter ball can do you a lot of good that way, if you can show your home team that you're getting your stuff back. It could work against you, too, though. You could go down there and get rocked, maybe put some questions in your organization's mind. You really have to go down there with the right mindset."

Even though there are risks, winter ball can be a great opportunity for players to experience a different style of baseball and gain valuable playing opportunities they may not experience during the regular season. "Sometimes organizations may want a player to hone certain skills," Adam comments. "They might encourage players, especially younger prospects, to go down and get some more innings. They'll be in contact with your winter ball coaches to check on your progress, or make sure you're not getting overused."

Although winter ball teams consist of more Latin players and coaches, an American influence and presence continues to grow, especially as major league baseball's influence in Latin countries continues to grow. Today, the baseball connection between Latin America and the United States is stronger than ever, especially because teams have expanded their scouting to many Latin countries, particularly the Dominican Republic.

Compared to Americans, most Latinos come from humble backgrounds. Like America, Latin American countries were formerly ruled by Europeans who brought with them an imperial sense of entitlement. Rather than admiring the foreign cultures they were encountering they did all they could to massacre and shape the land into European replicas. Instead of replicas, however, places like the Dominican Republic (Columbus's original landing point when he sailed from Spain in 1492) became shadows, places cowering under European rule, strong but inexperienced according to Western standards.

America came out successfully from the British. All Latin American nations eventually did the same (from places like Spain and France), but not with as much success. Some places, like the Dominican Republic, invited the return of Spanish rule (then promptly rebelled against it the year after) because their land and people had been so confused by imperial domination. Cuba found solace in the arms of communism, a triumph politically that won stability and power, but cold comfort for the people whose lives are restricted, regulated, and bullied by their own sovereign. Traditions and customs are strong in Latin countries, but they are often subject to forces beyond anyone's control.

Like America, baseball was born early in Latin America, running a narrative parallel to Babe Ruth, the Brooklyn Dodgers, Cracker Jack and the seventh-inning stretch. Cuba, which fought the earliest and the hardest to overthrow Spanish rule, became the instigator of baseball in places like Puerto Rico, the Dominican Republic, and Venezuela. The first Cuban league game took place in 1878 and "amateur leagues flourished around the island's sugar mills—a tradition that would later be duplicated to great success in the Dominican Republic."[1] Shortly after the Cuban league formed, a winter league began which included competition among players from traveling American squads. Although the Negro League was the only option for players of color during the first half of the twentieth century, a number of Cuban players (those with fairer complexions) began to star in major league baseball. Once Jackie Robinson broke the color line in 1947, Latinos (the majority still Cuban) joined the American game, yet not without the rejection and disdain of a society still reluctant to accommodate non-white players.

When Fidel Castro rose to power, the relationship between Cuba and America rapidly deteriorated; tensions played out during the 1960s through the Cuban Missile Crisis and the Bay of Pigs Invasion, during which the United States feared communist domination powered by nuclear weapons. Eventually political tensions cooled but Castro's regime no longer allowed Cubans to purse careers in American baseball. Baseball still flourishes on the island, yet now a world entirely unto itself. Each year, there are a handful of Cuban players who manage to escape the island (a recent example being Aroldis Chapman of the Cincinnati Reds) in order for a chance to play in the major leagues. In a place like Cuba, a baseball-crazed island, players understand what it means to be able to play the best of the best.

Tim Wendel makes the connection: "Perhaps that's the best reason why so many come from outside our borders to play in the U.S. major leagues: to play against the best. Too often we assume everything is about the money, the chance to land a big contract."[2]

Around the same time that Cuba closed its doors to American baseball, major league baseball instituted the amateur, or Rule 4, draft, which limited teams from scouting, signing, and developing players for their system. The purpose of the amateur draft was to prevent big-market teams from monopolizing talented prospects. With the draft in place, teams no longer felt the need to spend time and resources developing prospects when they had no guarantee they would be able to sign them.

According to Joanna Shepherd Bailey, an attorney and professor at Emory University, "This is when teams started looking outside the United States for opportunities, where they could continue to scout, sign, and develop players for their system. Basically, teams moved their operations from America to Latin countries; in America, players needed to get on good teams, play at top colleges, to get noticed for the draft."

This meant that as time went on, American players from low-income families (primarily African-Americans) felt the disadvantage and struggled to compete for draft selection.

Conversely, players in foreign countries who remained outside the draft flourished as teams began signing Latino players *en masse*. A natural starting place for scouts, now that Cuba was out of the picture, was Puerto Rico because of its status as an American territory. During the 1970s and 1980s, many great Puerto Rican players emerged, foremost among them Roberto Clemente, a player who went unacknowledged during the early years of his career regardless of his power hitting and his strong arm. Clemente remains an icon for Latino players not only because of his Hall of Fame career, but also for his acts of charity and public show of pride for his homeland.

Early Latino players like Clemente and Orlando Cepeda who flourished during their careers were mostly the exception to the rule, however. What many teams did not realize, or at least failed to accommodate, was that Latino players in many cases were struggling to adjust to American culture.

"It wasn't a matter of them lacking talent," says Breton. "They were struggling to communicate, living far away from home, and adjusting to American style discipline. These were the challenges they carried with them onto the field, and in many cases, these factors inhibited their performances."

Alvin Colina, a Venezuelan native who signed with the Rockies at age sixteen, arrived in the United States to play rookie ball when he was eighteen. Because he was so young and did not speak very good English, he remembers his first couple of months being a difficult adjustment: "Being far away from home was really hard at first. We relied a lot on the veteran players to help us get calling cards, drive us places, help us order food. The baseball was a lot more structured than what we were used to, also."

Adjusting to American routines—getting to the ballpark on time, conforming to group settings—can be a tremendous challenge for Latin players.

"These things come second nature to Americans," explains Breton. "But most players from Latin America come from very humble backgrounds; they're not growing up in homes where time management and decision making are emphasized like they are in America."

Adam Jonas, former Latin liaison with the Brewers who currently works at the International Academy of Professional Baseball in the Dominican Republic, finds that "many players are street smart but they find it difficult to adjust to a program and the rules of a program in the States."

Jonas feels that the pressure these players face is magnified because at age sixteen, they are shouldering the entire financial well being of their families.

"They're still kids, and yet many of them are responsible for the future of their families," he explains. "It's very complex. Many of them are underdeveloped socially—they only know what they see on TV or hear from people in their barrios. When they come to the States, a sixteen-year-old Dominican may not think it's odd to date a fourteen-year-old American girl, but of course in the States, that's going to be a serious problem. Without preparation, it can be a rough transition for these guys."

Many Latin players have never flown before, and when they first arrive in the States, they start their careers in mid-sized American cities, usually with strong local flair such as Chattanooga, Tennessee, and Zebulon, North Carolina.

"Many times," says Breton, "they begin playing rookie league ball in places where they scarcely have black people, let alone black people who speak Spanish. It's April in Grand Rapids, Michigan—they're freezing cold for the first time, they've never experienced temperatures below 75 degrees before—they can't express themselves, they get frustrated."

Finally, towards the late 1970s, teams began to realize that many Latin players struggled with the cultural adjustment when they came to America. According to Breton, "That's when teams started developing baseball academies overseas, places where they not only could develop players' baseball skills, but also prepare them for the cultural adjustment they would face when they came to America."

Most people credit Andres Reiner, former scout for the Houston Astros, for spearheading the idea of scouting, signing, and developing players within an academy setting. Reiner's initial academy in Venezuela led other teams to establish similar outposts in Latin countries.

According to Breton, once academies started taking hold, more and more Latino players began to shine in major league baseball: "Beginning in the late '80s and early '90s, if you look at a baseball almanac, you'll start to see the Gold Glove and batting-champion players emerge. How did this happen? It happened because a few teams had the idea to refine the talent before they arrived, and other teams began copying. Today, baseball is the sport where you see the strongest connection to Latin America."

That connection to Puerto Rico diminished greatly, however, beginning in 1989 when Major League Baseball included Puerto Rico (along with Canada) in the amateur player draft. Because teams no longer had freedom to sign the players they spent time developing, scouts spent less time looking at Puerto Rican prospects and more time scouting in other Latin countries that remained excluded from the draft.

Puerto Rican players, much like African Americans, have declined in numbers over the last twenty years for similar reasons: at an economic disadvantage, they do not have the resources to dedicate to playing baseball, and therefore cannot compete with middle class Americans. According to a *New York Times* article, "Puerto Ricans, as United States citizens, must wait until their high school class graduates or they turn 18 to enter the draft. Yet Puerto Ricans have no high school leagues and are limited to amateur teams that play on weekends."[3]

Puerto Ricans who are serious about baseball usually leave the island in order to enroll in American schools and thereby have access to better baseball training; this only makes the situation on the island even more grim.

Puerto Rico hasn't been the only Latin American country to face recent struggles. Venezuela, a country that produces scores of baseball players each year, has lost the majority of its baseball academies over the past twenty years, primarily due to an uncooperative president, Hugo Chavez, as well as tremendously high crime rates. Although teams still employ scouts throughout the country, most teams feel the risk of operating academies does not outweigh the return on their investments.

When Reiner originally planted the Astros' academy outside Caracas in the early 1970s, Venezuelans were prospering due to an emerging and lucrative oil industry. Ironically, Reiner had a difficult time convincing parents during this prosperous era, a time when Venezuela was labeled the "Latin version of Saudi Arabia," to play baseball.

However, attitudes changed when oil prices collapsed in the early 1980s and unemployment rates skyrocketed. As the nation's economy shifted drastically, so did its class structure, which polarized into two groups of people—rich and poor—with 80 percent of the nation living below the poverty line. Since that time, the economy has been unable to recover, and the problems have only compounded as violent crime has grown rampant across the country.

One *New York Times* article reported that the death toll in Venezuela in 2009 was significantly higher than in war-torn Iraq: "In Iraq, a country with about the same population as Venezuela, there were 4,644 civilian deaths from violence in 2009 according to Iraq body count; in Venezuela that year, the number of murders climbed above 16,000."[4]

Sadly, of those murders, 90 percent of them go unsolved. In law enforcement, police are underpaid and do not hesitate to supplement their incomes with bribery and kidnapping.

The problems in Venezuela have only intensified the people's passion for baseball over the years. In a place where many young men consider baseball their only option in life, they are dedicating the time they might have been spending on work or school to honing their baseball skills. As a result, Venezuelans are second only to Dominicans in producing foreign-born major league talent (in 2009 the Dominican Republic had 81 major league players, Venezuela 52, and Puerto Rico 28).[5]

Still, the highest percentage of foreign-born major league players are Dominicans, in large part because teams have shifted their resources to the island. Currently, every team in major league baseball operates an academy in the Dominican Republic, a place that many teams have found to be an ideal environment for scouting, signing, and developing players. The government rarely interferes with baseball operations, and the cost of signing Dominican players is extremely low—teams can hire ten Dominicans at the price of one American. Likewise, over the years more and more Dominicans grew wise to the fact that baseball was introducing tremendous business opportunities for an island entrenched in poverty. This mutual relationship held much promise for both employers and employees, and success stories like Albert Pujols and Vladamir Guerrero are now the pride of the Dominican people.

Unfortunately, as the media slowly has been uncovering over the past ten years, there is much more to the story—so much more, in fact, that in 2010 Commissioner Bud Selig hired Sandy Alderson specifically to address a spectrum of unethical business practices. One of the top concerns was steroids.

In 2010, Major League Baseball suspended a number of Dominican prospects (Mets' Melvin Colon, Indians' Steven Lebron, and Yankees' Josue Rodriguez to name a few) who tested positive for steroid use. Although steroids undoubtedly have been a problem throughout the baseball world over the years, the Dominican Republic particularly remains unregulated. So when players sign and come to the United States, they get suspended for PEDs, which not only removes them temporarily from playing baseball, but also forces them to train naturally. The transition to American baseball already can be quite challenging for Latin players—but players who are suspended and no longer can rely on steroids are prone to face significant, even career-ending, setbacks.

Unfortunately, regulating steroids in the Dominican Republic has proven to be anything but routine for Major League Baseball. Many players have been raised to believe that in order for them to have a shot at American baseball, they have to cheat. This belief is only reinforced by local trainers or *buscones*, many of whom provide their wards with illegal substances. In order to wean players from their belief in steroids, many feel *buscones*, who are motivated to earn a cut of players' signing bonuses, need to be regulated or even eliminated from the recruitment process.

Yet *buscones* have been a valuable resource for baseball organizations because they are well connected to Dominican communities. They go beyond the island's perimeter, into the barrios and sugar cane plantations where people are eager to find a better life. They are something that former *Washington Post* editor Charles Farrell calls "a necessary evil," who adds, "The amount of money major league baseball would need to spend in order to find talent in the Dominican Republic would be enormous. Instead, the *buscones* provide that service. They do serve a purpose."

At the same time, many *buscones* do not make it any easier for young prospects to resist the temptation to use steroids, especially when millions of dollars may be at stake. Adam Wasch, a Florida-based attorney who has researched human rights issues in the Dominican Republic, can understand why the temptation to use steroids is strong: "If your only shot to make anything of yourself in your country is to be successful at baseball, there's a high incentive for kids to experiment, as well as a high incentive for *buscones* to provide."

Still, steroid use is no longer an issue Major League Baseball can ignore, as astronomical numbers of Dominican players have tested positive after signing with teams in recent years. One course of action Alderson hopes to enforce is a testing system that is performed before players sign.

Along with drug testing, he would like to require players to verify their identities and birth records before signing, as age and identity fraud likewise have run rampant throughout the island. According to Farrell, "There's tremendous incentive for Dominicans to lie about their ages."

Although Dominican players can sign at age sixteen, two years earlier than Americans, the country does not have any developmental leagues, no college teams, no dads coaching little league. So major league teams want young Dominicans so that they can develop them in the same amount of time (or less) than American players. Older Dominican players are more of a risk for teams, a reality that could completely eliminate a player's chances if he doesn't resort to age fraud.

Farrell comments: "It's like the scene in *Ben Hur* when they're on the ship rowing and one of the guys falls out—they get another guy and put him in his place. That's how it is for these Dominicans—you fall out of the ship, you get replaced. If you're not rowing well by the time you're nineteen, they'll find someone else who can row."

Often times *buscones* once again encourage players to use fraudulent names and ages in order to appear more appealing to teams.

Because of the growing concern for age and identity fraud, Major League Baseball made it a rule that anyone convicted of the crime (Daniel Arredondo is a recent example, who claimed to be sixteen when he signed with the Yankees for $800,000) has to wait a year before signing with another team.

Still, other problems exist. In many cases, *buscones* take advantage of players' lack of education and wherewithal when it comes to baseball operations by skimming a player's bonus or charging up to 50 percent for representing the player. Unfortunately, though, *buscones* are not the only people taking advantage of young Dominicans. Just as many cases of bonus skimming have been discovered on the team side, where scouts promise a player a certain bonus then skim up to 50 percent off the top. In some cases, a player's bonus is skimmed from both ends—from teams and *buscones*.

According to Alderson, "It's not a one-way street; there are mutual problems that have to be dealt with comprehensively. Not all the problems originate with the Dominican Republic and *buscones*. There are people on the team side who are playing a role in aiding this."[6]

Regardless of these many problems, there are many *buscones* with honest reputations who have the players' best interests in mind. Likewise, Major League Baseball realizes the valuable resource *buscones* are throughout the recruitment process. According to Adam Jonas, "Academies work with *buscones* because they have the talent to identify players at a much younger age than the academies."

One change Major League Baseball has considered has been creating a national registration system for street agents, similar to the system the Players Association uses to regulate agents in the United States.[7] In order for such a program to be successful, major league teams would have to agree to only do business with licensed agents. A recent move Alderson has instituted is a player registration system, in which players signed from the Dominican Republic must undergo a registration process which could include drug testing and a means for dissolving identity fraud, fingerprinting.

Even as Major League Baseball works to resolve criminal actions like steroid use, bonus skimming, and identity fraud, many people have other concerns with recruitment practices on the island, including the conflict frequently present between baseball and education.

In "Children Left Behind," Adam Wasch argues that Major League Baseball should provide a formal education to boys who pursue their baseball dreams: "Since the first baseball academy opened in the mid 1980s, tens of thousands of Dominican boys have not received a formal education in the Dominican school system due to *their love of the game*."[8]

For boys who do fulfill their dreams and become major league baseball players, forfeiting an education seems like a small cost considering what they were able to achieve. However, the number of success stories is minuscule compared to the number of boys who get released and return to the poverty-stricken Dominican society.

Wasch commented: "Of the hundreds of kids who leave school to train at academies, at least 98 percent of them don't get anywhere. So they're nineteen-years-old, jobless, and without a high school education. They have nothing to contribute to their societies."

Charles Farrell, co-founder of the Dominican Republic Sports and Education Academy, also feels that major league baseball has a social obligation to provide these children with education.

The real dilemma, however, is that the environment of most baseball academies—the opportunity to play baseball, to get three meals a day, and to have a comfortable place to sleep—provides for many boys in a way that their families cannot. Abandoning education not only to pursue a dream but also to meet basic needs seems like a worthy sacrifice to many families.

It is this sort of poverty, however, people feel teams have been taking advantage of, signing Dominican players for pennies on the dollar. Even though those "pennies" do give many Dominicans a type of wealth according to their country's standards, a signing bonus usually does not amount to long-term wealth for most Dominicans.

"We're selling these kids on a dream," says Farrell. "We're taking advantage of these kids' situations and giving back very little to the majority of families and their communities."

Regardless of these concerns, critics would argue that major league baseball is a business, not an entity capable of or responsible for social reform. In fact, American views towards education are not only foreign to most Dominicans but also unlikely to influence a culture where more than 80 percent of the population doesn't make it past the eighth grade. "One in 10 Dominicans never goes to school," says Farrell. "Among Latin American countries, the Dominican government spends the lowest annually on education (less than 3 percent of the GDP)."

The bid for education is further challenged, however, by the fact that Dominican society does not provide many opportunities for upward mobility, even for educated citizens. It is a nation where the GDP is $5,000 per family; most cities, including Santo Domingo, the capital, are dirty, run down, and filled with homeless people. While the government does not invest a great deal of money in education, it does pour money into the service and tourism industries. These industries have been good for the Dominican economy, yet they perpetuate a financial gap between those who work the industry and those who can afford to patronize it.

Regardless of these realities, advocates like Wasch feel Major League Baseball is partly responsible for bringing education to the players they see come through academies: "Major league baseball could at the very least help the kids at the academies by providing them with an education. It's not going to solve the country's problems, but it will help some of the kids and their families at least in a local sense. A handful of teams have already started educational programs for their students—the Padres, Mets, and Indians come to mind—and the other teams should follow the leader."

In an effort to turn this philosophy into reality, Wasch has served as a Board member and advisor to the Dominican Republic Sports and Education Academy (DRSEA), a Dominican-based high school founded by Farrell and Harold Mendez and presently under development. The mission of the DRSEA is to provide Dominican baseball players not only with a high school education, but also to prepare them academically in hopes that the DRSEA becomes a feeder system for Dominican boys to attend American colleges.

Farrell, who has worked on behalf of Major League Baseball to investigate the state of academies in the Dominican Republic, understands the appeal of baseball in the Dominican, as well as the social realities on the island: "We're talking about a third world country. Here you're handing a sixteen-year-old $100,000, which is the average signing bonus, and he doesn't even know how to open a bank account. How can you prepare your country for the future without educating your people? If we use the power and attraction of baseball, combined with education, then we can give these young men a future and we're doing good to their community."

Funded by private and public donations and grants, the DRSEA operates independently from Major League Baseball, but has received the cooperation and the support of Sandy Alderson and the baseball commissioner. "Based on conversations our people have had with Sandy Alderson, we believe he is on board with our mission," says Wasch. "He is in agreement that MLB should do more to provide the signed Dominican players with an education."

Although education is not a requirement at teams' academies in the Dominican Republic, many teams already provide an educational program for their players. The Pirates, who opened a new academy in 2009, maintain a mandatory education program. The Padres, likewise, maintain an education program, but on an optional basis; for players who want to enroll in courses, the Padres will cover the cost. For the most part, these programs come at a minimal cost to teams. Farrell explains, "The Pirates' education program costs $75,000 a year—about the cost of two public school teachers in America. This is not an astronomical amount of money."

In Farrell's DRSEA, students would on a typical day spend two hours of baseball instruction, four hours of academic instruction, along with physical education which teaches players about "how to build their bodies naturally, not relying on PEDs and other supplements." The day will also include a life skills component that teaches students about time management, financial planning, and community service. "Our academic curriculum will be NCAA approved," says Farrell, "so that college can be an option for more and more players."

Interestingly, the DRSEA has been modeled after an academy in Puerto Rico, the Puerto Rican Baseball Academy and High School. This institution was founded (and funded) by Edwin Correa, former major league pitcher, who hoped to revive Puerto Rican players' interest and potential in baseball after the commonwealth became subject to the draft in 1989. Through Correa's academy, Puerto Ricans have been able to earn a high school diploma and if they are not immediately considered in the amateur player draft, they can feed into Puerto Rican or American colleges. Ideally, this is the system Farrell hopes to establish through the DRSEA in the Dominican Republic. According to Farrell, "When baseball is developing a system in which 98 percent fail, you have a social responsibility to educate that 98 percent."

Similar independent academies, including the International Academy of Professional Baseball in the Dominican Republic where Adam Jonas coaches, make education a priority alongside the baseball training boys receive. When Jonas had worked as a Latin liaison with the Milwaukee Brewers, he saw firsthand some of the struggles Latin American kids faced.

"These kids come to the States for the first time, most of them have never been on an airplane before, and when they arrive they're just lost," Jonas explains. "The food is different—they won't eat anything but rice, beans, and chicken every night because that's the only food they like. They have to be productive on the baseball field and be able to deal with an entirely new culture—that's asking a lot."

Jonas's academy resembles Farrell's model with the intention of providing boys the education they might be "passing up" to play baseball, but does not necessarily aspire to be college-preparatory. "The reality is, MLB is pouring all this money into the DR because they produce professional baseball players, not because they make these great students," he says.

Likewise, preparing Dominican boys for American colleges can be a lofty endeavor, especially for a baseball-focused academy. Many Dominicans are still struggling to learn English during their high school years, and may not even have great speaking or writing skills in Spanish. For the most part, the Dominican school system does not prepare students for higher education; many would not be prepared to take SATs or ACTs, let alone handle college-level material.

Jonas comments: "Kids in the DR only go to class half the day, and even then they only need to attend 60 percent of the classes. Part of our work at the academy is to emphasize the importance of education, maybe influence some of the people's attitudes about education."

Another important objective of Jonas's academy is to give Dominican players an ethical, American alternative to some of the shady *buscones* who have been representing players. According to Jonas, "For the last twenty-five years, Dominicans have had *buscones* representing players while they played. Now our academy will represent players, and we hope to bring American business sense and ethical standards to Latin baseball on the amateur side."

Not only does the academy represent players to teams, but they also try to negotiate scholarship clauses in players' contracts so that they have the option of pursuing higher education. To prepare them for this education, the academy runs a government-based distance-learning program (CENAPEC) in which students learn a week's worth of academic material through an accelerated weekend course. Through this course, players earn a high school degree while training at the academy during the week.

For Jonas, his passion is not only baseball but also providing Dominican children with opportunities that many Americans take for granted: "Many of these kids come from awful situations, broken homes, they've been struggling to make it all their lives, they've never been comfortable. Some of them gain twenty-five pounds during the first couple months because they're finally eating regularly and working out. A lot of them when they get to the States just eat fast food for dinner all the time; to them that's a luxury. In America we have no idea what it means to be poor."

Ironically, it is because Dominican players are so poor that they can play baseball so well. When you are poor, you lose sight of what might be considered very important to some. In America, we become obsessed with fashion—clothing, hair products, and shoes. When you are poor, you wear clothes to stay warm, to be modest, and you wear the same clothes again and again. Keeping them clean and in good repair—not deciding each morning what to wear—becomes the biggest challenge.

Each year Americans buy flowers, fertilizer, and lawn ornaments to make our yards beautiful during the summer. We put up colored lights (and pay for their electricity) in the winter. Stores like Lowe's and Home Depot have gained celebrity prominence over the years, filled with creative solutions for painting walls, building decks, and remodeling kitchens. When you are poor, you don't think about colors. You cannot be concerned with modern designs, and you may not have lights—*any* lights—if the electric quota has been used for the day. Your roof is tin; it leaks. Nothing is beautiful.

Then there is baseball. Baseball with the rich and the poor is different, too. When you have money you can read *Sports Illustrated*, watch games on TV, and maybe run a fantasy team online. You have access to modern ways of improving your game—better equipment, strength and conditioning routines, and proper nutrition. When you are poor you may have some of this, but not on a consistent basis. You don't always know the American box scores, and sometimes, after it rains, the fields are too muddy for practice. You eat usually the same thing every day, and who knows with how many calories and how much protein. If your bat breaks you do not get another, or maybe somebody steals it. You don't really have a lot of choices.

Still, when you are poor, you aren't distracted by options like video games, movies, or music. Your only option, most of the time, is to play baseball. You learn how to cultivate a singular pursuit and how to pour all of your passion and energy into that one thing. Being poor was never a bad situation for a baseball player.

This is especially true for baseball players in the Dominican Republic. As Adam Jonas remarks, "The kids who are the most talented in the Dominican Republic for the most part are not the wealthiest. Pedro Martinez once remarked that baseball in the Dominican is a poor man's game—the most successful players are from the poorest communities."

Adam Wasch likewise sees this trend in the country: "Look at the success rate of Dominican teenagers that were given million dollar bonuses. It is a short list. Dominican baseball insiders have told me that when a Dominican teenager is given a million-plus dollar bonus, that player feels like he doesn't need to earn any more money and that he is set for life so his perspective on the game changes. Those who don't sign for as much money know they still need to work very hard, and the majority of the time, those players are the success stories."

You don't have to be poor to understand the importance of discipline in a game like baseball.

"Absolutely, organizations want players who will work hard," says Adam Pettyjohn. "It can be hard for guys to put in the work they need to do in the off season, especially if they've always been the best on the team. But it comes down to work ethic, and being able to see beyond the moment. If you put in the work, you might be able to experience some very special things in your career and your life."

One of the special experiences that baseball provides is the opportunity for players to interact with people from different cultures. Latin players, especially when they first come to America, have many things to learn. With the help of their American teammates, they can make a smooth transition.

Ozzie Chavez remarks, "It was difficult being away from family. Sometimes when you're in trouble you need your family. But a lot of American guys helped with speaking English, food, everything."

At the same time, American players have many things to learn from their Latin teammates. For instance, according to Alvin Colina, "Many people think all Latin Americans are the same, but the cultures are very different. I might be on a team with other players who speak Spanish, but they're not from my country. That makes a difference."

Something else that Latin American countries have, that has been slipping away from American baseball, is the purity of the game. Marcos Breton comments, "In Latin America, 99 percent of the population plays baseball. It's the singular passion in those countries. In America, there was a time when baseball was the number one sport, but not anymore. In Latin America, no other sports rival baseball."

Throughout history, Major League Baseball's relationship with Latin American countries has been sometimes complex, sometimes unreasonable, and still sometimes glorious. In today's game, America's ties to Latin American baseball are stronger than ever, and the Latin American game provides many opportunities for players during the winter months for excellent competition. It is also an opportunity for every person to share the same dream: making it to the big leagues.

"The Show," says Marcos Breton, "once you get there, this is a fraternity of a very select group. It's the best of the best. Whether you're American or not, you've spent a certain amount of time surviving the weeding out process. So once you get there, you're in the club."

EIGHT

The Show

Those that don't got it, can't show it. Those that got it, can't hide it.
—Zora Neale Hurston

In order to get all the way to the top, you have to fight hard for what you want, but also adjust to the opportunities that are available.

Adam Pettyjohn understood through years of experience how to be open-minded to possibilities. In 2010, during his first full season pitching for the Mets' AAA affiliate, the Buffalo Bisons, his pitching coach asked him to move out of a starting role with the team.

"Since my surgery I've been a reliever more and more, but have always considered myself a starter, especially because I'm not a hard thrower," Adam says. "But I had this opportunity with the Bisons to be a situational guy out of the bullpen, and I've been doing well with it."

To prepare for his new role, Adam made some adjustments to his delivery, dropping his arm angle in order to be more deceptive. As Adam explains, "I don't have a power arm so I'm happy to move into a specialist role. If I went out there and just pitched with normal mechanics, I'd probably be biding my time. But with deception or quirkiness, I can play a useful role."

Adam adjusted well to his new role throughout the season, ending with a 4.94 ERA mostly in relief appearances.

As a minor league free agent, he realized that he needed to prove his value to a team that already had numerous major league and minor league prospects in the ranks. He was no longer controlled by an organization, yet this did not necessarily create better opportunity. Some years he had had multiple offers from teams, and some years he had to take what he could get. Like all players, his lifeline was the 40-man roster; if his name was fixed on the list of the team's major league possibilities, then he still might be able to avoid the trap of becoming an organizational player, a veteran that teams use for the purpose of advancing their prospects.

Of course, best case scenario, after all the big contracts have been signed, teams may find a few diamonds in the rough when scouring the list of minor league free agents. This is when players like Adam hope to find their opportunities, and in some cases, these opportunities have been pivotal in players' careers. Garrett Jones is an example of a minor league free agent whom the Pirates gave a chance during the 2009 season, and he rewarded them with a breakout rookie season. Clay Hensley of the Marlins and Chris Capuano of the Brewers likewise proved effective on the mound for their teams.

As always, however, nothing is certain, especially for players still looking to break into the big leagues. "You wait and see what kind of offers you get. It could range from getting no offers to having a couple offers to choose from. It just depends on what teams are looking for," Adam says. From Adam's perspective, a little bit of uncertainty doesn't change the way he trains in the offseason, saying, "You never know what you're going to get, so you've got to be ready."

If you love the game enough, you'll respect the game, even when nobody is watching—lifting, throwing, and preparing for what lies ahead in the spring. You'll prepare, as always, to win.

During the start of the 2009 season, Justin Lehr began to consider whether he was close to retiring. He'd been pitching in AAA the last two years, posting impressive numbers and earning the PCL Pitcher of the Year Award in 2009. Still, he was not getting any opportunities with the big league club. Meanwhile, the mental skills training Justin had begun a couple years prior was helping him to achieve good results on the mound: "It was kind of a frustrating process because in 2006, the year I started working on my mental game, I was designated for assignment. It took a little while, but by the next season I started seeing some good results from the mental training."

With a determination to return to the big leagues, Justin signed with a team in Korea, the Doosan Bears. With high hopes to earn some money and gain some valuable experience, the two-month stint proved unfruitful.

"I got buried in the bullpen," says Justin. "Something about it wasn't right. I was 0 and 6 in 6 starts. Combined with the other American on the team, we went 0 and 12. How do we go over there and go 0 and 12? Both of us came from playoff-contending teams in the States."

In Justin's experience, his team in Korea didn't show up every day to play. What he thought might have been an opportunity became frustrating. Within two months he asked for his release.

When he returned home, the Phillies picked up his contract. After pitching seven games with the AAA team in Lehigh, Pennsylvania, he didn't see much opportunity with their big league club and so asked for his release. The club acquiesced and traded him back to Cincinnati. Fortunately for

Justin, that was the move he had been waiting for. In July, the Reds called him up and he ended up pitching 11 games throughout the remainder of the season, with a winning record of 5 and 3. "It was like my reward for sticking it out," Justin concludes. "That season put me in a position to earn a starting spot in the rotation the next year."

That offseason Justin trained hard. He felt good but when he started throwing in spring training, he wasn't throwing as hard. "I'd been pitching with elbow problems since 2006 but I never went on the DL. I just pitched through it and still competed, even with not very good stuff," he says. That spring training, though, he felt like he just "fell apart" and could no longer compete. "Some players have that one pitch that snaps their ligament. I didn't have that, but my arm was very close to being gone last year. I was compensating because my elbow was so unstable."

At age thirty-three, Justin had to decide whether he still had a career left—if it would be worth it to undergo Tommy John surgery. His other option: retire and bypass the surgery.

"The Reds were willing to extend me a contract through the 2011 season, so at least I knew I could use their facilities to do the rehab. With that opportunity, I knew I still had a chance at least of coming back."

Justin chose the surgery. While he spent time at the Reds complex in Phoenix doing his rehab, Justin also assisted the pitching coach for the rookie league team, even filling in occasionally to work with the young pitching prospects. "It gave me a chance to stay in the game while I was separated from my team. I had a chance to contribute while letting my arm rest."

Like other players who have suffered injury, Justin's future remained uncertain. Still, he was willing to hold on: "Baseball has been good to me and my family—it's given me a lot. To me it's worth it to hold on. I feel optimistic about my future."

Brandon Snyder knew that 2010 would be an important season for him— a season when he could establish himself as a hitter and maybe work his way to the big league team.

During the first half of his season, Brandon got off to a good start, culminating in the month of June when he hit .330. However, to his disappointment, he suffered an injury mid-season that sidelined him for a little over a month.

"After one of the bus rides, we got to the stadium and I had a hard time getting loose," Brandon recalls. "Then when I got up to the plate, I could feel a pop when I swung. I tried to play it off but I knew it wasn't good. They ended up taking me out."

Although the injury didn't require surgery, Brandon was limited in his baseball activities for the weeks ahead. There was nothing he could do to speed the process—he applied ice and heat, and simply gave his ribs time to heal. According to Brandon, "It was tough dealing with that during the middle of the season, especially since I'd really been performing well in the first half. Then trying to come back after that, after being cold for over a month, you lose your momentum."

Brandon's numbers in August reflected his slow return, his average settling around the .250s. Nevertheless, once September arrived, he got the call from his manager: "I was getting off the bus after a thirteen-hour bus ride. It was like five o'clock in the morning, so I was half asleep, but then my manager came up to me and said, 'Hey, you're going to the big leagues tomorrow!' That woke me up a bit."

He didn't leave immediately to join the Orioles, but instead played a game that evening in Norfolk, then drove to Baltimore the next morning. When he joined the team, he felt comfortable because he'd played with most of the team at the last few spring trainings, and some of the guys had played with him in Norfolk. The Orioles manager, however, was a new face: "Buck Schowalter was a really great guy—down to earth, he knew the game, I felt very comfortable with him."

Under Schowalter's management, which began late in the 2010 season, the Orioles finished their season with an impressive winning streak, something new and exciting for the franchise. "That was a really fun time to be with the team. It was really exciting," Brandon says.

Once Brandon arrived in Baltimore, though, he had to wait a while before playing his first big league game, mainly because he joined the team when they were playing some of the hottest teams in the AL East. In order to maintain the integrity of the game, Schowalter didn't want to put unproven players in the lineup.

Eventually, Brandon saw his name in the lineup, starting at first base. Although the game was the same, albeit a little bit quicker, Brandon reveled in his opportunity to see how he would handle a major league venue: "It's nice to get into that atmosphere and see how you match up with a lot of those guys. I started seeing what I needed to work on in order to get better."

During the duration of his call-up, Brandon had 20 at-bats and ended with a .300 average; his most exciting moment was when he hit a chopper down the third base line and legged out a base hit. His most daunting moment, perhaps, was his first road trip to Yankee Stadium: "That's a really awesome ball park and a great city. I'd say it's pretty intimidating, though. That's the hardest thing to get over once you reach the big leagues—getting comfortable with the stage it's on. You're playing in front of 40,000 people rather than 5,000."

With his first big league experience under his belt, Brandon had high hopes for the next season, but didn't have any guarantees about where he'd be. "Now that I got a call-up, I feel like I'm a little bit closer to my goal,"

Brandon concludes. "Still, it's going to be an uphill battle to get back up there. And that's the goal: to get to the big leagues and stay there."

Vinny Rottino took on the majority of catching duties during 2008 because Nashville's everyday catcher went down with an injury. Although catching everyday was a grind, Vinny saw it as a great opportunity to prove to the organization that he could handle it. Rumors were stirring that the organization had intentions of preparing Vinny for a backup role with the Brewers in the future. He received another call-up in 2008 but very limited playing time because the team was making a playoff run.

Turning to the 2009 season, Vinny realized that the team's plans had changed. They told him he would have limited playing time in Nashville that season, so he requested to be sent to the AA team in Huntsville where once again he'd be catching full-time. Then, just before the July trade deadline, the Brewers traded Vinny to the Dodgers for pitcher Claudio Vargas. Vinny's analysis: "The Brewers obviously were looking in a different direction at that point. They needed pitching and the Dodgers needed more catching depth."

At one point, Vinny was hopeful to become the Brewers' next catching prospect. However, the organization, like many organizations, went through many twists and turns with their staff. They signed Jason Kendall, a veteran catcher who had a great reputation with pitchers, along with Mike Rivera, another veteran, to assist with backup duties. Behind them the Brewers had selected other catching prospects, Angel Salome and Jonathan Lucroy, in the amateur draft. Although a catcher with major league talent, Vinny was stung by circumstances that shifted him once again to the edge of opportunity.

The trade opened a new chapter for Vinny, even though it may not have been the chapter he was hoping for. Still, he had the opportunity to start fresh and prove himself to another team.

During that offseason, he received an offer from the Florida Marlins that included an invitation to big league spring training. According to Vinny, "The Dodgers wanted me back, but I would have started with them in minor league camp. I wanted to be in an opportunity to compete for a roster spot, and that's what the Marlins provided."

Earning a roster spot can be tough, though, especially when an organization hasn't seen you play. If they don't know you, they may look at other tangibles—draft selection, age, or college program. Vinny had none of those to recommend him. Still, he continued looking at something in the distance—the possibility that at some point what he had to give would be exactly what a team needed.

For Vinny, the 2010 season began much in the same fashion as his baseball career—low profile. Starting at AAA, he requested a move to AA after he realized he wouldn't have regular playing time in New Orleans. Although he'd always seen himself as a catcher, he had learned not to cling too tightly to anything—not a position, not a city or a baseball organization. So his manager moved him around, from first base to left field, sometimes backstop, sometimes third base. He began the season swinging a hot bat, consistently flirting with a .300 average, and ended as a team leader in on-base percentage and RBIs. That season he was nominated to the Southern League's postseason all-star team for utility player, and contributed abundantly to the Suns' post-season campaign which resulted in a championship.

Although minor league success was sweet (the Suns had won the championship for two years in a row) what Vinny wanted more, of course, was a chance to prove himself with the major league team. That season, he had put up numbers that proved he was major league ready.

"I was swinging a hot bat—I definitely proved I could play with the big league team," Vinny says. "But I'm not one of the team's prospects. Teams are always going to want to give playing time to their prospects above the older guys."

Yet, even though teams like to prove themselves right by their prospects, they also will take credit for discovering treasure in unlikely places. These unlikely places are sometimes filled with veteran players, players returning from injury, the undrafted, the high drafted, and everything else in between. Regardless, it is up to the team's fancy where they will turn for their talent. As Vinny explains, "If you're not a team's prospect, all you can do is put up numbers and hopefully some day catch a break."

Once again, Vinny's name had been on the lips of managers, media, and front office staff—once again he would have to continue to wait.

Like most players, Vinny was a pawn, at the mercy of the impersonal forces of baseball. He had another way of looking at it, though: "I know I'm exactly where I'm supposed to be. There's a reason for everything that's happened in my career, and I believe that whatever happens in the future, God will use it for something good in my life."

It would seem so much easier if we could just change the things in our lives that stand in our way—play God, make life cooperate with *us*. But life isn't any different from baseball that way. There are rules governing how we go about our business—foul poles, a strike zone, and nine innings. The rules make it possible to win, and they make winning worthwhile. Some days it would be nice to have four outs instead of three, just one more chance. But in the end, even one more chance wouldn't be enough.

When a person positions his life to pursue a lofty goal—particularly a goal that has to be met at a young age—it can be strange and difficult to understand how to want anything else. A baseball player of all people must put a great deal of time and energy into his journey to The Show. However, the same reality is true of a player who has had a fifteen-year major league career, a few call-ups, or a career in the minor leagues: his window of opportunity, his one moment in time, is fleeting, and over in an instant.

Still, nothing can ever replace playing baseball in the major leagues. Although minor league baseball puts up very stiff competition at the higher levels, most people have never heard of teams like the Sacramento River Cats or the Toledo Mud Hens. When players reach the major leagues, they step onto a stage where many more people see them, recognize them, and appreciate their talent. By reaching the major leagues, a player joins very elite company, not only with his present team, but also in a historical sense. Most people reminisce about the greatest players in the game; some players have the privilege of playing on the same team as their heroes; an even smaller number actually have the opportunity to play with those great players. By getting to the major leagues, a player positions himself one step closer to the inner circle, the place where he doesn't just observe the greatest people in the game, but he walks alongside them. When you put the game in terms of people—hitting behind Michael Young, catching someone like Roy Halladay, or learning the game from someone like Dusty Baker—the purpose of baseball becomes very clear.

Everyone wants his opportunity to shine on a big stage. More importantly, everyone wants someone to admire—a hero who has worked hard, a person who has made a statement to his hometown, to the entire *country*. Baseball is a team sport, and it is filled with opportunities for people to share their experiences. In such a highly competitive environment, the experiences become richer and richer, as the funnel of competition becomes narrower and narrower. Joining that conversation of competition, whether a player has three months, three years, or an entire career in the major leagues, may be the greatest privilege of someone's life.

Yet, it can be dangerous for someone to view the major leagues as an end, rather than another step along the journey. The entire time he is pursuing his career, a baseball player has to see beyond his baseball life. No matter how great the reward of baseball, especially major league baseball, it is a temporary situation, a situation most players find themselves separated from when they are still young men. For most baseball players, the majority of their lives will unfold *after* their baseball careers. The baseball years may contain pinnacle moments, but they are only short scenes in a person's entire life. One of the greatest challenges for a baseball player, or any person who has achieved greatness at a young age, is to discover how to apply what he has learned through baseball—how to be disciplined, dedicated, and passionate in his pursuit—to the rest of his life.

Like many things in life, players must spend some time in a major league atmosphere before they can understand the sort of pressure that accompanies such a high-profile career. It is easy to imagine the benefits of such a situation—everything is first class, you're getting paid a lot more money, and millions of people *care* about what you're doing. You're being televised, broadcasted, and interviewed. Fans hold up signs with your name, they cheer for you, and you realize suddenly that you're impacting so many people.

How many players would trade it all away, though, once they begin to feel the cost of being in such a position?

That is, they have to face reporters postgame after they got shelled in the first inning, or they have to work their way up to the plate once again, surrounded by an entire stadium of fans, while battling a relentless 0-for-15 hitless streak. Most of us like to handle our struggles privately, where nobody can see us, and then face the world again once we've righted the ship.

Not so in baseball, and definitely not so in major league baseball. Once the curtain rises, anyone wearing a big league uniform must be ready to fight, he must be in the mood (whether he wants to be or not) to win.

Obviously, *nobody* would trade away the opportunity to play major league baseball. No matter what the cost, any player would willingly pay it.

At the same time, playing major league baseball can play tricks with a person's mind. Like soldiers who go to war, baseball players can prepare for situations. But all the preparation in the world means nothing if, when the real situation unfolds, they are unable to perform. This can weigh heavily on a person's mind, and this weight is only multiplied as the spectacle of a player's performance increases—40,000 fans, 40,000 fans in New York, 45,000 fans (because some are willing to stand) during Game Seven of the World Series. If a player has not fortified his mind for such situations, he may find himself victim to the antagonistic forces at work within the walls of a stadium.

This experience, in many ways, is mysterious. Finally, someone has accomplished his dream, he's playing the game he loves, he's in the situation where he feels most comfortable, most completely *himself*—yet it has all turned against him.

Joey Votto describes this experience in an interview he gave following a stint on the disabled list in 2009 due to emotional struggles. In Votto's case, his emotional struggles were circumstantial—he was grieving the untimely death of his father—yet they were unresolved. Although he had hoped to throw himself into the game that season, he discovered that the pressures of being on the field started to feel overwhelming: "I was hoping that baseball would be the necessary distraction I needed to take me away from all the loneliness I was feeling."[1]

This worked for a certain amount of time, until Votto got a case of the flu, which led to an ear infection. At that time, manager Dusty Baker advised Votto to take some time to heal, and it was the first time he had been separated from the team and baseball since he'd returned in spring training. "All of a sudden, all of the emotions I'd been suppressing came crushing down on me," says Votto.

Once he returned to the game, Votto went to the hospital on more than one occasion, still feeling as if something was wrong, but doctors continued to give him a clean bill of health. Finally, during two games—once in San Diego and once in Milwaukee—he had to be removed from the game because he did not feel fit to play.

"I was having anxiety and panic attacks," Votto explains. "One time, in the middle of the night, I had to go to the hospital because I feared for my life. It was a really, really difficult thing to go through. There were moments when I couldn't see the game. I couldn't see the game and I couldn't feel what was going on and I couldn't focus. And still, that was the *easiest* part. It got worse when I felt like I couldn't breathe and like I was having a heart attack. It was really scary."

The game, for Votto, had turned against him, not because he no longer loved playing baseball, and certainly not because he was no longer capable. He had momentarily lost his perspective—he was momentarily unfit for the sort of battle major league baseball presented.

"Taking a step away and discussing what I've been suppressing has been a really necessary step for me," Votto concludes. "I spoke with the team and I've been speaking to the fans about what happened. Talking about it has been a tremendous help. I'm trying to help people understand that—what happened—I couldn't help it. It was so overwhelming that the normal version of me couldn't make sense of it and solve it."

Again, Votto's case was circumstantial, and yet it clearly demonstrates the challenges that major league players face. Like everyone else, they have to handle normal life issues—issues that include deaths of loved ones, marriage quarrels, and rebellious children—and then, when feeling vulnerable, subject themselves to public display on the field.

The public exposure, asserted Votto, was the biggest challenge during his emotional struggles: "Playing the game is the easiest part. But getting on the field, standing out there for nine innings, was the most difficult part."

In some cases, performance anxiety is not circumstantial.

Take Zack Greinke, for instance, who was diagnosed with social anxiety disorder after a DL stint in 2006 that nearly knocked him out of the game. Some may ask, What place does the person battling social anxiety disorder have in major league baseball? Greinke proved that he *did* belong, social anxiety and all. He was such a talented pitcher that it was impossible for the Royals to consider releasing him when they saw him battle with the postgame interviews, with the masses huddled around him in a stadium, a million miles away yet suffocating him.

Ironically, as Greinke has soundly demonstrated, baseball players come in all shapes and sizes, physically and mentally. Greinke is an odd mixture of extreme talent packaged in a fragile composure. Fragile does not mean weak, though—rather, more exquisite, more complex, and tremendously valuable. After missing most of the 2006 season, Greinke was able to return to major league baseball in 2007, having sought counsel and medication that allowed him to handle the game without any of his former distractions. Greinke's story has proven, too, that with the help of psychology, the mechanisms of a tremendously powerful machine could be set right—so right, in fact, that Greinke received the AL Cy Young Award in 2009.

During the 2010 winter meetings, many people questioned whether Greinke would consider a move to a big-market team, foremost New York, if he received a viable offer. Although Greinke had pledged no allegiance to Kansas City, he of all people understood that he had to carefully protect his talent should he make a decision to go to a different team. Many a player has gone to New York and folded under the media scrutiny coupled with the intense atmosphere at Yankee Stadium. Unlike most players, though, Greinke has a clear picture of what situations he can handle, emotionally and socially speaking. Because of the adversity he faced during the 2006 season, Greinke has become a baseball player very skilled at handling himself, a talent that many players do not develop until much later in their careers, if then.

Because of players like Greinke, however, major league baseball has made tremendous strides in supporting players' mental health, an aspect of performance that throughout the majority of baseball's history went unacknowledged. According to Stan Conte, the Dodgers' head trainer and director of medical services, "If [any] guy had a mental issue before, you'd just say, 'Get him out of here, the guy's nuts.' Now we try to look at it more objectively. We don't just throw him away."[2]

In fact, following Greinke's DL stint in 2006, Daniel R. Halem, baseball's senior VP and general counsel for labor, clearly established guidelines that teams should use for placing players on the disabled list due to emotional disorders. This was in April 2009, the same year Greinke earned his Cy Young Award; it was also the same year that a record number of players (five total) were placed on the DL for emotional reasons (Dontrelle Willis, Justin Duchscherer, Khalil Greene, Scott Schoeneweis, and Joey Votto).

Players like Greinke and Votto are a one-two punch of evidence that proves treating emotional disorders (rather than concealing them) ultimately develops better, even phenomenal, players.

At the same time, players do not need to have a "problem" in order to struggle with the conditions of major league competition. Any person who enters such a competitive arena is bound to struggle with the pressures. And some handle the pressures of the game more gracefully than others.

Brandon Snyder comments, "You can either be the person who deals with the challenges of the game, or someone who doesn't accept those challenges. You won't last very long, though, if you don't face the pressure head on."

Performance coach Jim Murphy believes that it is in the nature of the best athletes to crave high pressure situations: "I don't know any pro baseball player who has not dreamed of the highest pressure situation in a game. They've done this their whole life, since they were six years old. Rather than seeing that dream as their biggest fear, they look at it as what could be their greatest achievement."

Justin Lehr recalls an opportunity he had when he was pitching out of the bullpen for Oakland. It was June 2004, Justin's first experience in the big leagues, and the manager called for Justin to get warmed up. They were playing St. Louis, it was the eighth inning, and St. Louis was down by just one run with the bases loaded.

"It was insane—it was bases loaded, nobody out, on the road, with the potential to get walked off—and this would have been my first time pitching in the majors," Justin recalls. In the next at bat, St. Louis drove in another run, tying the score. When the bullpen call came again, Justin expected to head onto the field. Instead, the manager decided against bringing him in. "I still wanted to go in," Justin says. "I could have gotten walked off, but it was also an opportunity to get the team out of the situation. It would have been an awesome moment."

Likewise, Brandon Snyder enjoys when a manager calls on him to help the team in a high-pressure situation, like pinch-hitting when the game's on the line: "It's definitely something I embrace—I think, this is my time to be in the newspaper."

Every player is going to have to face high-pressure situations throughout his career, usually on a regular basis. In order to develop confidence, a player must train himself to view these situations as opportunities to grow and flourish, rather than stumbling blocks or moments to avoid. When a player has trained his mind to embrace adversity, he looks at the next obstacle as simply another avenue for him to achieve his greatest moment.

Naturally, a player's ability to achieve peak performance will fluctuate based on a variety of factors, many of which may be out of his control. However, an athlete who has a well-trained mind is much more capable of achieving moments of peak performance. Those moments of greatness, although recognized as physical achievements, are most completely characterized by an athlete's mental achievement.

The best players in the game have been in high-pressure situations and have proven to their teams they can deliver during those key moments. When players can distinguish themselves as clutch players, there's a strong possibility they will be able to maintain major league longevity.

Joey Votto, for instance, even with his 2009 struggles, swung a powerful bat, ending with a .322 average. In 2010, he only got better, playing a major role in the Reds' postseason campaign, and ultimately earning the NL MVP Award. Smokey Garrett, who had coached Votto in AAA, comments, "He's one of the most confident hitters I've ever seen."

Vinny Rottino speaks in similar terms of Ryan Braun: "He can be so confident because he's had so much success. He's just that much better than everyone else. That's just a gift."

Because of their success, players like Votto and Braun define the game today, bringing it new life, fresh records to compete against, and spectacular moments. As for everyone else, however, it's not quite so automatic to find distinction amid a sea of prospects.

Jim Wohlford managed to find distinction during his fifteen-year major league career through playing an effective backup role on his teams. Managers particularly served Wohlford out to hit against left-handed pitchers, and although he never achieved the status of an everyday player, he enjoyed a productive career on his own stage. According to Wohlford, "It's tough to get into the lineup because there's always plenty of guys waiting behind you who are just as good. To my credit, I never got injured. If you get injured, you can lose your spot very quickly, too."

Of course another approach players can take is to develop their mental tools, especially when trying to secure a spot on the major league roster. In most cases, there is very little players can do to improve their talent level on the field; what they can control, however, is their mental approach to the game, which can render them just as effective (if not more so) than more talented players.

When Greg O'Halloran played with the Marlins in 1994, the team had the services of sport psychologist Harvey Dorfman, someone who trained players to realize that failure was an inevitable component of the game rather than, as some perceive, a show-stopper.

"Dorfman tried to instill in us the power of positive thought," O'Halloran says. "Baseball is such an individual sport played in a team setting. So whatever you do right or wrong, you have to face the consequences. If you don't control your thoughts, that stuff can pile up on you pretty quickly."

Morgan Ensberg, who enjoyed an eight-year major league career, believes he was finally faced with retirement because he had lost his confident mental approach: "Looking back now, I thought my situation was much worse than it actually was. I was putting too much pressure on myself, and I was concentrating too much on things I couldn't control. Towards the end I was trying so hard to get a hit, but you can't control whether you get a hit. All you can do is put yourself in a position to try to get a hit."

In the moment, however, athletes can easily lose a sense of perspective.

Like a plane without a navigation system, an athlete without a sound mind to guide him can easily get blown off course. He can begin to think things and believe things that are not true. When caught in this unstable frame of mind, an athlete may be prone to visualize disaster and, just as positive imagery can condition an athlete to perform to his greatest potential, negative imagery has the power to fulfill an athlete's worst nightmare. If an athlete gets into a pattern of catastrophizing his performance (i.e., always expecting disaster), he is much more prone to fulfilling what his mind already believes.

Similarly, an athlete who falls into negative thinking patterns is in danger of magnifying the intensity of a problem. Rather than considering his situation rationally, he feels failure more intensely so that anything bad becomes loud, large, and overwhelming. Small mistakes become tragic failures; minor suggestions become scathing criticism. If a player does not take the time to correct this mental approach, he will always step onto the field with a constant sense of defeat. It's hard enough for an athlete to perform—but when an athlete has to perform with defeat draped over his shoulders, victory can feel impossible to reach.

In order for a player to get to the major leagues and *stay* there, that can be half the battle: believing that's where he belongs.

Morgan Ensburg is not alone in the struggles he faced: "I never had the feeling I was completely a team's only option—I never felt settled. I didn't feel like this was mine for sure; that made me feel like I had to constantly do something *right now* in order to keep my spot."

In reality, few if any players can exist in the major leagues with certainty. Although so much of someone's career depends on talent, an equally large part depends on the opportunities and timing available to him.

Adam Pettyjohn comments, "The number one factor for a major league player is opportunity, and the people with the opportunity are the ones who are able to get the most comfortable. When you get called up in September, you play maybe once a week, that's tough. Baseball is so based on repetition—when you're out there once a week, it's hard to get into a groove."

Finding that opportunity for regular play can be critical, then, in order for a player to stay sharp.

It was for this reason that Vinny Rottino requested to play in AA during the 2009 and 2010 seasons: "Even if a veteran guy is hitting better than a twenty-three-year-old prospect in AAA, the team's going to play the prospect. That's just how it works. For me, I wanted to prove to the team I could play every day, and that I could play at the major league level. So I requested to play at AA."

Ultimately, players are at the mercy of their team in order to be given an opportunity. The public sees 750 major league players each year—but in reality there are many more players who, given the chance, would be just as capable playing in the big leagues.

According to Adam Pettyjohn, "At least half of all AAA players if placed in a major league atmosphere, and given the opportunity to get comfortable, would eventually settle in and put up decent numbers, numbers that half the major league players are putting up. In the same way, many major league players would struggle on a AAA field. But because they've got seven years' playing experience, a $15 million contract, because of those factors they get to play every day."

That can be a tough reality to face, especially for players who have dedicated years and years of their lives to achieving their goal of reaching the major leagues.

Brett Butler had been told many times as a young player that his chances of making it were slim to none, yet he didn't allow those voices to sway him. Even though the odds seemed to be against him, he believed he had the potential to play. In his view, the most important thing a player can do is decide if baseball is what he loves to do, then do it to the best of his ability: "You don't know if you'll get the opportunity, but what you need to do is place yourself in a position where it can be possible."

Even though every player's goal is to make it to the major leagues, the opportunity to play professional baseball alone can be deeply rewarding. Playing baseball for a living—whether it be at Yankee Stadium or somewhere in the middle of Tennessee—seems like a dream, a luxury in a country where we can accommodate and gather around a pastime where everyone speaks the common language of the game.

"Absolutely, every player wants to get to the major leagues," says Adam Pettyjohn. "But most pro players, even if they don't carve out a major league career, can feel proud of what they did accomplish. They realize the numbers they're up against. It's an honor even to be playing pro ball—most guys don't even get that far."

Vinny Rottino agrees that his goal is to develop a career in the major leagues; yet, he believes he has a purpose as a player and a person even if he doesn't reach the goal he designed: "It doesn't matter if you play ten years in the big leagues and win a World Series and sign a $10 million contract— that wouldn't satisfy me. That's not why we're put on this earth. I've played on these teams with these guys for a reason—they've impacted me and hopefully I've given them a little something, too."

Having this sort of long-term perspective—one that sees beyond the immediate demands of the game—can help players see the bigger picture, that their lives consist of much more than baseball.

Yet, players who make it to pro ball and the major leagues have been playing baseball all their lives. When it comes time for them to stop playing—maybe they've been plagued by an injury, don't have any more offers from teams, or, best case scenario, have played out all of their baseball years—it can be tremendously challenging.

Greg O'Halloran comments, "Anybody who's playing pro ball doesn't want to talk about other careers. You're confident in what you're doing and you're focused on getting to the top. But all of that could change in an instant—it could change so fast and then you've got to figure out a plan B."

Naturally, players don't want to be distracted while they're in the game, weighed down by concerns for their future. At the same time, it is worthwhile for players to consider their options, and important to realize that once they retire from baseball, they still have a lot more life to live. More importantly, players have the opportunity to use what they've learned during their baseball years to impact those around them.

Some players are in better positions than others to move on to the next part of their lives. For instance, some players may have made more money than others, or some may have finished (or nearly finished) their college degrees whereas others may not have even started college. Depending on their success during baseball, some may have opportunities to remain in the game as coaches or other staff members, which can create a natural transition from one career to the next.

There are players, too, who have to start from scratch, forging a second career with few "marketable" skills according to traditional job market standards.

Greg O'Halloran, who retired from pro ball in 1994, found (like many pro athletes) that the transition was tough: "I'm not going to say it was easy. Pro ball is one of the greatest teachers of life, yet it's a fantasy world, too. When you're good, people will do anything for you, they'll give you things. You develop so many contacts. But then when you're done, people are willing to talk to you, but not necessarily willing to hire you."

Although baseball players may be considered some of the most highly-trained workers in the modern world, it can be quite a leap for many employers to understand how years of playing baseball can be worth anything to a business. What good is a split-finger fastball if a pitcher doesn't have a game in which to throw it? How can a home-run swing help someone sitting in an interview, telling an employer what he can contribute to his company?

This line of thinking can bring many former players to the point of frustration. Not only do their achievements in baseball seem unrecognized in the "real world," but they also appear unprepared to move into a new career.

In reality, as many have attested, a baseball career provides players with an artillery of skills and experiences they can bring into the rest of their lives. The challenge may be understanding how those skills connect to the job market, as well as conveying to employers what skills beyond hitting a baseball he possesses.

Greg O'Halloran has gone through the process and understands the frustrations: "You don't have any transferable skills—are you kidding me? Do you know what kind of confidence you need to have to face a stadium of 40,000 people booing you? Maybe you don't have knowledge of certain computer programs—still, you can learn it. You had to make adjustments all the time in baseball—you of all people should be able to learn something new and do what it takes to be successful."

In another sense, being out of the game can be difficult because players are no longer connected to the community that has supported them for so many years. O'Halloran comments, "All of a sudden your friends are all over the country and it gets really tough to stay in contact. That's why it's really important to stay close to people back home, no matter how much success you have as a player. Eventually, you'll end up back where you started."

Many players have found consolation in staying connected to the game in some way, or else developing a new community in the next career they develop.

Scott Sanderson, for instance, after a nineteen-year major league career, went right on to his next project—becoming a sports agent. Even when he was still playing, Sanderson began contemplating his next career. He realized that if he were a sports agent, he would have a great deal of practical experience to offer players: "I not only wanted to help players with the legal aspects of their careers, but I also wanted to be ready to give them advice from a baseball perspective."

Jim Wohlford retired after fifteen years in the major leagues and was fortunate enough to enter his family's business as a financial planner. Both Wohlford and Sanderson were able to move into their careers without completing their college degrees.

Some players make the effort to finish their degrees, like Morgan Ensberg, who returned to UC Santa Barbara to complete his degree in finance. Like many former players, however, Morgan has kept his baseball options open, writing a blog that speaks openly about his baseball experiences. His hope is to stay connected to baseball by landing a job in the field—as a broadcaster, writer, or coach—but he is also realistic about how slender the job market is in those professions, as well. It can be a long road starting at the bottom again, fighting your way to the top of a high profile, highly competitive field.

"The transition can be difficult," admits Morgan. "I had been competing in baseball since I was five. That was the only thing I knew. Then all of a sudden you have to go out and get a job. How do you do that? I guess I go out and make a resume?"

Many players would like to stay in baseball as coaches or managers, but those jobs are even scarcer than roster spots.

For somebody like Brett Butler, a person with great success at the major league level, coaching and then managing came as a natural transition to his career. Not only did he have the name recognition from his esteemed baseball career, but he also could afford to take the "pay cut" of a minor league coaching salary before working his way up the system.

Because of the low pay in minor league coaching jobs, some players who hope to coach look towards college as a better opportunity.

To Adam Pettyjohn, college coaching sounds more desirable because it requires less traveling: "The minor league schedule is difficult to maintain on a long-term basis. It's especially hard when you've got a family."

Tom Trebelhorn, who's been in the system traveling for over forty years, feels the road has become a comfortable lifestyle: "I'm a road dog now. You find you get restless when you're in one place for too long. You get used to the rush of always being on the go."

For somebody like Bob Tewksbury, his way of coping with the transition out of baseball was to learn a new skill—in his case, sport psychology: "Career transitions are difficult, no matter how someone prepares for it. It's never quite what you'd expect. It's like parenting—people tell you what it's like, but until you have your own kids, you don't know."

After retiring from baseball, Tewksbury earned a degree in psychology from Boston University and then went on to get his masters in sport psychology. Like Scott Sanderson, he wanted to combine his knowledge of baseball with a second career that could be useful to players.

"My motive to pursue psychology was that I wanted to help myself work through the change while I helped others," Tewksbury says. "Once I left baseball it was hard. That's because I was uncomfortable with my new reality. Because I dedicated myself to a new skill, it helped me work through that transitional time."

Morgan Ensberg hopes to reach out to others through his experiences, too: "I've been in very high pressure situations—it's a unique experience hearing 40,000 people either praise you or boo you. It's pretty easy to lose your perspective—I want to help the next person understand how to keep his perspective."

Keeping one's perspective can be challenging, especially in today's game when so many more young people are pursuing baseball careers than ever before. There are ways to find distractions, though.

Brandon Snyder, in the offseason, bought his first home. He goes hunting with his family, and with a new puppy in the house, has established somewhat of a different routine. "Now I'm learning about getting up early."

Adam Pettyjohn finds distraction with his toddler son, Truett; likewise

Justin Lehr helps his daughter Avery and son Reed with their homework, and tells them stories about baseball.

Vinny Rottino, when he's not thinking about baseball, is "the busiest guy ever," substitute teaching at his alma mater, Racine St. Catherine's, working at coach Jack Schiestle's hitting facility, spending time with family and his twelve nieces and nephews.

No matter what kind of success players achieve on the field, what happens off the field holds great significance, as well.

Still, in the end, everyone knows the records will speak for themselves, and the records matter to those who love the game. Trevor Hoffman with his 600 saves. Nolan Ryan the strikeout leader. Pete Rose with the most hits. The lure of the game not only lies in its traditions, but also in the names that players establish for themselves through their legendary performances.

The greatest players will be remembered throughout the generations, and their accomplishments will be retold again and again. In the ancient world, this was how the Greeks defined immortality: when, even after someone is dead, his praises are sung from generation to generation because of his great deeds. These heroes did not flinch in the face of adversity, they wanted to gain every experience, because then they would have more opportunities to achieve greatness.

And then there's everyone else. People who walk in the shadows of giants but wonder what their lives amount to when they cannot possibly leave behind World Series rings and MVP trophies.

It's true, the records and the awards stand as mountains looming over the inconsequential places below. But even the greatest records cannot possibly contain the glory that every player can wear as his crown—that he has fought with his teammates, believed in a common goal, and expressed in innings and bases the human struggle to achieve victory.

The names in the record books are not the only names that inspire us. We are also inspired by the person who, because he loves something so much, is willing to change the shape of his life in order to accommodate it. He is completely converted, a person who can sacrifice himself, at last, in the name of something higher, a selfless act.

To finally get beyond the self—the worries, concerns, pains, and disillusionments of this life—truly is a mark of greatness.

Appendix A

Psychological Characteristics of Peak Performance

If you know what you are striving for, you are more likely to achieve it.

> "Peak performances are those magic moments when an athlete puts it all together—both mentally and physically. Competitively, these performances often result in a personal best. They are the ultimate high, the thrilling moment that athletes and coaches work for in their pursuit of excellence. Unfortunately, they are also relatively rare."—Jean M. Williams

Mental and Physical Characteristics in the Psychological Profile of Peak Performance

Ready and Relaxed: Mentally you feel a sense of inner calm and a high degree of concentration. You may experience disorientation of time and space, a sense that things are moving in slow motion. This is when you really "see" the game. Physically your muscles feel loose and your movements are fluid and sure. You are capable of both precision and power. The mechanics of your technique don't feel mechanical ... they feel natural.

Confidence/Optimism: You possess a positive and adaptive attitude, along with the ability to maintain poise, courage, and control even during potentially threatening, pressure-filled situations. You welcome the opportunity when the event's outcome rests in your hands. You have no fear— "you just know it."

Focus on the Present Moment: You feel a sense of harmony that comes from body and mind working as one. You can narrowly focus your attention without being distracted by thoughts of the past or future. There are no worries about what just happened or what is going to happen next. Past mistakes and potential future failures are no longer part of the equation. Your body performs automatically, without conscious or deliberate mental effort. You are totally immersed in the task at hand.

A High Energy State: You feel eager, invigorated, joyful, and elated— the ultimate thrill. These are the moments where you truly know what it means to be alive. You are putting forth great effort but your performance feels effortless. You do not experience fatigue ... just fun.

Extraordinary Awareness: You have an acute awareness of your own body and your surroundings. You have an uncanny ability to stay one step ahead of the game. With this you have a sense of what is going to happen next and you act accordingly so that you are completely in sync with your environment.

A Sense of Control: You feel totally in command of both your mind and body. The mind sets the body in motion and the body follows through with exact precision. You are in complete control yet it feels automatic— there is no sense of exerting or imposing control. You just feel it.

In the Moment/In the Zone/Flow: You feel completely detached from your environment so that potential distractions just melt away. You can't hear the crowd. You don't feel pain. You have complete access to all of your powers and skills. In this moment, you are unstoppable. Everything just feels right.

Mental Skills Commonly Used by Elite Athletes While Achieving Peak Performance

- Imagery
- Thought Control Strategies
- Arousal Management
- Competition Plans
- Pre-Competition Plans

- Post-Performance Evaluation
- Attention/Focus Control
- Muscle-to-Mind Technique
- Mind-to-Muscle Technique

Self-Evaluation Activity

Try to recall your best and worst experiences in sport. Focus on the moment of performance itself, not on what you accomplished because of this moment. See if you can identify how you felt in every way during your finest moment. In detail, try to identify what was going through your mind, how this made you feel, how your body responded, and what you were aware of during this moment. After providing an account of your finest moment, do the same for your darkest hour (i.e., your worst experience in sport). After describing these two extremes, think about the key points associated with both your best and worst performances. You will likely find these experiences to be opposite in nature and in direct contrast to one another.

My Finest Hour

Description of my thoughts/feelings/sensations during my best performance:

_____

_____

_____

_____

_____

_____

My Darkest Hour

Description of my feelings/thoughts/sensations during my worst performance:

_____

_____

_____

_____

_____

_____

APPENDIX B

Understanding and Using Imagery in Sport

Imagery is defined as using all the senses to recreate or create an experience in the mind. It is a mental technique that programs the mind to respond as programmed—to see and believe.

Understanding Imagery

Creation or Recreation: Imagery is based on memory, so to practice imagery, you are reconstructing external events in your mind. In order to reconstruct these events, you need to evaluate your performance and gain awareness into your strengths and weakness. Then by recalling previous outstanding performances, and re-creating these experiences, you can increase your confidence. You can also use imagery to create new experiences in your mind. Once your mind believes something, your body can follow through to carry out those beliefs.

Any Time—Any Place: Imagery is a sensory experience that occurs in the mind without environmental props. When you engage in vivid imagery and absorb yourself into the context of your image, your brain interprets these images as identical to the actual event. The power of imagery allows you to practice sport techniques and strategies without physically being in the athletic environment.

The Six Senses: Imagery can and should involve all the senses, making it a polysensory experience (sight, sound, touch, taste, smell, and the kinesthetic sense). Kinesthetic sense or sense of motion is the feel or sensation of the body as it moves. Incorporating this sixth sense is essential in creating a real image, especially for an athlete. The more vivid the image, the more effective it is.

Key Elements in Using Imagery

Perspective: Internal perspective imagery means that you see the image from behind your own eyes as if you are actually engaging in the event. External perspective imagery is when you see the image from outside your body, as with a video camera. Internal imagery has been shown to produce more neuromuscular activity than external imagery, but using the perspective you are most comfortable with will have the greatest impact.

Vividness: As you practice and begin to master the skill of imagery you will be able to produce more vivid images. You will progress from an old black-and-white television with static to an HD screen with surround sound that you can pause, fast forward, or rewind. Increasing the vividness of the image will result in a deeper, more genuine, experience.

Controllability: Great images are controllable. You want images that will do what you want them to. You will need to be able to effectively manipulate images to have a positive influence on your athletic performance. Just like any other skill you will learn in the athletic environment, this takes practice.

Self-Awareness: It is helpful to become more aware of the things that happen during competition that either inhibit or promote your performance. If you can pinpoint specific factors that negatively influence your performance, you can imagine strategies to keep them from interfering with your performance again. The same can be done with repeating techniques and strategies necessary for athletic excellence as well.

Imagery Activity

Think back now to your finest hour as an athlete. As you imagine this moment, incorporate the six dimensions of vivid images. First, pay special attention to the visual, auditory, and kinesthetic senses. Jot down your ideas in the space provided.

Sight: Try to recall the image of how you looked during your finest hour. Not only will you notice what you look like when engaged in superior technique and strategy, but you also will recognize that your body language changes during these moments of excellence. Your confidence will be reflected in your appearance on the outside, just as you feel it on the inside.

Viewing tape of your successful performances also may help you create vivid images.

_____

_____

_____

_____

_____

_____

Sound: Focus on the sounds you heard during this moment. Listen to yourself and your inner dialogue. What was going through your mind during your finest hour? Then attempt to identify what you were hearing in the environment. Try to be specific. Sometimes your best performance is accompanied by silence. Listen to that silence. Try to recreate all of these sounds as clearly as you can.

_____

_____

_____

_____

_____

_____

Sense of Motion: Recreate the kinesthetic sensations you experience during your best performance. Do you have a soft touch? Is there a sense power and speed? Can you feel the intensity you experience when physically exerting yourself? Focus on the feeling of fluid movement. Incorporate any feeling of relaxed confidence or high energy as appropriate.

_____

_____

_____

_____

_____

_____

Touch, Taste, Smell: Finally, try to complete the image by including the senses of touch, taste, and smell. What type of fabric is used in the uniform?

Is there any required equipment for your sport that has a unique feel? Do you play indoors or outdoors? Are there any unique smells associated with the playing field or arena? Smell can provide a visceral link to your moment of greatness. Use it if you can. Incorporating taste may be difficult ... you'll have to be creative!

_____

_____

_____

_____

_____

_____

Now put it all together. Continue to practice using your imagery so it is there when you need it.

Relaxation Techniques for Regulating Arousal

"An anxious mind cannot exist in a relaxed body."—Edmund Jacobson

From a physical standpoint, you regularly bring the same tools to competition: your fitness and physical status, skill level, technique, and knowledge of the game. There is often no marked change in these areas from event to event. Despite this you can see great variation in performance. This lack of consistency is usually caused by a lack of mental and emotional discipline, resulting in fluctuation of your arousal levels. One night you go out flat while another you feel all jacked up. Still another, you might actually find "the zone." How will you know what to expect?

It is important to know that we think and feel not only with our mind but also with our entire body. If we embrace this we can learn to master and control our thoughts, feelings, and actions. Many athletes respond well to the "muscle to mind" techniques due to a physical lifestyle. When learning these relaxation techniques, you should be in a comfortable and quiet environment. Once skilled in these techniques, you should be able to relax in almost any environment under almost any condition.

Don't Breathe Just to Survive—Breathe to Gain the Advantage in the Moment

Breathing with purpose—Proper breathing comes from the diaphragm. This is the thin muscle that separates the lung and the abdominal muscle. This complete breath begins when the diaphragm pulls down and your belly pushes out. This draws air into the lungs and the bottom third of the lung begins to fill. As you continue your chest expands and the intercostal muscles and your rib cage begin to stretch. The middle third of your lungs is now filling up. Finally, the top third of your lungs fills up and your shoulders rise. You can feel the strain just before the sweet release when you exhale. When engaging in the process it is helpful to inhale through the nose and exhale through the mouth in order to regulate your intake and to avoid hyperventilation. (Avoid the nose/mouth approach when competing ... you'll pass out!) Not only does this technique provide you with the much-needed oxygen your muscles require, but it is also the first step to regulating your level of arousal. This technique can be used before, during, or after competition.

"In the Moment" Relaxation—This is a very important skill because it can be used to reduce overstimulation at any time during practice or competition. Anxiety fights against smooth, coordinated effort and performance suffers. By being able to relax in the moment you can minimize excessive muscle tension and mechanical movements. When this anxiety is removed it feels natural and your kinesthetic sense is able to function at the optimum level. This allows for a sense of control and balance thus promoting concentration, focus, confidence, awareness, as well as precision and power, quickness and speed, and so on. Just a breath or two can have a great impact.

Muscle Relaxation Techniques

Progressive Muscle Relaxation—This consists of a series of exercises that involve contracting a specific muscle group, holding the contraction for several seconds, and then relaxing. The exercises progress from one muscle group to another. The contraction phase teaches an awareness of what muscular tension feels like. The relaxation phase promotes sensitivity to the letting go process and what it feels like to be free of tension. This tends to have a calming effect on the mind as well. For example, you can simply clench your fist and take a moment to feel the physical strain. Then let it go and feel the tension flow from your finger tips as it is replaced by a feeling of relaxation.

Body Scan—This is a much-abbreviated progressive muscle relaxation technique that can be used in the moment. Quickly scan the body from head to toe. Stop only at the muscle groups where the tension level is too high. Release the tension and, time permitting, continue to scan. Practice focusing on the spot where you hold your tension, then release this tension. Once you learn to spot tension and relax, you can reduce your anxiety with greater efficiency.

APPENDIX D

Vital Skills for Generating Energy

Breathing—Establish a regular, relaxed breathing rhythm using the technique of the "complete breath." Now consciously increase that rhythm and imagine with each inhalation that you are generating more energy and activation. With each exhalation, imagine you are getting rid of any waste products or fatigue that might prevent you from being at your best. Slowly increase your breathing rate as you continue to generate more energy.

Energizing Imagery—Using all five senses along with the kinesthetic sense of motion, there are many images you can utilize to generate energy at will. For example, imagine you are a train building up steam, gaining momentum and power until you feel unstoppable. There are countless images that can be used as cues for generating energy, such as animal images, machine images, and forces of nature. Developing a supply of imagery cues that work for you in different situations can provide you with an edge when fatigue sets in, when you need a burst of energy, or when you just feel flat.

Energizing Verbal Cues—In the midst of a performance, when time is limited, word cues and phrases can quickly be used to help in buildup of energy and confidence. The words should come from you so you can relate and easily connect with their meaning. This can help generate a genuine and personal response.

Combine Energizing Cues, Images, and Breathing—Gain awareness of what types of thoughts, images, and cue words can serve to activate and energize you during practice and competition. For the most powerful effect, combine a verbal phrase with energizing imagery and a specific breathing pattern.

Transfer Energy—Learn to convert energy from other emotional sources into an adaptive and useful force for performance. If you are able to harness and channel arousal associated with anger, frustration, or some other emotion that may typically interfere with performance, you can turn this emotional energy into performance energy.

Storing Excess Energy for Later Use—The strategy of storing excess energy that is frequently generated just prior to competition can provide you with a means of transferring that energy somewhere else. It also provides a well of energy from which to draw upon at some later point. If over-aroused, store away that energy and use it later when you feel fatigued or discouraged.

Use the Environment—Draw energy from the spectators or the spectacle of the event. This can and often does provide you with the advantage while at home. You can learn to use all types of energy available in the sport environment and use it for your own purpose through imagery, word cues, and self-talk. You can even draw energy from the opponent or opposing fans.

Music—Music can be a great way to create an energetic mood when needed. It can also be used for relaxation. Using headphones, you easily can select and listen to the music that works best for you. This should be done on an individual basis, however, as one song may elicit completely different emotions in different players.

Awareness of Body Language—Fatigue is often caused by inappropriate pacing and unnecessary or unknown sources of energy drain. Becoming aware of your own body language and being sensitive to how you hold anxiety/tension/stress can help you minimize the drain in order to ration out your energy over time. Eliminating muscle tension, maladaptive emotional responses, and general anxiety or worry over performance issues will increase energy, confidence, and much more.

Use Distraction—Focus away from the state of fatigue or fear you experience. Many athletes do just the opposite; the more fatigued or fearful they become, the more they focus on it. This increases your sense of fatigue and will likely decrease your level of performance. Apply your skills of concentration and focus on the task at hand. Break it down into the fundamentals. Simple means safe. Focus on what you are doing rather than on how you are feeling.

Goal Setting:
The Game Within the Game

Systematic goal setting is a powerful technique that will increase motivation, commitment, and performance.

Why Goal Setting Makes a Difference

Goals Focus and Direct Your Attention—Goals direct your attention and action to important aspects of the game or areas that need improvement. With a narrow focus directed on a single aspect of performance you can achieve more.

Goals Mobilize Effort and Increase Persistence—Not only do goals increase immediate effort but they also help to prolong effort during obstacles and setbacks. They serve as markers along the way so you know how far you have come and how much further you have to go.

Goals Help Develop New Learning Strategies—Research shows that performers often develop and employ new learning strategies through the process of goal setting. Real, vivid, living goals will help you stay on target.

How To Set Goals

Set Specific Goals in Measurable Terms—Specific goals are more effective in improving performance than are general "do your best" goals or no goals at all. Goals must be expressed in specific, measurable behaviors so it is clear exactly what you hope to achieve.

Set Difficult but Realistic Goals—Difficult or challenging goals produce better performance than moderate or easy goals. But they must be achievable. This helps you to recognize your limits and push beyond them.

Set Short-Term as well as Long-Term Goals—Short-term goals allow you to see immediate improvement and increase motivation. They also help you keep sight of your long-term goals and what you ultimately hope to achieve. (Visualize a staircase. Without the steps in place, how do you progress from one level to the next?)

Set Performance/Process Goals—This helps you focus on task-relevant strategies and gain a greater sense of control without the distraction or anxiety that comes with winning and losing. Don't focus on winning, focus on what it takes to win.

Express Goals in Positive Rather Than Negative Terms—Focus on what needs to be done rather than what you are trying to avoid.

Identify Specific Goal Achievement Strategies—Once you develop a strategy for achieving a particular goal, you will be able to start taking tangible steps to achieve that goal.

Record Goals, Achievement Strategies, and Target Dates for Attaining Goals—It is useful to keep goals in written form where you will see them regularly. Somehow this type of "contract" means more when it is written down. Ink it, don't think it.

Feedback and Evaluation—This is absolutely necessary if goals are to enhance performance. Statistics can be helpful but in some cases coaches and teammates must make special efforts to provide their opinions. Work with someone you trust.

Support and Accountability—Discuss your goal-setting strategies with coaches and teammates so that you can receive understanding and encouragement. Being held accountable to others can also be very powerful. If you "put it out there" the incentive to follow through is stronger.

Goal-Setting Activity

My overall goal for competition:
Three strategies to use in practice to help me achieve my competitive goal:

1. _____

_____

_____

2. _____

_____

_____

3. (Mental Approach)_____

_____

_____

Comments on how I did:

_____

_____

_____

_____

_____

_____

Patterns of Distorted Thought and Maladaptive Thinking

Often athletes fall short of their goals and perform below their expectations because they engage in maladaptive thinking that results in self-defeating, distorted beliefs. These types of thoughts can create psychological obstacles as they have a negative impact on thoughts, feelings, and performance.

The Perfectionist—Some athletes proclaim they are perfectionists as if this is the best way to approach life and athletics. Though you can accomplish much with this attitude, you can do better. A perfectionist will never reach his goal or feel a sense of self-satisfaction because perfection cannot be attained. When you feel the need to be perfect you will blame yourself for every defeat and every setback. Your self-concept will likely suffer and you may begin to develop a fear of failure. You will put such pressure on yourself that both your enjoyment and performance will suffer. You are dominated by thoughts of "should." When others don't do what they "should" the response is anger, and when you don't do what you "should" guilt is the response. There is value in striving for perfection. Striving for excellence will not only assist you in achieving your goals, you might actually enjoy the ride.

That's Not Fair—"Fair" is often a mask for hiding your desires and preferences. When you don't get what you want you claim it isn't fair. Ideal conditions are rare and the path to success is filled with bias and inequality. It is unrealistic to expect that the world of sport should somehow be fair—that all your time and effort should always pay off or that everyone on a team should be treated the same. In reality, coaches definitely treat players differently; your efforts and achievements are not always recognized; and the breaks of the game do seem to favor the opposition. The sooner you realize the world is not "Fair" the better. Coming to grips with this and learning to stay composed is one of sport's many valuable lessons.

Filtering—You focus on the negative details while ignoring the positive aspects of a situation. This is characterized by a tunnel vision that dials in on only negative aspects of a situation to the exclusion of more positive events. Memory can also be very selective. The filtering pattern results in self-defeating thoughts by pulling negative events out of context and magnifying them, while ignoring positive experiences. Your fears, frustrations, and defeats are emphasized and exaggerated in importance because they fill your awareness to the exclusion of contradictory evidence.

Polarized Thinking—This refers to the tendency to view your experiences in absolute terms. All-or-none, black-and-white thinking leads to categorizing everything as either success or failure, good or bad, rather than learning from each and every experience. There is no middle ground, no room for mistakes. Such thinking often leads to judgmental, derogatory labels. This can be detrimental because negative labels are often internalized and disabling. This ultimately ends in your own character assassination.

Blaming—Nothing is gained by making excuses or assigning fault to others. This type of thinking allows you to shirk any or all responsibility and prevents you from taking adaptive action. It is important to be able to accurately identify what is and what is not within your control. The more you realize you are personally responsible for your experience and your performance, the more control you will have over gaining confidence from good performances. You also will develop the confidence needed to turn current failure into future success.

Mind Reading—This occurs when you commit time and effort in order to "try" to read the minds of others. You want to know what they are thinking and feeling, why they act the way they do, and in particular what they are thinking about you. In so doing, you tend to project your own insecurities onto them, leaving you with even more anxiety, frustration, and self-doubt. Mind reading is also counter-productive because your assumptions are typically wrong, causing more confusion and miscommunication. Finally, your time and energy can be dedicated to pursuits that are much more worthwhile.

Catastrophizing—You expect the worst possible outcome or a catastrophic result. Unfortunately, expecting disaster often leads to disaster. You become plagued by what-ifs. "What if I fail?" When you engage in this type of thinking it becomes a self-fulfilling prophecy when your fears come to fruition.

Overgeneralizing and Magnifying—You reach a general conclusion based on a single incident or piece of evidence. You link that one event with the outcome. You exaggerate the frequency and relevance of the problem resulting in negative global labels that far exceed the original event. When you magnify you exaggerate the degree or intensity of a problem. You turn up the volume on anything bad, making it louder, larger, and more overwhelming. Small mistakes will become tragic failures and minor suggestions will become scathing criticism.

Achievement Dictating Self-Worth—You believe that your own self-worth depends on your level of achievement. You feel you are only as good as your last performance, good or bad. Furthermore, you may begin to think you must excel in order to please others. Ask yourself who you are without your sport or your achievement. Try to focus on the personal qualities and characteristics it takes to achieve rather than the achievement itself. Your worth as a human being and as an athlete should be based on more than wins and losses.

Personalizing—The assumption that self-worth depends solely on achievement is often linked with the self-defeating tendency to personalize everything. You assume that everything people do or say is some kind of reaction to you. People who do this believe that they are the cause and focus of all the activities and action around them. You also may constantly compare yourself to others, trying to determine who is a better player. It is very difficult to develop a stable sense of self when you engage in personalizing. There is too much of a focus on the environment when trying to define self. Don't look "out there" for the answers, look within.

Appendix G

The Performance Triad: Thought, Feeling and Action

The arts and sciences have known for ages that the thoughts we have of our ability, of the demands we face, and of the environment in which we exist determine to a large extent the way we feel at any given moment.

Our thoughts, feelings, and actions are always interacting and impacting one another. Understanding how this progression impacts performance can be very helpful in terms of providing you with a greater awareness and increased ability to influence the positive wave of confidence or the negative undertow of anxiety.

The ideas we have and the thoughts running through our mind have a direct impact on our feelings and emotions. Our immediate feelings, in turn, directly affect our actions because they produce verifiable changes in muscle tension, blood flow, hormone production, and focus. For example, thoughts that anticipate failure lead to feelings of anxiety that result in overall muscle tension. Thoughts that expect victory lead to feelings of confidence that result in smooth, coordinated movement. With the use of muscle-to-mind or mind-to-muscle techniques, you have the power to intervene at any point in the triangle.

Performance Triad Activity

The following is an example of a negative thought that leads to a negative feeling, resulting in poor performance.

When the thought is, "I don't think I can hit against this guy," the feeling associated with this is one of mild anxiety. The action related to this feeling is one of muscle tension and holding on to the bat too tightly. This tension then influences your thought with more negativity: "This guy is good and I'm just not feeling it. I just want to get back to the dugout." This increases the experience of anxiety to the point where you start to feel desperation and fear. The action that follows is a grip so tight that your knuckles turn white and the excess tension spreads to the rest of your body. You look back to the dugout and lose your focus. Your performance ultimately suffers. You are paralyzed with fear after you strike out without even swinging the bat.

Use the preceding example to help you identify your own thoughts, feelings, and actions in the space below. Then go back and apply the mind-to-muscle or muscle-to-mind technique and see how you might impact the final outcome.

First thought: _____

_____

_____

First feeling: _____

_____

_____

First action: _____

_____

_____

Final thought: _____

_____

_____

Final feeling: _____

_____

_____

Final action: _____

_____

Overall Performance: _____

_____

_____

Bibliography

Arnold, Patrick. Phone interview. 2/1/10.

Belson, Ken. "Puerto Rico's pipeline has been running low." *New York Times*. 6/28/10. *www.nytimes.com*.

Berry, Adam. "Team chemistry Maddon's sticking point." MLB Advanced Media. July 29, 2010. *www.raysbaseball.com*.

Bigler, Ken. Phone interview. 1/8/10.

Bolek, Ken. Phone interview. 9/12/09.

Breton, Marcos. Phone interview. 9/5/10.

Burwell, Bryan. "Some inconsiderate fans act as badly as athletes." *St. Louis Post-Dispatch*. March 22, 2010. *www.stlouispostdispatch.com*.

Butler, Brett, and Jerry B. Jenkins. *Field of Hope*. Nashville: Thomas Nelson, 1997.

_____. Phone interview. 10/12/09.

Carroll, David. Phone interview. 1/20/10, 2/5/10.

Cerrato, Raphael. Phone interview. 7/22/10.

Chavez, Ozzie. Phone interview. 8/5/10.

Coakly, Jay. *Sports in Society: Issues and Controversies*. 10th ed. New York: McGraw Hill, 2008.

_____. Phone interview. 2/3/10.

Colina, Alvin. Phone interview. 10/27/09.

Curtis, Jack. Personal interview. 10/22/09.

Edes, Gordon. "Hamilton's past may still haunt him." *Yahoo! Sports*. 6/9/2009. *www.sports.yahoo.com*.

Eklund, Robert, and Gershon Tenenbaum, eds. *Handbook of Sport Psychology*. 3d ed. New York: John Wiley and Sons, 2007.

Ensberg, Morgan. Phone interview. 4/6/10.

Epstein, Joseph. "The Perpetual Adolescent and the Triumph of the Youth Culture." *Weekly Standard* 9. March 15, 2004. *www.weeklystandard.com*.

Fainaru, Steve. "MLB looks to regulate Dominican agents." *Washington Post*. 9/17/2003. *www.washingtonpost.com*.

Farrey, Tom. *Game On: The All-American Race to Make Champions of Our Children*. New York: ESPN Books, 2008.

Forbes, PJ. Phone interview. 12/3/09.

Gardiner, Andy. "Heat on college baseball." *USA Today*. February 28, 2007. *www.usatoday.com*.

Garrett, Smokey. Phone interview. 10/5/09.

Hamilton, Josh. *Beyond Belief.* New York: Faith Words, 2008.

Jacobson, Edmund. *Progressive Relaxation.* Chicago: University of Chicago Press, 1930.

Jamail, Milton H. *Venezuelan Bust, Baseball Boom: Andrés Reiner and Scouting on the New Frontier.* Lincoln: University of Nebraska Press, 2008.

Jonas, Adam. Phone interview. 10/6/10.

Jones, Garrett. Phone interview. 11/24/09.

Kennedy, Ian. Phone interview. 11/8/09.

Kennon, Dan. Phone and personal interview. 10/12/09, 1/7/10.

Kirschenbaum, Dan. *Mind Matters: 7 Steps to Smarter Performance.* Carmel, IN: Cooper Publishing Group, 1997.

Krich, John. *El Beisbol: The Pleasures and Passions of the Latin American Game.* Chicago: Ivan R. Dee, 1989.

Kurlansky, Mark. *The Eastern Stars: How Baseball Changed the Dominican Town of San Pedro de Macorís.* New York: Riverhead Books, 2010.

Kustra, Robert. Conference. "Sports in Society." St. Norbert College. Green Bay, Wisconsin. 5/26/10.

Lehr, Justin. Phone interview. 10/4/09, 11/17/09, 12/29/09, 1/7/10, 1/19/10, 2/9/10, 6/28/10, 7/6/10, 7/21/10, 8/3/10, 8/19/10.

Mathieson, Scott. Phone interview. 11/3/09.

Miller, Ben. Phone interview. 3/22/10.

Moawad, Trevor. Phone interview. 9/21/09.

Montana, Mike. Phone interview. 2/24/10.

Moore, Adam. Phone interview. 2/1/2010.

Moras, Mike. Phone interview. 7/28/10.

Murphy, Jim. Phone interview. 3/4/10, 3/15/10, 5/29/10.

Murphy, JR. Personal interview. 1/7/10.

Murphy, Kyle. Phone interview. 3/19/10.

"Opening Day rosters feature 231 players born outside the U.S." Press Release. 4/7/2010. *www.mlb.com.*

Orlick, Terry. *In Pursuit of Excellence: How to Win in Sport and Life through Mental Training.* 4th ed. Champaign, IL: Human Kinetics, 2007.

Pettyjohn, Adam. Phone interview. 9/21/09, 11/20/09, 12/10/09, 1/12/10, 1/25/10, 3/10/10, 6/22/10, 8/9/10.

Paule, Amanda. Phone interview. 2/12/10.

Pindyck, Blake. Phone interview. 8/20/10, 8/31/10.

Power, Ted. Phone interview. 9/14/09.

Porter, Kay. *The Mental Athlete.* Champaign, IL: Human Kinetics, 2003.

Price, Ritch. Phone interview. 4/22/10.

Rhoden, William C. "College Sports; NCAA aims to keep out of politics." *New York Times.* 10/1/1989.

Rodriguez, Rick. Phone interview. 9/9/09.

Romero, Simon, and Maria Eugenia Diaz. "More Killings in Venezuela than in Iraq." *New York Times.* 8/23/2010. *www.nytimes.com.*

Rottino, Vinny. Phone interview. 7/26/09, 1/18/10, 1/19/10, 1/21/10, 1/28/10, 2/10/10, 6/25/10, 8/17/10.

Sack, Allen. *Counterfeit Amateurs.* University Park: University of Pennsylvania Press, 2008.

_____. Phone interview. 3/9/10.

Saggese, Rick. Phone interview. 12/23/09, 1/6/10, 1/8/10, 1/13/10.

Schmidt, Michael S. "Baseball emissary to review troubled Dominican pipeline." *New York Times.* 3/11/10. *www.nytimes.com.*

Shelburne, Ramona. "John Lindsey Waits for His Chance." 9/1/2010. *www.espn.com*.

Sheldon, Mark. "Psychology in Baseball: Heroes Are Human." 8/10/09. *www. mlb.com*.

Shenbaum, Steve. Phone interview. 9/30/09.

Shepherd Bailey, Joanna. Phone interview. 10/11/10.

Sheppers, Tanner. Phone interview. 11/3/09.

Smith, Stephen G. "Boarding Schools." *U.S. News & World Report* 130 (2001): 38–42.

Snyder, Brandon. Phone interview. 10/27/09, 12/11/09, 1/6/10, 1/12/10, 1/18/10, 1/21/10, 5/24/10, 8/11/10.

Synder, Brian. Phone interview. 12/29/09.

Sperber, Murray. *Beer and Circus: How Big-time College Sports Is Crippling Undergraduate Education*. New York: Holt, 2001.

Stark, Kyle. Phone interview. 10/15/09.

Suggs, Welch. "The Boys of Summer ... and Fall, Winter, and Spring." *Chronicle of Higher Education* 50 (2004): A30–A31.

Swift, E.M. "Dangerous Games." *Sports Illustrated*. November 18, 1991. *www.si.com*.

Taylor, Jim, Ph.D. *Positive Pushing: How to Raise a Successful and Happy Child*. New York: Hyperion, 2002.

Tewksbury, Bob. Phone interview. 8/10/10.

"Timeline of Baseball's Steroid Era." Online. 2006–2010. *www.baseballssteroidera.com*.

Torre, Pablo S. "A Light in the Darkness." *Sports Illustrated*. 6/21/2010. *www.si.com*.

Trebelhorn, Tom. Phone interview. 6/11/10.

Tulgan, Bruce. *Not Everyone Gets a Trophy: How to Manage Generation Y*. New York: Jossey-Bass, 2009.

Upton, Jodi, and Kristen Novak. "College athletes cluster majors at most schools." *USA Today*. 11/19/2008.

Verducci, Tom. "Totally Juiced." *Sports Illustrated*. June 3, 2002. *www.si.com*.

Vermillion, Mark. Phone interview. 5/7/10.

Votto, Joey. Interview. Fox Sports Ohio. Cincinnati. July 1, 2009.

Wasch, Adam. "Children Left Behind: The Effect of Major League Baseball on Education in the Dominican Republic." *University of Texas Review of Entertainment and Sports Law* 11 (2009): 99–124.

_____. Phone interview. 9/23/10.

Weldon, Kyle. Personal and phone interview. 1/7/10, 1/22/10.

Wendel, Tim, and Jose Luis Villegas. *Far from Home: Latino Baseball Players in America*. Washington, D.C.: National Geographic Society, 2008.

Wenner, Melinda. "The Serious Need for Play." *Scientific American Mind* 20 (2009): 22–29.

Williams, Jean M., ed. *Applied Sport Psychology: Personal Growth to Peak Performance*. 6th ed. New York: McGraw Hill, 2010.

Wolverton, Brad. "Athletes' Hours Renew Debate Over College Sports." *Chronicle of Higher Education* 54 (2008): A1–A23.

Zaiger, Allan Scher. "Exemptions Benefit Athletes." Associated Press. Dec. 30, 2009.

Index

Academics 53, 54, 55, 56, 57, 139
Academies 141, 143, 144, 145, 146, 147;
    Academy of Professional Baseball 139;
    Bigler Baseball Academy 37; D-Bat
    Baseball Academy 28; Dominican Re-
    public Sports and Education Academy
    (DRSEA) 144, 145, 156; IMG Academy
    22, 38, 39, 40, 41, 67; Puerto Rican Base-
    ball Academy and High School 146;
    Think Outside the Diamond 27
Academy of Professional Baseball 139
Adjustments 31, 90, 102, 103, 127
Adversity 32, 160
Agents 124
Alderson, Sandy 141, 143, 145
Amateur model 31, 52, 53
Amateur player draft 17, 48, 49, 51, 140
Anabolic Steroids Control Act 99
Anti-Drug Abuse Act 99
Anxiety 53, 80, 81, 82, 83, 121, 158, 177, 186
Aristotle 4
Arnold, Patrick 49

Bay Area Lab Co-Operative 100
Bigler, Ken 37–38
Bigler Baseball Academy 37
Boarding school 39, 40
Bolek, Ken 40–41
Braun, Ryan 161
Breathing 82, 83, 176, 178
Breton, Marcos 135, 138, 139, 149
Buscones 142, 143, 147
Business model (in amateur sports) 29, 52,
    65
Butler, Brett 105, 106, 112, 122, 123, 163, 166

Call-up 120, 123, 127, 129
Caminiti, Ken 86, 99
Caribbean League 135
Caribbean World Series 136

Carroll, David 32, 33, 34, 37
Cerrato, Raphael 109–110
Chavez, Ozzie 134, 135, 148
Clemente, Roberto 138
Coaches 91, 106–107
Coakley, Jay 29, 32, 33, 34, 37, 38
Colina, Alvin 138, 148
College 51; baseball 50; degree 49, 50, 53;
    divisions I, II, III 48, 50, 53, 55; recruit-
    ment 31
Communication 47, 67, 73, 76, 114, 190
Confidence 14, 15, 21, 34, 36, 52, 64, 65,
    80, 94, 97, 102, 104, 106, 121, 127, 161, 169
Consistency 80, 101–102
Cuba 137–138
Curtis, Jack 63, 77, 115, 116

D-Bat Baseball Academy 28
DiFrancesco, Tony 107–108
Disciplined mind 15–16
Distorted thinking 76, 183
Dominican Republic 131, 132–134, 135,
    136–137, 141–148
Dominican Republic Sports and Education
    Academy (DRSEA) 144, 145, 156
Dorman, Harvey 161
Drugs 91–92, 95, 98–99
Dualism 3

EMDR 105
Emotions 64, 95, 103, 104, 158, 159
Ensberg, Morgan 50–51, 54, 56, 58, 69, 74,
    82, 121, 126, 161, 162, 185
Entertainment industry (baseball) 18–19,
    26, 27, 69, 74
Epstein, Joseph 75

Failure 16, 31, 32, 74, 80, 81, 94, 103, 161
Fame 15, 71, 72, 73, 74, 75, 76
Fans 74

Farrell, Charles 142, 144, 145, 146
Farrey, Tom 30
Federal Graduation Rate 57
Fielder, Prince 39
Forbes, P.J. 69, 82
Front office 17

Gallardo, Yovanni 82
Garrett, Smokey 109, 127
Goals 53, 63, 125, 180
Graduation rates 55, 56, 57
Graduation Success Rate 57
Greinke, Zack 158–159

Hamilton, Josh 91–92, 95–96
Hypnosis 116

Identity 16, 33, 91
Identity fraud 143
Imagery 78, 79, 80, 97, 104–105, 170, 172, 178
Imagination 77, 78
IMG Academy 22, 38, 39, 40, 41, 67
Injury 91, 92, 93, 94, 95, 96, 97

Jonas, Adam 139, 143, 146, 148
Jones, Garrett 66, 67

Kennedy, Ian 97
Kennon, Dan 38–40
Kinesthetic intelligence 19
Kustra, Robert 53, 56–57

Latin players 79, 134, 136, 138, 139, 141, 149
Lehr, Justin 2, 8–9, 13, 14, 21, 22, 24–25, 27, 35, 41, 44–46, 60–61, 68, 81, 86–88, 96, 99, 100, 101, 102–103, 106, 107–108, 114–116, 121, 125, 127, 128, 131–132, 136, 151–152, 160, 167
Leonardo da Vinci 4
Life skills 41
Lindsey, John 125

Maddon, Joe 109
Managerial style 124
Managers 107–109
Mathieson, Scott 92–94, 102, 111
Media 15, 22, 41, 51–52, 54, 66, 71, 75, 99, 141
Mental challenges 13, 14, 66, 81
Mentorship 128
Mexico 130–131, 135
Miller, Ben 57
Minor league lifestyle 65, 68–71, 73, 75
Mitchell Report 100
Moawad, Trevor 22, 36
Molitor, Paul 78
Monism 4

Montana, Mike 49
Moore, Adam 28, 33
Moras, Mike 65
Murphy, Jim 50, 64–65, 78, 80–81, 105, 106, 108, 109, 160
Murphy, J.R. 40–41, 57
Murphy, Kyle 55, 56, 58

NCAA 53, 57
Negative thinking 17, 22, 81, 82, 98, 103–104, 115, 161–162, 186
Negro league 137

O'Halloran, Greg 161, 164, 165
Organizational player 68
Ownership (over sport) 29, 31, 32

Parents (role in players' development) 29, 30, 31, 32, 33–34, 36, 37
Paule, Amanda 31
Peak performance 169
Pedroia, Dustin 21
Personal fable 76
Pettyjohn, Adam 2, 7–8, 17, 23–24, 32, 43–44, 51, 57, 59–60, 69, 70, 72, 73, 84–86, 92, 94, 95, 101–102, 103, 107–108, 111, 113–114, 124, 128, 129, 130–131, 135, 136, 148, 150–151, 162, 163, 166, 167
Pindyck, Blake 128
Player development 53, 55, 56, 57, 64, 65, 66, 67
Power, Ted 13, 73, 101, 122, 123
Pressure 13, 21, 22, 27, 30, 36, 45, 46, 48, 51, 53, 90, 98, 118, 134, 139, 156, 160, 161
Price, Ritch 50, 51, 55
Professional model 31, 58
Prometheus 6
Puerto Rican Baseball Academy and High School 146
Puerto Rico 131, 132, 135, 137, 138, 140, 146
Punishment (coaching style) 34–35
Pythagoras 4

Reiner, Andres 139, 141
Relaxation 83, 176–177
Risky behavior 73, 75
Rodriguez, Rick 123
Rose, Pete 122
Rottino, Vinny 2, 11–13, 14, 15, 21, 25–26, 33, 36, 41, 47–48, 50, 62–64, 72–73, 76, 81, 82, 89–90, 101, 107, 110–111, 115, 118–119, 121, 124, 126, 127, 128, 132–134, 135, 136, 154–155, 162, 167

Sacrifices 20, 29, 106, 110
Saggese, Rick 27, 34, 35–36
Sanderson, Scott 25, 50, 165
Scheppers, Tanner 95

Schiestle, Jack 128
Shenbaum, Steve 16, 67
Shepherd Bailey, Joanna 138
Showcases 27, 28, 29, 31, 36, 37
Smith, Stephen 40
Snell, Ian 81
Snyder, Brandon 2, 9–11, 18, 20, 25, 31–32, 36, 46–47, 54, 61–62, 69–70, 88–89, 94, 97, 108, 110, 116–118, 128, 152–154, 160, 166
Snyder, Brian 17, 29, 36, 48
Special admits 54
Specializing 32–33
Sport psychology 1, 2, 3, 4, 5, 6, 14
Stark, Kyle 67
Steroids 6, 87, 88, 99–101, 102, 141–142
Student athlete 51, 53, 55, 57
Subconscious 104–105

Team chemistry 109, 110, 111
Tewksbury, Bob 121, 166

Think Outside the Diamond 27
Trebelhorn, Tom 64, 72, 77, 78, 79, 80, 82, 121, 126, 127, 166

Unfair conditions 18

Venezuela 131, 135, 136, 137, 138, 139, 140–141
Vermillion, Mark 74
Veteran players 68, 72, 110, 125, 126, 127, 128, 155, 162
Vitruvian man 4
Votto, Joey 2, 157–158, 161

Wasch, Adam 142, 143, 144, 145, 148
Weaver, Jeff 124
Weldon, Kyle 20
Wendel, Tim 137
Wenner, Melinda 18
Wohlford, Jim 161, 165